# My Child is Going to be Rich & Famous

## How To Successfully Balance Family, Parenting and Entertainment

### Angela J. Williams

TGBTG PUBLISHING

**Mental Health, Legal and Financial Disclaimer**

The author of this book does not dispense medical, legal or financial advice or prescribe the use of any technique as a form of treatment for physical, emotional, medical, legal or financial problems, either directly or indirectly. The intent of the author is only to offer information of a general nature to help you in your journey for well-being. In the event you use any of the information in this book for yourself or others, the author and publisher assume no responsibility for your actions.

*To my sons…*

*Tyler, you make me proud because you are wise.*
*Tyrel, you bring me joy because you are kind.*
*Tylen, you make me smile because you are genuine.*

*Jeremiah 29:11*

*"I know the plans I have for you, declares the Lord. Plans to prosper you, and not to harm you; to give you hope, and a future."*

*In memory of my Mother, my Mentor, my Moses – Angela Upshur*

*In honor of the greatest daddy a little girl could ever ask for – James C. Upshur*
*That little girl still thinks you are superman! I love you!*

# Table of Contents

# Insight from the Industry

# Preface

*I* wrote *My Child Is Going To Be Rich & Famous* as a guide and a resource for parents. It is written for the benefit of the children who will be involved, inspired, affected or infected by experiences in the entertainment industry. The insights I share in this book can be applied to all stages of a child's creative development and discovery in the arts, and for all areas of entertainment, including sports, music, modeling and other creative endeavors. That being said, the focus of this book is on the commercial, print, theater, film and television worlds. I will be speaking to you from a mother's perspective, not to discourage or impress you or your children, but to inform you and help you make better decisions. I have never embraced the label "stage-mom" and I do not live vicariously through my children, although I spend a lot of quality time with them. For reasons that I will elaborate upon later, I am not my sons' talent "momager," manager or agent. I am their mother. However, I am also the creative, business, personal and financial overseer of their lives, businesses and careers.

Although I am their parent, I (along with my husband) found purpose in raising them to know that they matter. Just like any other child, they have unique thoughts, great ideas, dreams, feelings, fears, flaws, positive and negative qualities, doubts and questions. All of these things matter deeply, and as a parent, I wanted to respect that. The goal was never to be a perfect mother or to raise perfect children. Nevertheless, I am and will always be their mother first. So I chose to be present, aware, discerning, hands on and involved with all areas of their lives because I love them. I have great confidence in them and I want them to accomplish all that they are purposed to achieve. However, I also have a life outside of overseeing my children's

1

lives and what they do for a living. This "life" does not include striving to be a super-star, socialite, or actress, although I consider myself to be a closeted character actor. I am a Christian Minister (by calling), a personal/business manager (by experience), a writer/producer (by profession), and a life coach/spiritual parent and mentor (by purpose). I have a Bachelors Degree in Business Management and a Masters in Psychology. As a family, all of our many responsibilities keep us very busy, but the key is finding the balance we need to accomplish everything, collectively and individually. Sometimes discovering that balance means shifting from what worked just a few months ago, to finding a "new way" forward, but the adjustments are always worth it in the end. By achieving this careful balance, my sons have the opportunity, within reason, to use their individual voices to make choices that help them exercise certain areas of leadership related to and concerning their careers, businesses and lives (according to what is age appropriate for the situation, of course). This helps us all to keep a clear focus on what our responsibilities are and it allows us to stay in our respective lanes, so to speak.

Throughout the last 18 years (at the time of writing this book) in the entertainment industry with my sons, many parents have asked me countless questions about my experiences. Some genuinely wanted advice. Others desperately wanted to learn about the business. Some wanted to take advantage of my freedom to share and others wanted me to guide their child's career. Nevertheless, it is an honor to now share the many things I have learned. One of my greatest desires is to help parents to understand what is possible. Still, most parents will discover on their own, and very quickly that every child's journey is unique. There are certain paths along the way that most parents will obviously take. However, the roads begin to splinter and become more specific for that child's path when doors begin to open or close. This book will serve as a potent dose of reality (good, bad, crazy, funny, adventurous, exciting and sad) for some. For others, it will be a much needed resource guide and source of assistance. It will challenge yet others to assess motives, ethics, integrity, parenting skills or styles as they proceed forward with their lives and the quest for "riches and fame."

# Introduction

*My* Child is Going to be Rich & Famous is meant to enlighten, teach and educate you. The root of all of the great lessons I have learned (and am still learning), the survival skills and strategies, and the principles that have ensured that my family succeeds are biblically based and extremely effective if applied diligently, consistently, and deliberately. This root has been a constant source of peace of mind and balance for my family and me. It has helped me keep my sanity, avoid booby-traps and landmines, maintain communication in my household and keep my family focused on our purpose for working in the entertainment industry. This journey can be an exciting experience, and of course along the way, there are many distractions. However, some of these are easier to recognize than others. I am convinced that my children may not have reached certain levels of personal and professional growth had it not been for them being grounded, discerning and disciplined in the life applications of certain biblical principles. As they are becoming and growing into young men and maturing adults, I believe that as long as they continue to follow these applications they will be just fine, no matter how life unfolds for them.

Hopefully by the time you finish reading this book, you will have some of the necessary information and tools needed to make sound personal, financial, creative, emotional and parenting decisions for your child and your family regarding entertainment issues. This book is not well suited for parents who also want to pursue a career in the industry along with helping his or her child find their footing. That's another conversation entirely because it requires a bi-focal or forked perspective that has many gray areas - although I'm sure it can be done. Here, I will be sharing my stories and insights in a candid, comical, and passionate manner, as if we were out to lunch and speaking one on one. I will give you answers, advice, resources and suggestions. You may not like my answers, want my advice, need my resources or even feel that this information is relevant for your situation. However, some of you may find that this is exactly the type of book you were looking for. My goal was to write the book I wished was available when we started on our journey over 18 years ago.

I will be talking to you as if the tables were turned and I wanted this information from you. It doesn't matter what your child's gift, goal or talent is; the information I am sharing is relevant and applicable. Be it sports, music, arts, science, technology, academics, stocks, baking, fashion, cosmetology, or the debate team - the advice is still palatable. I invite you to break off the pieces of information that work best for you or that seem helpful to you, and use it as a guide for your specific situation. My experiences over the last 18+ years have presented a wealth of knowledge gathered in the areas of television, movies, print, and commercials. I will be addressing everything from casting, business, management and production to studio sets, including exclusive interviews with agents. Many parents have questions about managers, producers, studio teachers, Coogan (trust) Accounts, interacting with stage parents, child work permits, understanding work hours, education/school options, balancing family life and similar issues. Instead of having a FAQ section in this book, I decided to share my answers to these questions via specific scenarios, personal examples and professional situations. Over the years, I have found that parents are most concerned about a handful of specific issues: proper parenting, marriage, pitfalls, success stories, failures, sibling issues, money matters, prayer, communication, leeches, sick kids on set, taxes and extended family drama.

I write this book for parents who have already made mistakes, parents who want fame for their children, parents who are considering the possibilities of fame, parents who are reluctantly skeptical and everyone in between. I purpose to be an integral, ethical and honest person. So, while sharing with you, I will not speak negatively against any specific person, groups, networks, studios, systems, structures or the like because your experience may be different from mine, and I don't want to influence your judgment one way or another. Nevertheless, I will be specific enough so that if you find yourself in a particular or similar situation, you will be able to reference sections of this book for assistance. I will make general statements and comments but still be vague enough so that you can make up your own unbiased opinion. I will give you no gossip, no shortcuts to fame, or manipulative insider tricks of the entertainment trade, because there aren't any. Throughout this book, I may use words like "they," "their" or "them" when referencing the entertainment system or structure. It is not directed or reflective of a particular person or select group of people. It is solely meant to establish my perspective of the spirit, personality, or disposition of the entertainment industry and its many moving parts, as I, and others that I know, have experienced.

Let me give you an example. I am a native New Yorker. Some people think that the typical New Yorker is rude, always in a hurry and aloof. I would like to believe that I represent the essence of the average New Yorker's personality. I am friendly (most often), guarded (when I sense I should be), outspoken (when necessary), candid and oftentimes terse (to make a point), swift on my feet at times (because I have somewhere to go) but rarely harsh, disregarding or aloof (unless the atmosphere warrants it). I am sure that there are New Yorkers who fit the negative description or interpretation, but hopefully this remnant represents the exception and not the typical New Yorker at heart. Suffice it to say that you will rarely walk away from one of us on the street, after asking for our opinion, and ask yourself, "I wonder what they meant by that?" We are generally straightforward. Out-of-towners tend to say things like, "They sure do have a way of getting to the point." That being said, "they" and "them" will be the words used to describe many (but not all) dimensions of the entertainment industry. I will also be defining specific and seemingly obvious words in order to clarify or further explain an example or an experience. For instance, an entertainer, by definition, is simply, one who entertains and amuses.

With this book, I intend to celebrate the "amusement" industry as a whole, in the same way that I would celebrate the medical profession, educational system, and other public servants, if one of these were my chosen field. I celebrate the structure of creativity and everyone who represents entertainment well. By the time anyone watches a commercial, movie or television show or listens to a song on the radio, behind the scenes were hundreds of people who were instrumental in sharing their expertise along the way to create the finished product the world is allowed to enjoy. I will introduce you to just a few of these awesome people later in this book. Just as many believe that it takes a village to raise a child, it takes a village of creative people to make what eventually comes to life on the big or small screen or the stage. "They" are one big collective reason why so many people want to do what entertainers do, and I celebrate all of them.

However, as with all industries, these creative folks experience both negative and positive dimensions along the way. Some of them didn't know what to expect or how to navigate within the system and are left with many regrets and scars. If folks are not careful, this industry has a way of changing them or their mindsets for the worse. I have often heard people say, "If I only knew then, what I know now, my choices would have been different." If more people were aware of the realities ahead of time, I'm convinced they would be better prepared. As a result, my goal is to catch as many parents as I can before they head in the wrong direction. If I can help one family, one child, or one parent, then this book was worth all of the time, energy, sacrifice and life experience that it took to write it. So, if you are ready, I welcome you to take a metaphoric seat and turn the page.

# 1

## *Cold Open*

$\mathcal{J}$ am the mother of three sons: Tyler James, Tyrel Jackson and Tylen Jacob Williams, who are 22, 18 and 13, respectively at the time of finishing this book. They are all professional actors, producers, writers and musicians. Before entering the entertainment industry with them, I was a Gospel and R&B singer/songwriter, author, literary/music publisher, and minister. One evening, 18 years ago, my four-year-old son, Tyler and I sat back on the couch in our living room in New York to watch the feature film "Men In Black," starring Will Smith. Tyler was looking forward to this movie because he had seen so many of the action-packed movie trailers. After the movie was over and the end credits began to quickly scroll atop the black television screen, he sat still as if he was recording every scene in his mind. His gaze was distracting but familiar. I got up from the couch attempting to go about the rest of the evening when I noticed that he had not moved and was still staring at the television, as if he were daydreaming. After five minutes or so, Tyler – wise beyond his years even back then - called to me, pointed at the black screen and said, "Mom, that's what I'm supposed to do." Naturally, I said something supportive (but aloof) like, "Oh really? You'd be a good actor too." I assumed that was going to be the end of our little "I want to be on TV" chat. Subsequently, every day after that one, he asked if he could watch "Men In Black" "one more time." Each time, immediately after the movie was over, he would say, "Mom, that's what I am supposed to do" or "I want to be an actor like Will Smith," which caused me to begin contemplating the gravity of his comments as I maintained my supportive response. I knew he was serious.

One day while reviewing a few spelling flash cards, he once again reminded me, "Mom, I really want to be an actor like Will Smith." By nature, four-year-old Tyler was wiser-than-his-years, selectively social, talkative around the house, dry-witted, observant and focused. He didn't really "perform" at home but he did like to read (or have me read) stories. We'd act out the characters and turn the tale into big, over-the-top, "story-time" productions. He loved watching television, going to the movies and listening to all genres of music. We would watch television and listen to music as if the program or song were a homework assignment that needed to be analyzed. We would dissect movies like we were just hired as replacements for the famous movie critics, the late Gene Siskel and late Roger Ebert. After watching our movie, we would have a discussion, peeling away layer after layer. As a toddler, he was obsessed with Barney the Dinosaur! At about two-years-old he could not get enough of the animated Disney movie "Fox and the Hound," Michael Jackson videos, especially the video "Scream" (which featured Michael's sister, Janet Jackson), and The Lion King (the movie, the video, the book, the sound track, the stuffed animal, the slippers, the pencils, the bubble bath…well, you get the point). So from the sincerity in my four-year-old son's voice, I knew it was time for us to have a discussion about his current "acting phase."

In the past, I'd made it a point to have daily conversations with my three sons. Even while I was pregnant with them, I would rub my growing belly and say things like, "Good morning baby, it's time to wake up. What do you want to do today?" Or "Ok baby, it's bedtime. Are you ready to say your prayers?" The goal was to talk with them about everyday occurrences and activities to teach them how to develop a vocabulary, communicate and process information properly. I wanted them to know how to embrace and express life from their little perspectives. Because I envisioned that they were going to be academic scholars, I wanted to teach them how to discern their environment, ask questions, find the answers and develop a conscious voice. I noticed that many of the kids around me at the time didn't have these qualities, so I wanted to help my children as best as I could to use that voice to make wise choices (later in life of course). So this pending conversation with my four year old was no different.

While he was drawing one day, I asked Tyler to explain to me what he thought the movie "Men In Black" was about. I wanted to know how watching the movie made him feel. I continued by asking him questions like, "What do you think acting is? Why do you want to be an actor? How do you know you really want to be an actor after watching just one movie?" I told him to take some time and think about his answers, and when he was ready to talk about them, we could talk. He left the room and returned about an hour or two later with a serious look on his face and answers to the questions as he remembered them. "The movie is about Will Smith who fights aliens, and he is tough and funny," he said. "The movie made me feel like I can be tough and funny too. I think acting is pretending to be different people. I want to be an actor because I know that's what I am supposed to do. I don't know that I want to be an actor because I just watched *that* movie; I feel that way when I watch all movies, all the time. When I watch movies, I can see myself in the movie doing what Will Smith is doing, and I am doing a good job." At first, I was taken aback by his comments. He stared at me, waiting for me to say something. I quickly realized that I either had to close my mouth or let a couple words fly out of it. I responded, "I thought all of your answers were really good. Good job!" Even though I was not in the mood to consider what my next steps would be, I could not deny or ignore the passion I heard coming from his heart and out of his mouth. After our quick Q & A, I told him, "Let's have a family meeting with daddy and your baby brother." My son Tyrel was a few months old at the time. "After that, we will pray about it then I will let you know what the final decision is." He was very excited but tried not to show it because he was in his "I'm a big boy" stage. So he just simply said, "Ok" and walked away, trying hard not to blush.

Needless to say, the tentative family discussion and time in prayer went well because a week or so later I suddenly found myself in research mode. I had an idea of what to expect from this journey because when I was around six years old, along with voice classes and tap dancing classes, my mom took me on several commercial auditions in Manhattan. I remember sitting in long, crowded hallways full of nervous moms and their energetic children holding scripts in front of their faces. They would take turns reciting little phrases like "Wow…these cookies taste great, Mom!" and "Thanks, Mrs. Johnson, you're the greatest!" while waiting for someone from inside the closed casting room to step outside and call the next child whose name was on the long waiting list. As a six year old, there was nothing about the experience that was exciting or fun for me. I didn't like feeling extra dressed up with extra bows hanging from my ponytails, or wearing perfect looking socks and polished shoes just to sit in this dreary room with a bunch of boring people. I felt like I had to look my best for these strangers as if I needed their approval. I remember feeling about as indifferent as any six year old could feel, especially when the alternative was playing outside.

My mother thought that I was hilarious, and as a kid I loved making her laugh and watching her roll over on the couch holding her stomach as if I was Lucille Ball or Carol Burnett, two of my favorite childhood comedians. So, to pass time at the audition, I would tell her made up stories of how the rest of the kids at the audition were from other planets because they were too perky, smiled too much and didn't act like any of the kids that I played double-dutch with in the South Bronx. I would sit next to my mother, watching the kids who seemed almost robot-ish as they rehearsed their weird lines. Once my name was called, my mother would nod as I approached the casting director and turned on the charm, with a big smile and polite handshake. I'd look back at my mom who was smiling, calm but proud, then I'd walk into the empty room where there was a huge video camera sitting on a very large tripod at one end of the room. A few emotionless strangers sat at the opposite side of the room behind a long wooden table. The table had a tall stack of photographs of children on it, and each stranger took notes on sheets of white or yellow paper while they stared at me. I felt like they were glaring at me, waiting for me to do something to amuse them, and I didn't like that. I felt like they were evaluating me as if they were observing an animal's behavior in a research lab.

The casting director would politely ask me a few simple questions like, "What's your favorite color? What's your favorite animal? Do you like ice cream?" They would then ask me to recite the lines that I had just memorized in the hallway. I didn't feel nervous or intimidated, but the experience felt intrusive to me, and I was not happy about feeling imposed upon by strangers. Every now and then, I'd enjoy reciting the lines or eating the products from the commercials that I was auditioning for (like vanilla pudding, jellybeans, chocolate, or apple juice). For some reason, I always seemed to think of a line or two that was funnier or better (so I thought) than the ones that were on the auditioning paper. At times, when I decided to throw caution to the wind and say my "funnier line," the casting folks would politely smile and send me on my way. They didn't appreciate my little improvisations. After a few months of these boring and uncomfortable experiences and taking some cute headshots (professional industry pictures) of myself smiling widely and exposing my missing front tooth, I had had enough. I told my mother that I didn't want to do it anymore. Before quitting, I did manage to land a background spot in a cereal commercial starring the late great Vincent Price. No one could see my face in the commercial, but I knew that I was one of the many kids screaming inside the big box on the floor off camera! And just like that, my acting career was happily over.

I believe that my mom secretly danced a "Happy Dance" in private at my unexpected news of wanting to quit the acting business. I know that she did not enjoy the countless impromptu trips from the Bronx to Manhattan, hopping on and off trains and buses, especially during the winter months, going from building to building due to last minute phone calls from agents and managers for an audition that "just came in to his or her office." The auditioning schedule and process was unpredictable, rarely resulting in a booking. It was time consuming and quite bothersome because I didn't want to be pulled away from playing with my friends, hanging out with my sisters, or watching television. I didn't want to stop playing jump-rope, or having relay races outside with the neighborhood kids just to go into the house to get cleaned up and take that long trip to the city. I believe another reason my mom was relieved was because she was a homemaker and the mother of two older daughters who needed her attention too. Having to stop everything that she was doing at the time to gather me, our coats and her bag and run to auditions with one daughter at a moment's notice must have been frazzling for her at times. So as quickly as my childhood "acting journey" started, it ended without a fuss.

However, I must admit that to this day, I can remember those cold days when the trains were running behind schedule and we were late for an audition. Instead of my mom getting upset, she would look down at me and ask, "You want some hot chocolate?" I would happily nod and smile widely as she opened the large double glass doors that led into a warm coffee shop with bright red countertops and silver spinning barstools. I can almost smell that sweet marriage between fresh brewed coffee and fresh creamy hot chocolate as if I were thrown back in time to that very moment. It was the greatest experience ever! I can just see my mom and me sitting at the counter, shivering from the cold outside but drinking hot chocolate and coffee (for her) with my little legs swinging off of my shiny barstool. I felt rich, safe and important. We chitchatted and laughed together as if we were old girlfriends with nowhere to go and nothing to do but create a memory that would last a lifetime! I would look at her from the corner of my eye while she would carefully toss a couple of sugar cubes into her coffee and think, "I have the best mom ever and I make her laugh!" That is my sweetest, warmest, most cherished memory of my very short acting career!

I digress. A few days after my initial research - which included reading every book that I could find on children and the entertainment industry - I sat Tyler down on the couch and explained a few things to him. I told him that we had to make an agreement before proceeding. "Okay, I am only going to say this once," I said. "Nothing is more important than school.

If you really want to do this, you have to put 100% effort into this and all of your other responsibilities at the same time. No matter what happens, remember this is what you are doing right now. It is not who you are. You are no better or worse than anyone else. Except for a few family members and close friends, we will not be telling anyone what you are doing. Do you understand?" He was so young and I doubt he completely appreciated the gravity of what I was saying, but he knew his mom very well. For some reason I knew telling too many people about what we were going to do would become problematic (more on that later).

Although he was just in nursery school for half of the day and at home using the Hooked on Phonics learning program the other part of the day, he agreed. The next day, I ended my initial research with the most current auditioning handbooks and other industry resource materials I could find. It would have been great to simply ask my mom how she got started with me when I was a little girl, but she unfortunately died of breast cancer two years before Tyler was born (she would have gotten a kick out of the irony of the moment). About an hour into reading a few books, I realized that this venture was going to be just as time consuming as I remembered as a child. The only difference was; I was now standing in my mom's shoes. What? How did that happen? I'm sure you can imagine the excitement I must have been feeling. I silently thought, as I forced a pleasant yet excited looking smile on my face, "I better get some hot chocolate out of this deal!"

Speaking of motherhood, I also needed to carefully consider how I was going to balance this new venture into my already full schedule that also included my infant son, Tyrel Jackson, the new release of my first book (an autobiography about my mother's life and battle with breast cancer), book signings, speaking engagements, countless hours in the recording studio, writing and recording new music, and performing. Nevertheless, every time I looked at four-year-old Tyler's face, I committed to continuing my research and gave it a try anyway, at least for a while (I thought). The good news was that our family was fortunate to live in a city that had access to the wonderful culture of arts that incorporated the theater, radio, television, music, movies and performing communities and many other entertainment industry experiences of New York City. It was now just a matter of time, patience, traffic, knowledge, sacrifice, focus, perseverance, and countless hours on the road, strategic navigation, confidence, prayer, discernment, time management, talent and diligence. I was convinced it would all pay off.

Sounds simple enough, right?

The auditioning locations were familiar to me because many of the recording studios, supper clubs and singer/songwriter outlets were in the same area. While walking the busy and fast paced streets of the city on our first auditioning field trip to Manhattan, I picked up an entertainment resource magazine called *Backstage* from one of the newsstands and looked for any auditions or workshops that would fit my son's description. At the time, *Backstage*, for me at least, was an overwhelming informational research booklet that served to show readers, along with everyone else who wanted to be a "star," how to avoid getting swallowed up in the industry scene and spend unnecessary money. This guide, I imagined, was especially overwhelming for those who were new to the experience, desperate for fame, from out of town, or from a small town. This informational guide featured auditions for plays, musicals, commercials, television shows, feature films, voiceover work and the like. It provided discount coupons on everything from workshops and acting classes to photo shoots, music lessons and anything else related to entertainment.

Depending on the reasons, hunger, motives, hopes, dreams and level of determination for entering this world of endless possibilities and pitfalls, a person can learn life-changing lessons – starting with who to (or not to) trust, how to persevere, how to pay dues (literally, creatively, personally, and financially), how to commit to the craft, when to walk away, and which doors to walk through (or out of). Fortunately for me, I had many eye-opening experiences in the music industry as a Gospel and R&B artist. I have met and had great moments with some of the most wonderful people. However, I have also encountered the sharks, liars, pimps, hustlers, scam artists and unethical people. So I was somewhat ready mentally and

14

emotionally. I just applied the lessons that I learned in music to *this* side of the entertainment industry.

While reading *Backstage*, in the midst of all of the visually stimulating announcements competing for my attention, I found a listing in the audition section for a very low budget gospel musical drama, entitled "Murderers." I thought, "Yes, this is it! This is how and where we should start, with stage plays!" The play was written, produced, and directed by one person. The listing stated that the casting director was looking for a cute, mature, four-year-old boy, with lots of personality. I thought, "Hey, I've got one of those!" After speaking to the casting director on the phone and getting a copy of the sides (lines or scenes from the script to study to prepare for the audition) for my son later in the week, we were on our way to our first official audition! He was so excited and I was thrilled for him! The audition was in the heart of Manhattan in a big brownstone apartment building on the east side of town. I felt as if he was on the road to paying his "acting dues" because the play was not going to be on Broadway, but it was a step in the right direction. I thought, "What a great way for him to sharpen his craft, if he actually has a craft to sharpen." As we walked into the poorly lit and airy room, it felt like some of the small music rehearsal studios that musicians and singing buddies of mine used quite often. I immediately noticed that my son was the only four-year-old boy in the room at the time. I laughingly thought, "Well, the odds are in his favor for booking this role!" We walked toward the casting table, and I introduced myself to the friendly woman sitting at the desk. I didn't know at the time that this woman was actually the writer, producer, director, casting director, one of the main characters in the play, and the woman that I spoke with over the phone. Did I mention that this was a low budget, off-off-Broadway play?

I had no idea what was about to happen but the confident look on Tyler's little face was enough for me to find somewhere for us to sit and wait for his name to be called. He was determined to succeed at his first audition. He sat quietly while swinging his legs back and forth in his wooden chair. I asked him if he wanted to go over his lines but he said that he didn't need to because he remembered them. He learned to read at the same time he learned to talk, so I knew that words and memorizing would not be a problem for him. Once his name was called, he walked into a very small room with the casting woman, and the door closed behind him. While he was inside, I prayed, "Lord, if this role is for him, show me how to balance this with everything else that I have to do because I will not let this stress me or us out." I was sitting close enough to the door to hear what was happening with the audition and was proud to hear the sound of self-assurance in his voice as he auditioned.

After the quick audition was over, we talked about his experience as we walked back to our car. We picked up a snack, turned on the radio and listened to music during our long drive home in traffic. I casually told him that we had to wait a few days to find out if he had booked the role. He simply said, "Ok" in his hopeful, big boy voice. To take the pressure off of the impending call, once we got home, we had a very short conversation about what would happen if he didn't get the role and what would happen if he did. Since we didn't know either way, we decided that if he was supposed to book the role, it was already his; but if he was not supposed to get the part, it was already for someone else. We still attempt to hold that mindset today. So I gave him a high five in advance (for whatever the news would be), and we gave another high five in the air to the boy who got the role instead of him (if that was the case). After that day, we didn't bring up the audition again and just went about our normal daily routine. A few days later, "The Call" came! Tyler booked his very first audition! He was excited, but naturally pretended to be very cool and low key about it.

Tyler had a dramatic role in the gospel-centered play. His character's father was a drug dealer who didn't want to change his ways. One day while little Tyler's family was at home eating dinner, they got an unexpected visit from the father. During the confrontation with his character's grandfather, gunshots rang out and Tyler's character and his pretend mother was shot and killed. Tyler learned to deliver the emotion needed for his role, each night, for an entire summer. I remember watching the look on his face from back stage (I was eventually hired to be the stage manager for the play) every night, right before he responded to the sound of the fake gunshots. He was focused and ready to tell his part of the story. He didn't care that he only had a few lines and that he got paid a couple hundred dollars from his first acting experience. He learned how to fall to the ground and lie still on stage, while listening to the "Oh No!" surprised responses from the audience. While watching him during hours of rehearsal, I knew he had found one of his passions - and that's all that mattered to him. I realized then that this was a part of what he was supposed to accomplish in his life. This was a part of his purpose! He loved the long rehearsals, learning his lines, finding new ways to deliver them, and working with the other actors. He didn't even mind the cramped dressing rooms or the long trips in traffic to and from rehearsal. He just wanted to do what he saw Will Smith doing in MIB. He just wanted to act. It was as if he knew at four years old that he was laying the foundation for bigger things to come.

Since then, his younger brothers Tyrel Jackson and Tylen Jacob have followed in his footsteps voluntarily. They started even earlier than he did, Tyrel at 18 months old and Tylen at three months old. All of my sons' natural talents, hard work, discipline, and opportunities have opened doors for them. I didn't know, 18 years ago, that watching one movie would change the course of our family's life. I had no idea that this industry would be such a large part of all of my sons' lives or our family's day-to-day existence. Nor did I know that my brief moment auditioning as a child and more than 25 years in the music industry would be just the reference and "entertainment" support I needed to begin this journey. I now know that it was always a part of their purpose and that the information I learned throughout the years would be gathered to help you now.

At the end of this book, I trust that you will know and understand a little more about the entertainment industry and how to apply what you have learned so that you can navigate and parent well within it. Please feel free to highlight and take notes or even journal as you read this book. These notes can serve as breadcrumbs for you, your child and your family to follow along your journey. I believe that by the time you finish reading, you will be able to answer questions that will serve as safeguards for your path in show business. I will leave you with a two-part question at the end of the book that can be used as a starting point to keep you focused as you proceed.

# 2

## My Child is Going to be Rich & Famous!

You might be absolutely right! However, this statement, in itself, is a mouthful. These words may also be a trap. I truly believe that words, statements and declarations have power. Declarations like "My child is going to be rich and famous" can inspire us to motivate our children. It can also motivate parents to continue making sacrifices for the sake of our children. Positive statements can help to move us in specific and desired directions depending upon our understanding or perception of the use, definition or interpretation of them. The dictionary defines "rich" as having abundant possessions and material wealth, having high value or quality, and being well supplied or endowed. The dictionary describes "famous" as widely known, or honored for achievement. I can imagine that when most people think about being rich and famous, they think about possessing all the money they will ever need. They expect one day to own yachts, airplanes, big homes, boats, and possess the finest cars, jewelry, and clothes that money can buy. They imagine themselves eating at the finest restaurants, attending grand and affluent parties, and having lunch with celebrities and famous socialites.

We can imagine ourselves receiving accolades, listening to fans applaud as we enter a room, or being honored at a luncheon or an award show while watching performances of other famous people celebrating our achievements. Some people visualize ribbon-cutting ceremonies to celebrate the opening of a chain of stores, or sitting by humbly, while glowing and watching as the faculty of a library or school announces the renaming of a building (which now spells your name in big bold letters, across the top of the doorway). Some people even fantasize about getting a star on the Hollywood Walk of Fame. I can imagine that, even as you are reading this, you can vividly imagine your own unique idea or perspective of what being rich and famous looks like and have probably shared the idea with close friends, family and colleagues.

Similarly, many of us dream about our child or children being rich and famous as well. We can imagine our child on stage performing, standing out in a crowd of other talented children, playing a particular role or instrument, or becoming most valuable player. We can also see them in our mind's eyes walking on stage to accept his or her achievement awards, getting endorsement deals, nailing that Oscar winning performance or signing that much anticipated and lucrative contract. Most parents and caregivers can almost see their child's face raised high and plastered on billboards all over the country hoping that he or she will one day be featured or interviewed on "Entertainment Tonight" and CNN. Some hope that just maybe an exclusive interview by Barbara Walters will prompt critics to write favorable articles and reviews about them in the New York Times. All of these experiences are attainable and are just as wonderful as they sound. Many children have been preparing, practicing, sacrificing, and dreaming about these same things, too. Some children will actually experience this life and some of these experiences. When they do, it will be a "Dream Come True" for the child and the parent.

Being rich and famous has many positive benefits. Those that I just mentioned encompass the rippling effect of what being rich and famous gives one access to. I am sure that everyone can agree that having all the money one can ever want or need is quite freeing, wonderful and life changing. When I was younger, I enjoyed watching famous entertainers being interviewed – and I still do. One night, I watched the incomparable singer/actress/performer Pearl Bailey (1918-1990) being interviewed on a talk show. She said something that made me silently sit back for a minute and take a pause. She was responding to a question regarding her career and the way she measured success. She said with confidence and resolve, "I've been rich, and I've been poor and I like rich a whole lot better." I thought for a second, "Hmm, she's been rich and poor. I wonder what the biggest difference is?" It seemed as though - at least to me at the time - that she had assessed the disadvantages of poverty and the advantages of her level of riches and never planned to be poor again. Her words implied to me that she had found the financial escape from not having enough of anything and being surrounded by lack and she wasn't going back to where she had come from. I thought, "She sounds like she's free." I smiled in celebration for her, even though at the time I didn't quite understand the gravity of her words.

Certainly, there is a freedom that comes with financial abundance and being widely known that one will never attain from lack and obscurity. When a person is financially secure, the weight and stressors that lack brings with it are eliminated. The ability to take a sigh of relief and not have to constantly worry about food, shelter, safety, and unexpected emergencies or unforeseen monetary crises is liberating and stress reducing. That's why just about everyone we know wants riches and strives for them. Realistically speaking, the majority of people in the world have more experience with lack and obscurity than they do with abundance and notoriety. That is why the average person wants to be rich and famous, even though they have never experienced or considered the negative side of them both.

Those who don't have such fame and wealth are convinced that the alternative life has to be better than the one they are currently experiencing. In most cases, I would imagine, they are correct. There are places that rich people shop, eat, travel to, bask in, live in, explore, splurge on and experience that others never see. There are events that famous or influential people are invited to, socialize at, celebrate and get dressed up for that many people don't even know exist. Rich people typically have the best seats on airplanes and in theaters, and drive the most expensive cars. They get most of their meals, clothes and jewelry from places that others just look at through windows and in books to experience. Rich and famous people stay at expensive hotels and write the biggest checks for charities. They don't live from one paycheck to the next or save up for vacations, and they don't wait for furniture to go on sale before they can buy it.

Famous people generally don't ride buses, clip coupons, save money in order to shop for the holidays or stand in long lines at restaurants. They don't have to because they are privileged, financially secure, influential, regarded and fortunate. They clearly experience the type of life that others dream of. Rich and famous people are popular and have many "friends." Because of this wealth and notoriety, other rich and famous people want to be around them, know them, party with them, and have them as friends and associates as well. I have never heard a person who lives in obscurity say, "You know, I always wanted to be and feel impoverished, overlooked, disregarded and unimportant to others. I like living this way. I never wanted to be rich or famous. I have no desire to pursue it. That way of living is not for me. My life turned out just the way I imagined and hoped it would be." On the other hand, I have never heard a rich or famous person say, "I long for the days when I had to struggle to pay my bills, lived in an unsafe neighborhood and was ignored by others for the hard work that I accomplished every day." I have never met anyone who didn't want to be rich and famous, at least to some degree, whatever they imagined that might entail. They want to live a life of convenience, luxury, freedom, fulfillment, ease, excitement, abundance, and the like. Some want to live a rich and famous life so that they can help themselves and others who are less fortunate than they are. Others want to do it to make their lives better or to financially provide for their family and friends. There is a small population of people who selfishly want as much of it as they can get (legally or illegally) for themselves so that they can brag, live in excess and make themselves feel or appear superior to everyone else.

When parents make the declaration or even ponder the idea that their kids will be rich and famous, they think about most of what I have just mentioned. I don't believe that there is anything wrong with wanting or striving to live a well-known life of abundance as long as there is a benevolent or selfless purpose behind it. In a perfect world I would imagine just about everyone would accomplish his or her own interpretation of rich and famous. That is what the American Dream is suppose to represent, right? I understand and respect the pursuit of it. Many parents want to dream big for their children and that's normal. They want the best for them. They want their children's lives to be better, easier, more convenient, more exciting, safer, fuller, bigger, happier, more fun and less stressful than their lives were. I respect that. If you agree, please follow me to the next chapters so that we can explore this idea from more than one perspective.

# 3

## *Whose Dream is This?*

*M*any adults (me included) had childhood dreams of becoming rich and famous and living a life that we saw on television, read in magazines or watched in the movie theaters. As a child, I was convinced that I was going to have an exciting life and a fulfilling career of adventure, crime fighting, philanthropy and leisure. I had a very vivid imagination and I allowed that imagination to take me wherever it wanted me to go. This exciting life would resemble the images that left a lasting impression in my mind as I watched television and movies throughout the years. As a child, my imagination shaped what I thought my life, marriage and career would look like.

I dreamt of living the fictional lives of Wonder Woman - the ultimate DC comic heroine who made her way to my television screen via Lynda Carter - and Cleopatra Jones, the first black super heroine to appear in movie theaters, played by the late Tamara Dobson. For some reason, through both of their characters, these two women spoke to me and confirmed what I somehow already knew as a young girl about the strength of my "woman-ness." They reminded me that I was a strong, beautiful, multi-tasking force to be reckoned with. My dream continues. After introducing my "Super Woman-ness" to the world, I would eventually meet and marry one of my three favorite music/movie/television boyfriends (in my mind): the late, great Michael Jackson (the young, "I'll be There" Michael with the afro), Bernie Casey (the handsome former professional football player turned talented and cool-tempered Blaxploitation actor in the 70's), or Matt Houston, the private detective (whose real name was Lee Horsley) on the early 80's ABC television show.

After meeting one of my top three "boyfriends," we'd of course have a whirlwind romance, an over the top wedding and a marriage like Robert Wagner and Stefanie Powers on the ABC television show "Hart to Hart" (Yes, I liked watching television). Because of our rock solid marriage and successful careers, we'd spend hours cuddling and drinking champagne while playing with our two male and female German Shepherds on our private yacht while watching the sunset every night. Each morning, we'd step onto our deck (camera ready, of course), preparing to slow dance to any Barry White love song that came to my mind while listening to the sound of the sea beating against my one-of-a-kind boat named something deep but corny like "Eyes To The Sky." Afterwards, we'd get into our separate but matching chauffeured driven limousines or private jets headed to a breathtaking location to commence shooting our highly anticipated blockbuster movie by day, then fight crime together by night. I would, of course, enjoy these "fun-filled" and "realistic" experiences every day, for the rest of my life.

As children, many adults imagined themselves to be the toast of the town, the life of every party, and able to perform in front of millions of people. After their crowd-pleasing performance, they imagined quickly leaving the venue from the back door, wearing black sunglasses, surrounded by bodyguards, personal assistants, and a hand-picked entourage with photographers and interviewers following along, hounding and pulling on them for a picture or an interview. They could almost hear the crowd and watch their security team from a distance as they shielded them from the impending stampede while yelling out to the pressing crowd, "Excuse me, coming through, no pictures please!" As kids, some of us parents envisioned being eternally in demand and at the top of the "A" list of performers, forever.

However, as with most adults who had these dreams, they grew up and unfortunately their reality did not resemble the vivid dreams they once had. Somehow real life happened and replaced all of their fantasies.

Adulthood, long-term employment security, immaturity, mistakes, fractured relationships, high credit card balances, student loans, bills, less than glamorous jobs and lives, responsibilities, family, school, alternative careers, sickness, accidents and unforeseen circumstances took center stage. As a result, these new types of personal comedies and dramas became our platform. Even the best professional accomplishments never seemed to create the excitement or level of fame and notoriety that some adults were once convinced they'd achieve.

Most people make their peace with it and go on to live content and even fulfilling lives, although the sounds of applauding fans seem to be missing. Nevertheless, the former dreamers somehow peacefully resolve to perform to a much smaller audience at home, at work, or within their communities, and settle on entertaining or embarrassing their loved ones during the holidays and special occasions. Although at times, when they are watching their favorite television shows, they will imagine themselves as the characters on the screen or they will find themselves critiquing the actors as if their performances are disappointing. These parents soon realize that the actors weren't as bad as they initially thought and move on to watching the next show. Every now and then, however, they silently ask the "What if?" questions. Not long after, though, something remarkable would happen in their "normal lives" that would bring about one of those "I wouldn't trade my life for anything in the world" moments that puts everything into perspective.

However, a very small percentage of these adults, who were once dreamers as kids, will carry around those unspoken "hopes deferred" like baggage well into adulthood. Internally, there remains a hidden but burning flame to "make it big." Although the burning desire is now just a flicker, the child-turned-adult is still aware of its existence. Just when the adults thought it was too late to live their dream, they get the role of a lifetime to participate in the greatest project of all. They star in the production of "Parenthood" by becoming moms and dads. They think, *what an honor! The miracle of life! What could be better? Everything makes sense now! I have found my purpose! I am a parent, and nothing that I ever wanted can compare to this! I am now fulfilled!*

The new parents remain satisfied with their new role until they notice something that seems oh so familiar. As his or her baby begins to grow and develop, the parents sees a sparkle, a twinkle or a gesture that goes beyond the average cute little things that babies do. They notice that something is a little different. Their child seems to be just a little more talented than other kids and this "extra something" forces the parent to pay close attention. While doing so, the parents notice that their child seems to be a miniature reflection of themselves and the child unwittingly becomes a reminder of who the parents used to be, wanted to be, or could have been. The suppressed flicker of the past slowly but gradually turns into a small but unnoticeable flame again. Just as the phrase *"those who can - do, those who can't - teach,"* sometimes applies, so does *"those who could – did, those who couldn't – got their kids to do it."* Besides, the child is just as cute, just as talented and with the same amount of potential they once had. This is an obvious "no brainer" for those parents.

The parents then declare, "I missed my opportunities but I am NOT going to let the same thing happen to my child." That is a wonderful resolve and a moving gesture if the parents' motive is to give the child (not themselves) the opportunities they didn't get and if the child is interested and more excited about the idea than the parents are. If that is the case, then their journey can be an interesting and fulfilling one, full of lifelong memories to cherish between the two of them. However, if that is not the case, their time together can be a frustrating one, full of life long memories of regret between the two of them. But let's assume, for the sake of this topic, that this is the case of the latter scenario. The parents begin to gradually attempt to manipulate the child into the same extracurricular classes and activities that they once participated in.

The parents unfortunately start to share stories of their talented past with the child or even proceed to share regretful stories about how successful they could have been if their life would have turned out differently.

They never notice the child's body language as they are talking or notice that their child is less than interested. I have seen these parents and these children. If you ever care to watch an emotional train wreck in slow motion, this would be one of them. I have seen parents who manipulate or push their child by rewarding them with gifts, snacks, praise, money and future promises just to get them to audition or participate in an extracurricular activity. Even worse, they often punish the child with unreasonable physical threats, yelling at them in public, taking away toys and not speaking to them to get the child to audition, dance, sing, catwalk or play a certain instrument or sport. Sometimes these parents are hard to spot because most want their children to excel and do well with creative, physical and even academic activities. However, identifying them becomes easier over time.

In a short period of time, the truth begins to emerge. It can become a bit easier to recognize them because they are just a "little-too-much" at times. They are a "little too" stressed when they think their child is not doing their best. They are a "little too" aware of what the other kids who are also auditioning are doing. They are a "little too" mindful of how the director is responding to or directing their child. They are a "little too" aware of how many lines (more or less) his or her child has compared to the other kids. They are a "little too" knowledgeable about what the other kids have worked on in the past. They are a "little too" friendly to the directors, producers, writers and parents. They are a "little too" talkative, opinionated and present on set. These parents exist, and they are not necessarily all bad parents. They may not even realize what they are doing or how they are affecting their child or the environment around them. Also, sometimes it takes a while to adjust to these experiences, and no one has it all figured out. However, here are a few questions to ask yourself to determine if you are living vicariously through your child, or attempting to capture your own deferred dreams.

- *Am I unusually disappointed, upset, and verbally cold or condescending when my child loses, fails, doesn't score, is rejected, isn't selected, or misses the mark, etc?*

29

*Note:* All parents want their children to do the very best, and it is ok to be disappointed. But sometimes they may not be *at* their best. That's ok (sometimes) because they are not perfect and everyone has bad or off days. Someone else may be stronger or even better than they are in a certain area or on a particular day. If a parent expresses disappointment inappropriately, a child may interpret the parent's behavior negatively and develop negative self-esteem issues or resentment toward the parent. Parents must learn to control their emotions even if they are disappointed.

*Suggestion:* Learn how to balance your emotions. Don't get overly excited regarding a positive outcome or overly disappointed on a negative outcome. If your child sees that you are emotionally balanced (when getting good or bad news), you will be teaching them to be and stay emotionally balanced in the future.

*Example:* One of the words that I would use when one of the boys got either good news or bad news was "Ok!" That one word could mean: "Ok, congratulations here we go!" Or it could mean: "Ok, you didn't get this one, maybe next time!" The good news response or the bad news response is the same, and it wasn't blown out of proportion either way.

- *Do I ask a list of questions of my child before, during and after a performance, audition, exercise, etc?*

*Note:* Most parents want to know how their child performed at the audition and that is natural. But many ask questions mainly to see if they can determine if their child's performance was acceptable or likable by the casting director.

*Suggestion:* Be careful not to put a magnifying glass on the moment or the audition. Fight the urge to drill your child because if he or she doesn't accomplish what is expected, the rejection may be more difficult on the child than it needs to be only because you made such a big deal about the experience. Truthfully speaking, your reactions and questions are not going to change that reality one way or another. In most cases, the job was either your child's to book or it wasn't. Your questions or your child's answers after the audition will not change the reality of the booking. There is no way for you to determine what the casting agent is looking for anyway. So it's best to briefly talk about it rather than investigate the audition. It will make for a more peaceful trip home. Afterward, change the subject of the conversation and don't bring it up again so that the focus is on something other than the audition.

*Example:* One of the only questions I would ask after an audition was "How'd it go?" They had the choice to say very little or a lot about it. I followed their lead, and we then moved on to another conversation.

- *What is the countenance or body language of my child before, during and after a performance or activity? Do they seem indifferent or disconnected from the activity or toward me once they are finished?*

*Note:* Most kids are transparent and readable; they have not learned how to mask their emotions. A parent can see right through them if they know them well enough. Most parents know if their child wants to do something, likes an activity, or is interested in something, unless the parent is so focused on his or her agenda that they miss all of the signs.

*Suggestion:* Pay attention to your child. Even if your child is good at the activity, a negative attitude or body language may be a sign that you want this more than they do. That doesn't mean that a parent should not encourage or push a child or request that the child should stick to an activity for the sake of them learning lessons on dedication, perseverance and discipline. Teaching your child these fundamentals is one thing, but forcing your child to do something that he or she clearly doesn't want or like to do is another. It is the parent's job to discern the difference.

*Example:* My middle son Tyrel was taking piano lessons at about four years old, and he was a naturally gifted player. But he simply hated everything about playing the piano. He attended classes and played in recitals for about two years, but he hated practicing and piano class. After about two years of it, I noticed that I was still making him practice and he never volunteered to play on his own. There was no passion or look of enjoyment in his eyes. There were times when he would start to cry while he was playing. One day I told him it was time to practice, and I watched him from a distance drop his head and his shoulders and walk toward the piano, as if I were punishing him. His whole personality changed. I couldn't ignore what I saw. So I called him over to the couch to have a little chat. I asked him if he wanted to play the piano anymore or become a pianist? He looked up at me and simply but with honesty in his eyes said "No." At that moment, I was reminded of the day that my six-year-old self told my mom that I didn't want to go on auditions anymore. He convinced me that he was as sure that day as I was then. I immediately responded by giving him a hug and telling him that he didn't have to play anymore, ever. The look of relief on his face made me sad that I had forced him to practice. However, I was hopeful that, because he was a natural, he would eventually return to the piano or at least find an instrument that he really wanted to play. He is now 18 (at the time of writing this book) and hasn't returned to the piano. However, he now volunteers to play guitar and he is a talented music producer…by choice!

- *Is my child desperately looking for affirmation, validation or an immediate response from me once he/she is done?*

*Note:* Getting the approval from a parent is the coolest thing. The child feels validated when that happens. However, if the child is looking for approval because of the stressful or negative effects that will follow, that is not a good thing. If he doesn't get that immediate response he is expecting, he knows that the usual ride home is going to be a nightmare because the parent is going to pick apart every single moment of his performance. Some kids feel more comfortable and secure when their parents are front and center at a performance or taping, while other children prefer that they not see their parent or have eye contact with them while performing because it is distracting to them. Stressors are not good for adults and they are not good for kids either, especially if the stress and pressure to perform is looming over them and coming from the parent.

*Suggestion:* For children that are not comfortable when their parents are standing right in front of them, take the pressure off by not being noticeable during a performance. Always be in a place where you can keep your eyes on them but not so much so that they can see your reactions, especially if it's not a good reaction. If your child is more comfortable when you are front and center, to take the pressure off of both of you, have something productive or distracting (but not consuming) to do while you are sitting near them. Read a book, use your cell phone or laptop, start a hobby that requires you to concentrate on it rather than your child's every move. Although you are distracted by your activity, you can still hear and see your child in case you are needed. You can also create a signal (between the two of you) that lets your child know that you are watching, and everything is ok.

*Example:* Often times, I catch my sons' eyes from a distance and give them a thumbs up gesture or something else less noticeable to others to let them know that I am there and all is well. Other times, I just look up from whatever I'm doing and smile at them. Many times, I walk up to them during a break and give them a high five while asking them if they need anything – or I'll ask them a secret question that will let me know if they were comfortable in their surroundings or not. Remember to affirm your child because he or she is your child, not because you approve or disprove of the performance.

- *Do I only celebrate with my child when he/she wins, overshadows another child or excels in an activity?*

*Note:* We teach our children so much about how to behave by them watching how *we* behave. Realizing when, why and how you celebrate your child is just as important as the celebration itself.

*Suggestion:* Begin to make a mental list of when, why and how you celebrate with your child and make adjustments where needed. I am not suggesting that you celebrate failures instead of successes. I am suggesting to you to assess your motives. You may find that you are manipulating your child to excel or even worse, hope for the failure of other children.

*Example:* When my sons were just starting out in the industry, I purposely chose not to talk negatively about the kids who were auditioning with them. If I said something out loud about them, I tried to make it positive unless it was a behavior I didn't want the boys to imitate. If I had to say something negative about a behavior, I would (and still do with Tylen) attempt to subtly speak through public eye contact at the moment but make a comment of correction in private.

- *Do I belittle or devalue my child's competitors in front of my child?*

*Note:* Parents will compare their child's talents to those of the competitors and will sometimes comment on the competitor's skill level, physical differences, or similarities. Many parents think that their children are always the best, the most talented and most worthy of achievement. That's fine, but the reality is that every child is special and every child has his or her moment to shine. There is a positive way to teach children that they are special and unique without belittling others.

*Suggestion:* Be careful not to verbalize everything you are thinking. You may make one negative comment about a competitor but your child may interpret that belittling or devaluing others as acceptable and expected. Respect is not difficult to emulate. If the parent shows it, the child will learn it.

*Example:* We are comical people by nature and we can always find something in our environment to laugh at or about. I try hard not to let our perception of a situation be about a person specifically, but rather a funny behavior or situation. My boys eventually learned the difference, and try to do the same.

If you can answer "yes" to two or more of the questions above, I would suggest that you seriously reevaluate your motives or strongly consider making an about face until you are willing or able to make some changes in your behavior. You could be creating emotional discomfort for your child and he/she may grow to resent you for it. As a result, this could compromise your future relationship, or he/she could grow into the teen or young adult you never expected him/her to be. If you are still not sure, that's ok. You can test your motives via your child by looking into his or her eyes and waiting for an honest response as you ask a few questions. Some of the questions below can help you assess what your child's true feelings are. Make sure you reassure him or her that there is no right or wrong answer. Finally, be mindful, when asking the questions, not to manipulate him or her to answer a certain way, by the tone of your voice, your body language or your facial expressions. You all know what I mean by that.

- Are you having fun?
- If you could be doing anything else right now, what would it be?
- Do you want to do this when you grow up?
- Would you like to take a break from doing this?
- If there was one word to describe how you feel when you are doing this, what would it be?
- What do you like best about this?

- Is there anything you want to tell me about this even if you think I may get upset or may not want to hear it? There is no right or wrong answer.

Hopefully he/she will feel comfortable enough to answer honestly. If you feel that he/she was honest and he/she said things that you didn't expect to hear, please be willing to consider making the necessary adjustments, even if it means giving him/her permission to try another activity. You may be so glad you did…in the future.

# 4

## _The Price_

_S_ports uniforms, equipment, headshots, tap shoes, acting lessons, sports coaches, voice lessons, and the like can get quite expensive, but in order for your children to sharpen their skills or further develop gifts, talents and ambitions, all of these items may be necessary investments. That being said; there is no greater joy than watching your child run across a field and score after you have spent most of your life savings on sports camps and a uniform that he will probably outgrow by the end of the season. Just watching the smile on your child's face after he or she has accomplished something important, like a piano recital, is priceless.

Now that that's out of the way, have you taken into consideration how drastically your life would change if your child did become famous after all of the years of hard work, practice, and financial sacrifice? I'm sure that the parents of rich and famous kids (past and present) have many stories (good and bad) to tell you about. If we had to give these stories a title, I'm sure it would be something like "How My Child's Fame Changed Our Family's Life."

One of the first things that you and your family will have to sacrifice is _time_, because if your child is successful, he or she is also going to be pulled in many different directions. If your child is in demand, that means he or she has a very full schedule. Your daily routine will now include: photo shoots; interviews; early morning radio tours; daily creative decisions; wardrobe fittings and changes; non-stop flights; speaking engagements;

taking breaks to eat a little, nap a little and fit in countless hours of practice/ rehearsals/recordings while attempting to complete the mandatory minimum three hours of school every week day (hopefully the parent is making sure that happens); countless hours of driving/flying from one engagement to another; last minute meetings; additional hours of practice; red-eye airplane trips; and special appearances. Charity events, premieres, lunch meetings, autograph signings and trying to get enough sleep will dominate any leisure time. These are all exciting and fun things, and because the child is a minor (under 18) everywhere he or she goes, an adult must chaperone. From a contractual, legal, and parental standpoint, a young performer is not considered an adult until he or she turns 18. In most cases, the person accompanying a minor will most likely be a parent, grandparent or legal guardian. While your child is working on set, a studio teacher, who is also considered a welfare worker, must accompany your child as well, to make sure the state requirements of education and child labor laws are followed.

Usually, the only *two* exceptions to this rule are if the minor is either emancipated or has tested out of school before age 18. *Emancipation* is the legal severing of the parent's obligation to a minor. If emancipation happens, the minor is legally separated from the parent and is no longer dependent on the parent to sign legal documents or to provide a living environment. Some emancipation restrictions apply from state to state, but as it relates to the entertainment industry, in most cases, the emancipated child now has total control over his or her life. Testing out of school early (via the proficiency *CHSPE exam*) is another way that the minor doesn't have to abide by the rules of having a legal guardian on set, complete the mandatory three hours of school a day or have a studio teacher/welfare worker on set with them. If a minor takes the CHSPE exam and passes, in most cases, he or she is allowed by law to work in the industry as an adult, with unlimited work hours. With the exception of these two rules, once a minor turns 16, the guardian may not have to accompany him or her at all times. For the young performer, it would be the equivalent of having a summer job (of sorts). However, until then, the parent/legal guardian goes everywhere the child goes. This is necessary and beneficial for both parent and child, but over time the schedule can take its toll on both.

If a parent has a full-time day job that is not flexible to these demands, trying to juggle the child's extracurricular activities and your workload can be a very difficult, frustrating and an almost impossible task. Many parents try to juggle both and attempt to take days off of work, leave early or go to work late when an important audition comes around. Some of them put their jobs in jeopardy because of this. At times, parents will attempt to lie to an employer for the sake of an audition or possible booking. Some of them, unfortunately, lose their jobs because of this. Some parents even quit their day jobs so that they can be available for the child's unpredictable auditions. The thought process behind it is, "Well, my child can make more money in a month than I can make in a year. So I will quit my job and dedicate all of my time to getting my child's career started so it can happen faster."

In some rare cases, that is true, probable and possible. However, a parent, especially a single parent in a single income household, should seriously think about quitting a secure day job and steady income to gamble on a possible payday because the child's career and that payday may never happen. I am sure some of you might say, "Who would do something crazy like that?" There are more parents who have done it than you may think. For some of them, the child had already landed a role on a series but for most of them, the child didn't even have representation or the possibility of a pending job. There are parents who have taken a chance and everything worked out just fine. However, there are many more parents who tried it and it didn't work out very well. For the single parent who plans to keep his/her day job, it's ideal to have a strong support system - grandparents, friends, neighbors, or a set sitter (a person who is hired to sit on set with your child while you are at work) to divide the time with you. Let them help you if they are willing and you can trust them with the safety and daily responsibilities of your child. I will elaborate more on this later.

Another sacrifice is *privacy*. Fans, extended family members, people from your past, enemies, jealous people, strangers on social media, gossip outlets (printed, electronic or televised) and the general media may want to know everything there is to know about your child, your family, friends, enemies, health issues, cars, favorite restaurants, vacation trips, stores, clothes, favorite color, money matters, secrets, dysfunctional issues and medical history (even if it's not true). That's why some television shows, the growing social media world, gossip magazines and gossip television shows are so popular. Our society has become very voyeuristic, self-exploitive and nosy. In the world of entertainment, there is a need, a purpose and a productive way to market, promote and publicize using social media, which is very beneficial and valuable. But in general, our society has developed itchy ears and an appetite for telling too much of our business, voicing our thoughts and opinions (while some are hiding behind electronic anonymity), and wanting to know too much of other people's business. We have to be careful about sharing information and teach our children how to do the same. We are leaving behind traceable electronic fingerprints that can come back to haunt us. These technological footsteps can also be used to damage our reputations and our families. We have all heard of celebrities, professionals and average folks who have used social media and media outlets inappropriately and have gotten into trouble with their employers and others because they made certain comments. Some of them have even lost their jobs and careers.

It also seems that some individuals have become consumed or obsessed with the "ME" factor as well. Because of the explosion of the social "accessibility" factor via new and emerging forms of media and technology, information is more available than ever and nothing seems to be private. It is amazing but true that some people want to know everything they can about other people in general. I have several theories as to why that is, but I believe that the number one reason is to compare the other person's life to his or her own. But now there is a movement happening where people want to tell all of their business, and give detailed information about every move they make. They will release anything for the entire world to see without filters, discretion or even an understanding of the disadvantages in doing so. They will even add pictures for further proof, knowing that someone will be clicking, following and scrolling, interested in what they are sharing whether they know the person sharing it or not, or whether the information is a true representation of the person and their life or not. With that being said, social media is the perfect place to lie, pretend and embellish one's identity - but that comment is for another book.

A celebrity's life is even more alluring than that of the average person's. Look at how many magazines and websites are focused on the lives of famous people (even if the information is not true or just have measures of truth in them). In a general sense, this can be acceptable, helpful and informative if the targeted person is comfortable with having their information available or exposed. However, when the celebrity is not comfortable with it, it becomes bothersome, disrespectful and violating. Now that everyone seems to have a phone with a camera, video and recorder built-in, a person's everyday movements can be captured without his or her consent, knowledge or control. This is very beneficial in certain situations but not so beneficial in others. I would imagine that some people reading this would say, "Well if famous people or entertainers didn't want people taking pictures of them, they shouldn't be famous. That is just what happens when a person becomes a celebrity. That's the price they pay for making all that money and having the life that everyone else wants." My response to people who embrace this point of view is although you may have a valid point, it is not completely or necessarily justifiable.

Entertainment is the vehicle that allows a minority of people the opportunity to become *famous* (well or widely known), *successful* (having achieved popularity, profit or distinction) or *infamous* (well or widely known for a negative quality or action). However, before most of those who fall under the previous categories became famous, they had private lives that no one knew or really cared much about. When you or your child is the center of attention, or you or your child becomes famous, the luxury of privacy goes out the window. One of our first experiences with this was one afternoon when our family was eating lunch at a restaurant. We knew that there were people staring at us from other tables, but we had gotten used to the stares and whispers. We would generally try to politely smile and keep walking. This particular day, while we were in the midst of an engaging conversation, a woman and her two children walked over to our table and the woman interrupted our conversation and just began talking to my oldest son, who was about 13 years old at the time. She said, "I don't mean to bother you but my kids would like an autograph." Of course we were taken aback by the lack of respect for our family time but we let her continue talking. There was no apology for interrupting, and the parent just took it upon herself to address a minor instead of the minor's parent, but we didn't make a big deal about it because we assumed she just got caught up in the moment.

I said, "Excuse me, hi. I'm his mother. As you can see, we are eating. Thank you for watching the show. You can't have an autograph at this moment, but if you could wait until we are finished, I am sure he would be happy to give them one." At that point, she was a little taken aback, and realized how she must have looked with her kids standing in front of all of us in a restaurant where everyone else was seated except them. Sometimes fans are so excited or surprised when they see a celebrity that they don't consider their approach or excitement even if it is bad timing, inappropriate or intrusive to the celebrity. It is not entirely their fault, as there is no rule book on how to politely approach celebrities without being disrespectful or getting on their nerves so I try to help them understand the situation if I can - unless they are rude, pushy or demanding. Then, well…they get to meet me and may not like my introduction.

Some people are just rude and want what they can get from whoever they deem to be famous. They may want an autograph, a picture, or even information: the good, bad, personal, private, sensitive and the ugly. They assume that this information is a part of the famous person's entertainment or "famous" duty to share. Not true. The entertainer's "personal and private life" should not have to be sacrificed as a result, unless they choose or volunteer to share that side of themselves, which many celebrities often do. Some people would say, "Well, if I bought a ticket to his or her concert or movie, or bought their music, I have a right to take a picture, ask for an autograph or interrupt them in public while they spend time with their families. If it wasn't for people like me, they wouldn't be famous in the first place." That statement, to a degree, is correct.

Without fans and committed supporters of entertainment, there would be no successful basketball players, singers, actors and the like. But remember, entertainers are ordinary people who just happen to have extraordinary jobs. It is a privilege for entertainers to get paid for doing what they love to do. However, it is also a privilege for fans to reap the benefit of the entertainer's talent by being entertained by them. There is a two-fold, win-win situation for both the giver and the receiver. Each entertainer has to decide; sometimes by trial and error, how assessable they want to be to their fans. When it relates to children, this is the responsibility of the parents, caregivers and the support system that is in place to look after the minor. Hopefully it is a well functioning support system. You have to determine what accessibility looks like for your child and how safe your child feels in public. Parents have to be diligent with this because once a child feels unsafe they may internalize it negatively.

Entertainers provide a service and the entertained pay for services rendered. Beyond that, entertainers should have the right to choose if or how they want to extend the boundaries of this exchange. Here's an example: some entertainers don't sign autographs or take pictures with their fans. They feel as if that is too personal and uncomfortable for them. Other entertainers consider it an honor and love to do both. The same goes for fans. Some fans just buy the artist's music, respect his or her craft from afar and never go to live concerts. Other fans are 100% supportive. They will do it all and buy it all, concerts, t-shirts, CD's, DVD's, and the like. With that being said, the previous statement does not mean that the fans should not get or expect to get autographs or photos with the entertainer. It just means that depending on the situation, the entertainer or the circumstances, they may or may not get one. Much like the entertainer should never assume that every fan is going to buy every CD they release or go to every movie they star in. Depending on the day (just like everyone else), how the entertainer feels, or what they may be going through, they may seem off-putting, aloof, and anti-social or even mean.

The truth is, there isn't one entertainer who will ever make all of their fans happy all of the time and that is not his or her job. Much like the average person will never please or make everyone around him or her happy, and that's not his or her job either. But for a minute, it would be advantageous for fans to consider that everyone has good and bad days and there are days when many celebrities don't want to be noticed. But when the fan is in the moment and runs into a "famous" person, they are not thinking about how the celebrity feels. They are thinking about the thrill of meeting them. However, some fans won't accept this and will feel slighted by the entertainer if they don't make time for them. It is the adult's job to make sure that the child is shielded from the responses of fans, especially if they are negative. My immediate family (the five of us) has experienced countless situations where adults would pull at one of my sons to get his attention at airports, or walk up to them directly as if my kids were adults and begin asking for pictures and autographs.

Our family learned to develop a system in public (whenever there wasn't security traveling with us) where we would walk together in a way that an outsider couldn't run up and gain access to the son that they were reaching for. It took time but we developed eye contact, body gestures and secret words to let the others in the group know what was happening. We felt, at times, more like security than family when we were in public. By the time we arrived at our destination, we were exhausted just from trying to get from one destination to the other without incident. I would describe us as approachable but private people most of the time. However, my husband and I quickly learned that our unique situation (with family on television) presented advantages and disadvantages to us, and we had to accept the good and the bad and incorporate both into our new lifestyles.

This reality was a challenge for my oldest son Tyler when he was younger. He loved working and was willing to sacrifice sleep, hanging out with friends and free time to do so. However, he didn't like the attention that came along with his career choice. He wanted the work aspect of the success and had an exceptional work ethic at a very young age, but he was not interested in the "fame" aspect that resulted from it. For a long time, he didn't like or want to attend movie premieres, malls, amusement parks, or large family public outings because people would recognize him and begin pulling at him. He didn't like being noticed or being the center of attention. He just wanted to do the work but be treated like a normal kid. He wanted to go into the theater to watch a movie without walking the red carpet and doing interviews. He didn't like attending red carpet events and award ceremonies because of the interviews, photographers and everything else that accompanied celebrity attention. Many times he'd ask if we could sneak into the theater through the back door to avoid the paparazzi or photographers. Sometimes we did it as if we were playing a "hide-and-seek" game with everyone at the theater, except no one else knew about the game except us. He wasn't shy or anti-social, nor did he lack communication or social skills. He just preferred to be seen as an average kid who just happened to have an unusual job.

Over time he realized that walking the red carpets, participating in the special events, interviews, and appearances, were part of fulfilling his job description. Once he realized that this part of his career choice was just as significant as the part that he enjoyed, he changed his perspective. I am sure some people are reading this and saying, "Are you kidding? I would love all of that attention, being invited to red carpet events, hanging out with celebrities, television appearances, camera lights flashing in my face, photographers calling my name as I walk by, and people asking me questions about what I do." You would be in good company because many celebrities love all of the attention and show up to as many events as they can attend. There is nothing wrong with that if you have a legitimate reason for being there. However, sometimes it is better to be missed at an event or two than to be expected to show up everywhere. There are some events that you can't or don't want to pass up on though, because they are fun and exciting. I am sure some people will disagree with my last statement and say that a person who works or who wants to work in the industry should always be seen at industry events because you never know who you might meet. They have a very good point, but I have learned over the last 18 years that less is sometimes more. I have noticed, with some folks who seem to be at every event, that if you are seen everywhere, the novelty of what makes you special tends to wear off.

However, like my son, not all celebrities or entertainers want or enjoy the spotlight. There are wonderful and exciting elements to the entertainment industry. Some entertainers would prefer not to participate in many of them but understand that this is necessary to promote their current or future projects. For some of them, they are not interested in talking about anything but their work, the causes that they are passionate about and the community service that they are involved in. They would like to keep their private lives private. Some celebrities build enormous homes complete with movie theaters, bowling alleys, large basketball courts and many other forms of entertainment because they don't feel relaxed or comfortable in a public setting. Some feel that as long as they are seen as an entertainer, when they are out for an evening with family and friends they have to be "on" or "camera ready." They want to have a normal, uneventful night out at times. However, they feel like they are not going to enjoy the evening out as much as everyone else because of their notoriety. So they just hire a chef, order take out, or entertain at home. A parent has to be sensitive to how the child is feeling and must have regular discussions about this issue.

Once a person becomes famous on any level, their fans and other people want to have a measure of access to them - especially now that social media allows them to. They want to know where they live, what they eat, who they associate with, how much money they make, where they hang out, their personal and family secrets, who their family members are, the type of relationships they have with them, and anything else you can possibly imagine. Unfortunately, gossip and tabloid magazines, websites, television shows, and social media outlets know this and that is why they exist and are thriving. Their purpose is to get as much information out as possible to its targeted viewing audience (whether there is a measure of truth or not). These outlets cater to those people who are ready to buy, read, watch and believe anything and everything that is printed in the magazines, written on websites and flashed across their television screens.

I would like to throw in a valuable piece of advice right here. *Don't believe everything you read, scroll through, listen to, click on, or watch (good or bad).* There will be stories that are written, uploaded, and posted about your child (if fame is the journey) and you, for that matter. If you weigh and consider the positive and negative things that you read about others now, you won't freak out when you read something about someone you love in the future. Just because it is printed or posted doesn't mean it is true. Just because the information starts with "told to us by a reliable source," don't assume that the information is accurate. There are three sides to every story - your version, my version, and the truth, as God knows it. Unless you have all three versions confirmed by everyone involved and you are able to make a final analysis, assume that wherever you got the information from it may be a bit skewed. And when you read something about your child that is skewed, you will consider how many articles you read before about people that may not have been completely true. With that being said, there are many reputable, well written, produced, and ethical magazines, websites and television shows that serve as the veins that directly connect and affect the heart of the entertainment industry. How would one ever know about the great, awesome and exciting things anyone in this industry is doing without these outlets? I am grateful for them and the purpose that they serve. I applaud them and thank them for attempting to get the story right!

I will never forget reading the first article that supposedly featured a story (in our home town paper believe it or not) about my son's "Rags to Riches" journey. It was full of lies and I was livid as I read about my "made-up" life. According to the feature, I was a single mother from Brooklyn struggling to raise my "one" son, when he miraculously booked this television show that saved us from poverty. I was in shock when I read it the first time. So

I wrote down the writer's name and committed to call that magazine and give him a piece of my mind. After I got the family together (you know, my husband of 28 years and our three sons) to read it over again we began to laugh out loud. Once I vented, I felt a little better and quickly realized that people are going to write whatever they want to. The only good thing about the feature was that they actually found a great looking picture of Tyler and me on a red carpet somewhere. I thought, "At least it was actually a picture of the two of us."

# 5

## Be Careful What you Wish for...

This statement is a mouthful of caution and should be taken very seriously because most people can't foresee the reality of their aspirations while they are still dreaming. Let me explain. Although all of my sons are actors, I never desired for any of them to work in the entertainment industry, nor did I wish for them to become famous on television or in movies. However, I was confident that they would excel at whatever they decided to be in life because my husband and I purposed to raise them to be mentally, spiritually, and emotionally strong and focused. We wanted them to be benevolent, proactive, purposeful, and humble, yet confident in their abilities. We didn't walk into this industry naïve, excited, desperate, impressionable or clueless. We had a trunk full of life lessons stored away.

I had consolidated all of my music, publishing, ministry, and church leadership experience, conducted a great deal of research, spent a substantial amount of time in prayer and asking God, others and myself countless questions. I also purposed to surround my family with people who were smarter than we were. I have learned over the years (the hard way at times) that if you are the smartest person in your group of friends and associates, it's time for you to expand your group of friends and associates. I say this because everyone around you will be learning, growing and gleaning (and sometimes leeching) from you but they will not be able to return some type of knowledge or insight to you when you need it. If you are always the "go to" person, there is no one for you to "go to" when you are in need. So if you wish for your child to be in the industry, look for a group of positive people to surround you that you can learn from. If not, you will eventually become frustrated and drained realizing that you have been living your life on a treadmill of sorts. Your feet are in motion but you are not going anywhere.

On our very first day on a large studio lot, after my young sons and I had relocated to a new town, we found ourselves surrounded by a large group of unfamiliar industry people. I knew we would be staying for some time but had no idea how long. My son was working on a television project and while we had taken a break for lunch, a gifted artist began a conversation with me and shared some very interesting and sobering information that I have never forgotten. He said, "Get ready for your family and friends to surprise you."

I responded, "What do you mean?"

He continued, "People on the outside looking in always seem to think that entertainers have ten times as much fun, make ten times as much money, and live ten times more lavishly than we actually do. Those who work in the industry, once we become successful, don't really change much. We are who we are. It is other people's perceptions of who we are, or who they think we have become, that changes." I soon learned what he meant by that and he was absolutely right. Of course, there are many exceptions to this statement (example: entertainers and celebrities who seem to have forgotten that there was a time when they were not famous). However, even in those isolated cases, I believe that the match to the fire that engulfed those celebrities in the midst of their celebrity was lit years before and their celebrity status just fanned the flame. I will share more on that topic later.

I received a word of caution a few weeks later, while on set, from a veteran crewmember. He had worked behind the scenes on many projects. I was walking around the studio lot one day, attempting to take a breath from balancing home schooling my two younger sons in our trailer, running back and forth on set to look after my oldest son, trying to reserve a rental car, forcing myself to sit down long enough to eat and remembering that it was time to find new doctors so that I could make annual appointments for the family. I was given some solid advice. This awesome individual grabbed my hand, pulled me toward him, placed his arm around my shoulder and said softly, "Let's go for a walk and talk for a minute." He had to see how frazzled I was and knew that I didn't trust many people at the time, especially around my boys.

We chitchatted for a while, as I continued looking around to make sure all of my sons were where I left them. Then the conversation quickly shifted. He said, "Your life is about to change and some of the people around you will start to change, too. Don't let it bother you because they *will* try to affect you. You have three boys to take care of so don't let them get to you. People will soon be coming from everywhere asking for money. Everyone will be trying to get their hands in your pocket." His comments surprised me, but I kept listening. He said many valuable things that day that forced me to pay attention. Then he concluded with an interesting piece of advice. "I can tell that you are one of those generous Christian women who want to help people and make a difference in the world. Just remember that you can't rescue everyone and not everyone wants to do better. They don't want to do what you did to get it, but they do want to take what you have and suck you dry. They don't see what I see watching you on set every day, nor would they care to see this part. They just want to leech off of you." His terse words of wisdom were sobering. However, there was something about how he spoke to me that was comforting. I somehow knew that although we were in an unfamiliar town, around unfamiliar people, that we - me and especially, my boys - would be ok. I didn't really comment, because I had no idea what he was talking about. I just listened, thanked him and filed that large and uncomfortable nugget of information away in my long-term memory just in case I needed it.

Less than a week later, I was introduced to those sobering realities. Folks came knocking at my door, ringing my phone, sending me emails, leaving voice messages, sending me letters in the mail and sending me countless texts. Once it started, it never stopped. I must admit though, at first, I was surprised by a few of the people who came slithering by. Some I expected, but I must admit that others and their comments, logic, constant harassment and responses to my answers, challenged and tested my impulses and my character. In my teens and twenties, I didn't have a problem letting people know how I felt about them or any given situation, without a filter, especially if I thought they were wrong or disrespectful to my immediate family or me. But as I got older and matured, I learned to pick my words more carefully, so this was a challenging time for me. I began to hear from people asking for money for everything - startup businesses, rent, starting a record label, helping them get out of financial messes that they created, helping them resolve bad business deals, paying off house loans, taking over mortgages, plastic surgery, getting out of debt, buying a new car, paying for hospital bills, paying off mortgages and some things that are just too ridiculous to mention. I had some people sending messages via other people asking for money or a job working in Hollywood. For several years, I walked around feeling as if I had a hot dry towel wrapped around my face. I felt smothered, weighted and cornered, but I had to ignore the noise as best as I could because I had to protect and look after my sons. My focus needed to be on them.

During that time, emotional manipulation and chatter was intense. When you love people you want to help them, even if you don't realize at the time that you are being used, misunderstood and mistreated. Around this time I was totally overwhelmed, drained and I must admit, saddened by a couple of family members and associates. My thought was, "What is all of this? Where did all of this come from? When did I become so popular to you? When my immediate family and I needed money, we worked it out or did without as if we had no other options and eventually our situation worked itself out. No one ever considered how much money a month it takes to operate and maintain my family's life." I even tried saying that to a few folks and was surprisingly met by, "I can't believe you are talking to me this way. Your tone is so disrespectful. All I wanted was..." Over time, I became stressed, sleep deprived, resentful, bitter and no longer wanted to answer my phone, check my emails or return phone messages. What was most distressing was that these people weren't strangers.

I would look at my phone to check to see who was calling when it rang and hit the decline or silent button because the thought of talking to certain people would be exhausting and frustrating. I thought, "Did you ever stand back and think that you are asking this of a person who has three small children? You have no idea how much money we have, how many bills we have, how much savings we have, and you didn't even care enough to ask!" Many times, I felt so ridiculous as I listened to myself trying to explain to people why I was not giving them any money or any *more* money. Every time they would ask, the dollar amount got higher and higher as if just by them asking I was somehow obligated to explain my financial status to them. At that time, it became challenging for me to find the balance between helping, ignoring emotional manipulation, and supporting. It was happening so often that after a while, all of the voices asking to come over to visit, wanting to reconnect because it's been "such a long time since we spoke," begging, and leeching all sounded like one muffled sound. I thought, "This is all because you saw one of them on a commercial or on a television show? I wish it had never aired." I must admit that some of the harassment was my fault because I am generous by nature and would volunteer to help people if I could. At times, I knew that many of them could have done more to help themselves but I wanted to "encourage them" by helping a little. That was a bad idea.

All of this was happening while we relocated without my husband, who still had three more years left at his job before retiring in New York. We own a home in New York so we could not just uproot without a plan. So, I was actually living as if I was a single mom, even though my husband flew in every two weeks to visit. I was home schooling my sons (in trailers, an unfamiliar apartment, and on studio sets, getting to know new people whom I wasn't sure if I could trust), overseeing their business, legal, personal, and talent affairs, and establishing healthy environments for them to adjust to. Thank God my sister and a couple of girlfriends came out for a long while to help me balance home schooling and studio set life. One of my daughters in ministry had relocated about a year before we did and helped to make the transition easier; she helped out with the boys as well. Several friends, church members and family came out to visit, which helped so much to take the focus off of my stressors. However, eventually they all had to go back home. Then I was reminded again of the stressors but became stronger. During this time, I was amazed at how many of the wrong people would call or email to ask to come visit, meet certain entertainers, or get a role in a movie but would never, ever ask how we were doing. Only those friends and family members who never or rarely asked for anything for themselves would just call to say "I love you" or "How are you and the boys doing?" or "We are praying for you guys." I guess everyone else just assumed that since we were in the industry, we had to be doing quite well, so there was no need to ask.

Thankfully, we still had our core support system, or village, of family and friends who didn't care what we were doing (although they were proud of the accomplishments). They loved us, prayed with and for us, played hard with us and were there to listen and give sound advice. The number of our original core village of family and friends has diminished over the years, but God has sent many other loving, ethical, genuine and non-toxic people to replace them. The core didn't and still don't care about who we know, what the next project is and how much money my sons make. They never harassed us for money or wanted anything from us. These people were and still are breaths of fresh air in the midst of the toxic relationships that we eliminated, and I so appreciate them. When I see their numbers flash on my phone or their email pop up in the inbox, I just smile because I know that peace will meet me on the other side of the phone or email. I thank God for considerate people.

As far as the other folks were concerned, it took some time to learn how to deal with emotional, spiritual and relational manipulation, friendly fire, professional imposters, industry bullying and familial entitlement. However, I eventually figured it out through prayer, fasting and studying scriptures for discernment. While adjusting to our new life on the West Coast, creating a safe environment for myself and for my boys, and learning to balance our schedules, long work hours, school, down time, fun outings, and sleep, I began to learn how to deal with leeches and opportunists. I learned how to decode conversations, detect ulterior motives, and dissect the negative voices from the positive ones. After a while I started to feel like an empowered word-ninja without apology, explanation or guilt. I also shifted my footing, which repositioned my posture. My stance was different, my character stood front and center, my voice and words became more deliberate, terse, confident and sword-like, especially to one person who wouldn't take "no" for an answer. After a while, those experiences became fascinating teaching tools and life lessons to educate my sons about.

We learned how to make personal adjustments and determine that it is ok if everyone doesn't like you, understand or agree with what you are doing. My sons learned about all types of people and the power that came with using the word "NO" without explanation or apology. I told them (really my oldest at the time) specifically who certain people were, what they wanted and how they responded when they didn't get it. I did this because one day they would get older and the folks who are now harassing me (and others) may come to harass them. They needed to know how to handle these folks. I taught them, "Everyone deserves your respect; not everyone deserves your trust. Some people may surprise you, even hurt you, and try to make you feel guilty. However, if you don't have peace about doing something for someone, don't do it. Even if that person is your mom." I wanted them to know how serious this was. I wanted them to know that their voice is powerful and valuable and their choices should be respected. I wanted to use myself as an example, so that they would understand that no one is exempt from the point I was trying to make.

I told them, "If, in the future, I start to act the way these folks are acting, you are not obligated to accommodate me. I don't believe that you guys would leave me stranded on the street if I was destitute, so I am not worried about you disregarding me in the future. So, if you don't have peace about it, don't do it. You have the right and power to control what you do with your own money. Don't volunteer to put that burden on your shoulders. It's too heavy and will weigh you down." I often create scenarios and ask unexpected questions of them at the most random times to catch them off guard. Many times they look at me as if I'm crazy but most of the time they are ready and equipped to respond well. I usually give them a high-five or sing an awful impromptu song to let them know that I am pleased with their answers. They either video tape my unique performance, stand in amazement staring at me or just walk away, shaking their heads as if to say, "Yep...she's crazy." Just as long as they get the point I was trying to make, I'm happy.

On another note, some parents of child stars in this industry "guilt trip" their children into giving them money, buying them things and doing things with their money that they should not be doing. That is not fair. Parents should not be financial bullies because they have legal authority of the child. That is why there should be someone else (other than the parent) who is aware of a child's finances, like an accountant, for the sake of accountability (but more on that later). Please don't do this to your child. Don't be the person that stresses out your child. I have never seen a parent who raised their child properly (in or out of the industry) who made major sacrifices for their children but was left destitute because the child didn't take care of them when they got older. The good news is many parents have interests that are not related or connected to what their child does in the industry. That is a healthy and productive thing to do and it will keep the child (and the parent) from panicking as the child approaches legal age.

I digress... the gifted artist and crewmember shared their advice with me just in time. I learned very quickly, and carefully taught (and continue to teach) my sons and others, that people will *expect* you to provide them with careers, money, homes, cars, lead roles in films, relationships with stars, unlimited and unpaid visits to your events, access to parties, back stage passes, front row seats, first class flights, unlimited invitations to your house (to stay indefinitely), award shows, red carpet passes, agents, managers and executives' telephone numbers and email addresses. People whom you least expect may also disappoint you by proving to you that they can't or can no longer be trusted. Some people may expect a free ride to success without working for it or paying any dues of their own. However, don't get too discouraged. See the situation for what it really is, and try not to take it personally even though it may be challenging. Create boundaries for those types of relationships. Some of the toxic relationships may be severed forever but don't allow it to make you bitter towards them or other people, although it may be so very easy to do so. Many folks have no idea what it takes to maintain life or the responsibilities of being where you are or to get where you are going. So don't waste your time trying to explain it to them. Keep your focus because time has a way of working things out.

At times, all some of them care about is what they "think" they know about you and your current situation. They don't consider all of the many expenses you have, in-spite all of the money you may or may not make. Many people can easily see and assume that the grass is greener on the other side, but never seem to take the time to consider how much work it takes to get the grass as green as it is. And even if they did know or consider it, most people wouldn't care or be willing to follow your lead and make their own grass as green as yours. I have had some very sad conversations with people who were so focused on what they wanted, they didn't even want to know how we were doing or how hard we were working to make what they saw happen. They simply could not hear me past their own voices. The crazy part is, if the tables were turned and you were to ask them for a chunk of their paycheck (or their child's savings), they would look at you like you were crazy and say something like, *"Are you crazy? I didn't see you at my job last week earning this money, so why would you ask me something stupid like that? No!"* But wait, it get's crazier. They won't even realize (or care) that they are actually asking you for money that your *child* earned.

Speaking of your child, if by chance you have more than one child but one is getting more exposure than the others, you may find that folks around you will put more value on the more exposed child than the others.

We have had very unfortunate experiences where we would walk into a room and only my oldest son would be acknowledged (when he was the only one known to be on television). Or people would approach my oldest son as if my two younger sons, who were standing right next to him, were invisible. We have had experiences where people would only invite the son who was on television at the moment to events. I have gotten phone calls from people who only asked about the one who was most visible at the time. When they all became visible at the same time, it really became interesting. Phone calls were coming from folks I hadn't heard from in decades who wanted to keep in touch or see the boys. A few of the calls were genuine, but most of them were not. Then all of a sudden, according to them, I became "full of myself," or "too Hollywood." At the time these situations were sobering and disappointing, but they aren't anymore. They serve as great teaching tools.

Here is some more advice. You don't have to feel obligated, stressed out or pressured to let people into your world and family if you are not comfortable with it. You don't have to help people who are forcing you to give them money either. You are in control of how you give, and whom you give money to. In many cases, no matter how many people you attempt to help, some of them may keep coming back for more. Then, when you have had enough and say "no more" to any of them, you may then become (in their minds) full of yourself, a horrible person and stingy. They will resent you for it. It is at that very moment when you (according to their logic) "have changed" or "you just don't want anyone else to get ahead like you did." They never consider working, sacrificing or struggling just as hard as you did, for as long as you did. They just resolve that you are supposed to help them whenever they need or want you to. That type of relationship is toxic. Toxic relationships are dangerous.

Let me make something very clear. I believe that we are all blessed to be a blessing to others, no matter how much or how little money we make or how much we accomplish in life. I believe that we must all have a heart of generosity and benevolence, because if we live long enough, we will all need help from someone else, to some degree. However, my helpful advisors were not telling me not to help people or refrain from being generous. It wasn't until I was knee deep in my situation when I realized that there was a difference between being generous to those in need and giving money or my time away to a leech or someone who wanted an easy remedy to their situation. Over a short period of time, I began to pray for more discernment. I have always been a discerning person but at times it became difficult to determine a person's true motives through their tears, sad stories, emotional manipulation, and polite requests. Over time, I learned the difference in most cases. I have learned that I can remain benevolent and help as many people as I need to or can, but I have also learned how to say no without explanation or apology. It took some time to get there with some people, but I finally got there.

On another note, if you are going to financially help (certain) people, instead of *giving* that person money, *loan* it to them. This helps them to keep their dignity and also holds them accountable to pay you back, even if they never do. If by chance they never intended to pay you back, at least they will think twice about asking you for more money. However, there are some people (and I have experienced them too) who will continue to come back for more no matter how much they have gotten from you in the past, even though they promised to pay you back. So don't think you are crazy when that happens. One of the things that I do when I loan someone money is I quietly accept the fact that I will never see the money again so I won't be disappointed if I don't see it again. I will expect it back, of course, but I won't be sitting around looking, asking or waiting for it. I won't even ask for it back after I have made my initial point at the time that I gave them the money. If a person can remember to ask for it, he or she can also remember to pay it back. If the latter doesn't happen, the obligation to resolve the issue is on the person who asked for the money, not on me. From that point forward, I purpose to give the person the benefit of the doubt and go on with my life so as not to develop any bitterness or resentment towards them. Also, don't give/loan any amount of money away that you are going to need back. If giving/loaning the money will cause you to have a negative personal or financial outcome if you don't get it back, keep it in your wallet or bank account. You can help the person in other ways.

With that being said, there are several people, organizations, and others that I volunteer to give to consistently and help just because it is the right thing to do, not because I feel obligated to do so. Here is how I determine if I am giving to the right person or organization. If I don't have peace about giving it to them, they don't get it. If I feel pressured to give it to them, they don't get it. If they appear entitled to it, they don't get it. That goes for everyone…now. Finally, many times, money is not what a person really needs any way. Often times, people need money management skills, insight, discipline, or they simply need to stop spending money on things that they don't really need at the moment. Other people need to stop asking others for money and learn how to fend for themselves and still others need tools to help them accomplish this. I have learned the power behind an old proverb I once read as a young adult: "Give a man a fish, and he can eat for a day; teach him how to fish, and he can eat for a lifetime." I love helping people by teaching them what I have learned over the years. I have embraced, applied and am purposed to continue to execute it and it has been beneficial to so many. There have been others that don't want to put in the time and effort to do what it takes to "eat for a lifetime" so to speak, but if I can help one person, then I am grateful for the chance!

So as you begin wishing, consider the good and the bad that is connected to the manifestation of that wish. Your negative realities may not be the same as mine because your tests and lessons may be different. Life will always present challenges. Challenges are normal and I believe necessary because they stretch us and prompt us to rise to that challenge. However, as you are wishing and declaring consider how the world or environment around you will be different. Begin to posture and prepare yourself for it. Don't be afraid of the negative side of what your hopes bring, just be careful and prepare for them so that you can be ready to overcome them.

# 6

## What Type of Parent are you?

*I* have had the honor of meeting some of the most wonderful parents in the entertainment industry. Along with their families, they have been able to find a balance between the celebrity life and a normal life. It is both refreshing and inspiring. These families are healthy, and the kids are well developed and strive to keep that balance at the forefront of their lives. I celebrate these parents, because there is no tailored rulebook to follow for each family. Traveling this road is not an easy one, but it is possible for child entertainers to survive and thrive in all areas. With these parents, it is obvious to see that family comes first and the wellness and soundness of mind for the children is paramount. On the other hand, I have met parents who have made many mistakes and awful choices because they were ignorant to situations that confronted them. They were looking for the next big payday, networking with the next hot producer or staying relevant rather than finding a balance that works best for the child. Obviously if they had a chance to revisit certain moments and choose differently, I am sure these parents would. Nevertheless, some of these guardians have learned from their mistakes and have made the appropriate changes in their behaviors and decision-making. A few of them now have to watch their children (who are now young adults) make some of the same mistakes they did. The end result may not be the best for everyone involved, but eventually the life lessons will serve beneficial for something or someone else in the future.

## *The Pushy and Unethical Parent*

I have also met some parental disasters whose children are recipients of negative and destructive behavior and activities. Children are forced by their parents to do things that even the child knows is not appropriate. Children have come to me asking why their parents allow them to say certain lines, work in inappropriate scenes, or why they have to be put in certain situations when they clearly don't want to be there. Some parents don't realize that they are neglecting their child. These parents are endangering their welfare, not adhering to or even knowing the child labor laws by allowing their children to work long hours, or work in environments that are unsafe, immoral and inappropriate. Some are spending all of their child's money and are not paying taxes on income. When I initially spoke with a few parents about it, I was shocked by some of the responses. Some understand that they are breaking laws but don't want to make the necessary adjustments, speak up or get industry heads upset for fear that their child will be blackballed (secretly rejected or removed from future opportunities to work in the industry by people in powerful positions) or won't get to work with certain industry insiders again. Some of them never expected to obey the laws and planned to let producers see that they were willing to let their children do what other parent's wouldn't just in case there was another project coming along that their child could be hired for instead.

There are parents whose children are home schooled on paper but the children aren't learning anything. These children are academically deficient, because the parents are convinced that their child will have a successful career for the rest of their lives and don't need academics to fall back on. Instead of having lessons during the day, they are sleeping in late after a long night going to industry events that they should not be attending. Some parents forge school records and report cards so that the child can get a work permit renewed. They know that the child can't work without a current work permit, and a child can't get a current work permit unless they are in satisfactory academic standing. The parent is teaching the child (through their unethical actions) to do whatever it takes to get ahead. Some of the parents, who know that their children are behind in school, will focus on nothing but trying to get their children another booking. Even though they haven't done any school work for weeks and sometimes months, the parent will continue to drive their children to every audition in the hopes that they'll land the role of a lifetime that will escort them into adult stardom.

The truth is, based on my research, experience and estimations, less than 1% of child stars become adult stars. If you consider all of the children, in all of the neighborhoods, in all of the cities, in all of the states in America who are training, practicing and trying to make it to New York or Hollywood, the number of those kids who actually end up, at the very least, doing extra work on a successful television show is an extremely small number. This is not a pessimistic outlook but rather what the reality looks like for most children. I understand that some parents will think, "Well somebody has to be a part of the 1%, and I'm going to make sure it is my child." I celebrate and encourage that frame of mind. However, if you are wrong, then what? If the journey doesn't work out the way you thought it would, what happens next? I will talk more about this later. At any rate, because of this, the child, and the family for that matter, needs a plan "B" and most parents don't have one for their children because they don't feel like they need one. It is important that the child and the parent purpose to have a life outside of their quest for show business because life can get very stressful beating the stardom pavement day in and day out. The child needs to have something else going on besides auditioning. These parents need to have something else going on in their own lives outside of the child's as well.

## *The Neglecting and Partying Parent*

When I suggest that the parent should have a life outside of the child's life that doesn't mean for you, the parent, to neglect your child and leave him or her on set so that you can live a Hollywood lifestyle. Unfortunately, those parents exist too. There are parents who party just as much as, or even more, as everyone else in the industry. They will volunteer to show up for a premiere, promotional event, sometimes dressed ready to embarrass their kids. The child may get the invitation to an event but the parent is the first person out of the car and into the venue. That is a pitiful sight to see. Most parents are not like that, fortunately. Many of them are quiet from an industry standpoint. My family would probably fall in that category and we do it on purpose for the most part. We don't attend every event, every movie premiere, and definitely not every party. We have our events that we go to regularly, friends that we support and hang out with, annual outings that we attend, and charity/philanthropic events that we support and host. We have a wonderful and eclectic host of people that we associate with who are our circle of close friends, family and associates in the industry. We celebrate with them, support their events and causes and have a wonderful time hanging out with them. However, if you ask a socialite or regular party hopper who or which families are most likely to be seen at a party, our name will probably never be on that list. We tend to do a lot of our socializing where there aren't many media cameras. We have found that some times less is more and better to have people miss you than to expect to see you all the time. That mindset may not work for everyone, but it works for us.

The partying parents are a sad sight to see. They don't know when to go home and they don't realize how their appearance and behavior is affecting their child. There are parents who will use their child's name or celebrity to get into a venue that the child cannot even get into because of age restrictions. I will never forget my first experience seeing that. My heart broke for the child. We were at an award show after party. I had heard some unflattering things spoken about this parent but had not met them so I chose to give them the benefit of the doubt. Then I heard this loud commotion before I entered the green room. The parent was making a public, drunken spectacle of herself while the child tried to ignore the scene. Over the years, the child began to imitate the parent's behavior and they both became walking disasters. The saying, "The fruit doesn't fall far from the tree," is absolutely true in this case and now everyone in the industry knows what to expect when either of them walk in the room. This is not the type of parent to be if the goal is to be respected.

## The Dreaded Negative Stage Parent

Contrary to what you might believe, all is not well on television and movie sets. There is bullying (from children and parents), peer pressure, parent-to-parent strife and even physical fighting. The crazy stories that are told about kids and parents on the soccer and baseball fields also exist on television, movie, and commercial sets. There are some parents who have quit their jobs, and their child is the primary or the sole financial provider for the household. Sometimes the child knows he is supporting the family and the stress and pressure for him to perform is evident and almost criminal. At times the parent is spending all of the child's money, except the 15% of their gross income that must go into a blocked trust/Coogan account until the child turns 18 years old.

I attempt to get along with all parents because it is best for my child, the cast, crew, production and the other children. Generally speaking, it usually works out well. However, there are a few parents that make this difficult, and it is best to keep a distance from them but it never hurts to be cordial and say hello and goodbye. In most cases, the behavior of the parents set the tone for the behavior of the children. There are mean-spirited parents in the industry who are raising mean-spirited children. Nevertheless, there are lessons to learn from them too, even if the lesson is how not to act.

An important lesson to learn quickly is that each production project is a job and it is temporary. Even though it feels like the paycheck and the experience will last forever, it will come to an end at some point, usually sooner than later. When it does, there is no need to associate with the parents or children again, unless the children just happen to work together in the future. But you will have to tolerate certain mindsets and behaviors, as long as it doesn't get out of hand, until the production of the show comes to an end. This is necessary, at times, in order to keep the peace on set. However, there have been times when the production company and even the network have to get involved. That is never a good thing, and in many cases it will result in recasting a child, changes in production schedules or premature cancellation of a project.

Fortunately, most of my experiences have been good and some have even been wonderful! The good far outweighs the bad and many of the children and parents that are out of line don't work as much or as long as the others anyway. The casting and production companies soon learn to recognize these folks and won't hire the child even if he or she is the best kid for the role.

One of the reasons why I rarely "help" kids get into the business - unless I really feel a pull to do it - is because I don't know how emotionally healthy the child, the parents or the family is, and I don't know what the child's purpose is. The child may be very talented but might be more suited to perform at Community Theater, at school, doing something creative on the Internet or at a children's hospital. There are so many ways and avenues to take if a child is talented these days. It just so happens that the first thing most people think about when they think "Performing" or "Talent" is Hollywood, Broadway or show business. That is understandable, but it is not always the best choice. This business is not set up to fulfill everyone's purpose in life. If a person is pursuing a show business career and this is not the place for them, they will be wasting valuable time that they will never get back. If I knew that I helped someone get into the business and that very opportunity was the opened door that led to his or her or the family's demise, I would not be ok with that. That's why I prefer to give parents tools and information so that they can make their own decision by doing the work for the child that it takes to get and remain here.

If by chance they make the wrong decision, the blood is not on my hands and I will know that I tried to point them in the right direction. I have seen parents make bad decisions without a plan, safety guards, proper understanding or realistic expectations. I have seen parents' personalities change from being reserved and easy going to self-absorbed, stressed, competitive and petty, in a matter of months. They went from being child focused, cooperative, level headed and teachable newcomers, to becoming crazy parents! Don't be a crazy stage parent. The goal is to be your version of a sane and levelheaded parent who happens to have a child in the industry. It is not hard to do. It is a matter of focus, perspective, respect and choice. There are also a few key things to remember:

- The world doesn't revolve around you or your child.
- Accept the fact that you don't know everything about the project that your child is working on, so talk less and listen more.
- You, the parent, were probably not hired *by* the production company. So you are not on salary *with* the production company. So *your* opinion about the project is not warranted, requested, or welcomed.
- You are not the parent of other people's children. It is probable that you do not have all of the information about a situation so take a couple steps back, and consider that your take on the situation may be a bit skewed.
- Your child is not the most talented kid ever created.
- You are not the show runner or the department head so don't act like one.
- You must have a life outside of your child's entertainment life.
- Stop talking negatively about people or hanging around people who do. That is not a good look.
- You are your child's parent and it is important to stay in that lane and be the parent, unless unusual circumstances require something else from you.
- Children can be vicious and disrespectful to others. If this is your child, find out who taught him/her how to act that way (even if it was you), address it and deal with it quickly.

## *The Alert Parent*

Hopefully by now, you have started a personal inspection to determine what's best for your child. I am assuming that all families and households have rules, regulations, morals, statutes, or a particular lifestyle that they live by. Alert parents learn how to survey environments to determine if it is safe for the child or not. Alert parents know how to detect *yellow* or *red flags* that serve as *warning signs* of *dangers* ahead. What would be a red flag for my family dynamic may not be an issue for your family or vice versa. However, it is the parent's responsibility to know what the warning signs are and address them as soon as they are presented. Every child needs boundaries. When they are on a creative path in an adult world, these boundaries are even more important. They serve as bumper guards to keep your child going and growing in the right direction. The entertainment industry is set up as an adult industry that just happens to have minors employed as well. Primarily adults run the entertainment industry. It is the parent's responsibility to protect their children, provide a safe place for them, and teach them how to protect themselves. So what exactly are examples of a waving flag? A *waving flag* is an offer, opportunity or sugges-tion that instantly makes you feel uneasy or makes you second-guess your natural flow of forward motion. Sometimes the waving flag can come from production, or a key player on the project that your child is working on. If you feel uncomfortable about changes, lines, scenes, or the environment, speak up. Tell the studio teacher, who is also your child's welfare worker on the project, and call your agent or manager.

I will give you an example of a waving flag for one of my kids. As a Christian family we don't celebrate Halloween. We are not legalistic or religious about it; we just choose not to celebrate it. There are many reasons why but in general we don't participate in activities that promote satanic content, witchcraft or occult activity. Not everything Halloween-related falls under that category, and there are exceptions to all things, of course. With that being said, let's say that there is an exciting role in a new feature film that is rumored to be a box office hit that comes into the agent's office for a boy who practices witchcraft and the occult. Casting requests for my son to come in and says that this role could make his career and the movie is set to have at least one sequel. This is the role that all of the kids his age want to be considered for. There are super hero elements to it with lots of action, special effects, and adventure. The child actor who books the role will get to perform lots of cool stunts, cast spells, massacre a couple of bad guys and pretend to conjure up demons to acquire supernatural powers in the movie. It sounds like a great opportunity for one of my sons, but the storyline goes against our beliefs. Unless the story lines call for the character to be fighting or standing against the dark powers that be, or something along those lines, we would pass on it. The agent calls to say that casting understands our position but asks if my son would come in a read for it anyway. They may be able to alter a line or two. The flags are already waving because there are too many variables in the script that we are not going to do. So, if my son goes in and they like him, there is more of an obligation to sign on for the role even if my son is not comfortable doing it. So, it's best to pass on the audition and be glad that we did than to get tangled up in it and wish we had not.

There are exceptions to every rule and each script is different, but that is where we stand on the issue of Halloween, satanic practices or the occult. So, if a script or offer comes in with obvious satanic overtones, although these are subtle or the role is created as an animation or something innocent, this role will serve as a waving red flag for us not to do it. So instead of getting in too deep with the project or having to back out at the last minute because our assumptions are confirmed, my sons, especially the ones under age, will pass on the script, the audition or the offer. No matter what their agent, manager, lawyer or casting says (although they wouldn't say much because they know us very well by now), the answer is going to be no.

To be totally honest, I have purposed to recognize yellow flags instead of red ones because I have found that, at times, red flags are signs of imminent danger. Imminent danger suggests to me that something is fast approaching.

Depending on how fast a person is moving in the opposite direction of said danger, one may not move fast enough. I practice not to put others or myself in red flag situations; rather, I tend to address "yellow flag" situations. Obviously no one has control of every situation; that's where prayer comes into play. When I have control of the situation or environment, we have developed ways to recognize yellow flags. Recognizing yellow flags require discernment, wisdom and alertness. I believe that I developed these qualities during my time in the music business and in ministry. My previous experiences helped me to adjust a little better and faster, to my sons' celebrity in public. However, we were caught off guard a few times by fans or situations that we didn't see coming in or near our vicinity. We were at times caught off guard by behavior or certain comments. After several unexpected scenarios played out in public that threatened the safety or peace of mind of my boys or our family, we had to develop several different types of security systems depending on the environment we were in. We learned to anticipate red flag situations. For most anticipated red flag situations, we would avoid them altogether. However, for unavoidable yellow flag situations, we would put one of our security plans in place.

These situations can emerge through unexpected opportunities, unusual situations or unsafe environments. However, there are those red/yellow flags that can present themselves through people. Have you ever had one of those moments when you were casually talking with someone and something about the conversation rubbed you the wrong way or there was something about the person that made you feel uncomfortable? At the end of the conversation, the person asked you for your contact information and you reluctantly gave it to them, even though you really didn't want to. Then, over the course of time, you discovered why you felt uncomfortable during the conversation and why you should not have given them your contact information? That experience represents a yellow flag situation. I believe that we have all had situations, at some time in our lives, similar to this. I also believe that we all have an internal alarm that goes off when something is not quite right, but some of the alarms are louder or more obvious than others. I believe that this is because some people are more sensitive to them. Some folks are more aware because they practice listening or responding to them more than others.

- My advice to you is, listen to your gut, and don't dismiss a waving yellow flag.
- If you are not sure at times, ask your children how they feel in certain situations. You may be surprised by what they say.
- An alert parent is a good protector.

Again, I don't frequently help people "get into show business" - unless I feel that God is leading me to do so - because it serves as yellow flags for my sons and me. Many folks will assert themselves to reach out and ask for connections but they have not done or want to do the prep work and it is distracting because folks actually expect me to stop what I'm doing and "make them famous." Another reason is, I don't know what they're supposed to be doing in or out of the industry. They have to figure that out and finding their own way is the best way to do it. I have found that if this business is not a part of your purpose and you get tangled up in it, you will either waste a considerable amount of your time, lose your way or end up regretting it. I have total peace with staying alert and giving sound advice, encouragement and tools that will work no matter where a person ends up in life. Of course, some people, especially those who feel entitled, will get offended if I/we don't help them but they will either get over it or stay under it, the choice is theirs. I have learned the hard way that it is better not to "Hook People Up" and wish I had, than to "Hook Them Up" and wish I hadn't.

As with all situations and learning experiences, there are exceptions to every rule but in the world of entertainment, a parent needs to know what "type of parent" is best for his/her child. So please consider being the positive type of parent and learn to recognize the color of the flags, for the sake of your child. If you do, I don't believe you will regret it.

# 7

## *Scenarios*

*T*he hope for fame puts certain parents in an "at any cost" or a "do or die" frame of mind. Wanting your child to be famous is not an entirely bad or negative attitude to have. However, there needs to be realistic realms of consideration. I am a woman of proactive movement, but I believe that there is more than one way or road to accomplishing a goal. I am also an optimistic realist. I have learned that there comes a time when we have to reevaluate our plans and course of actions to adjust to certain realities. Some people allow the focus on a goal to overshadow everything else in their lives, and they lose sight of important matters that are staring them right in the face. These important matters need to be addressed, but some people may not notice them. Parents can get so preoccupied with fame, or what they perceive fame to be, that they leave a trail of emotional, relational and financial debris behind them in the process.

I have seen marriages destroyed, siblings neglected, families fractured, finances depleted, houses foreclosed, kids abused, and former child stars permanently damaged beyond repair. If you are having problems in your marriage before your child enters the industry or if your child has problems with discipline or issues with self-esteem, you have big problems on your hands. The entertainment system, and choices people make within it, seems to be set up to weaken the family structure instead of strengthen it. If there are marital problems beforehand, the stressors of the industry are set up to magnify them. Make sure that your family is healthy and your marriage is healthy or healthy enough before you proceed.

When the possibility of fame knocks on the door, some parents immediately quit their jobs prematurely for their new quest and soon learn that the knock was not fame but child prostitution. Other families even relocate to certain areas (usually New York or California) with hopes of fame. They have no pending jobs for the child or the parents. Some find themselves homeless, or living out of cars, in just a few short months. They listened to the advice of folks who told them how to get ahead. In a short time, their money is depleted due to extended hotel stays, acting and dance classes. Many parents have good intentions. But they don't have any direction, a plan for worse case scenarios, legitimate agent/manager representation, possible acting prospects, contractual jobs lined up or a support contact once they arrive.

Believe it or not, some people, many of whom I just described, will read this portion of the book and ignore what they just read and go for it anyway. I respect and applaud your spunk, courage, confidence and tenacity to throw caution to the wind. Let me ask you a question though. If you knew that it would take five years of auditions, close calls, disappointments and depleted funds before your child booked his first national commercial, would you be ok with that? If you are not ok with that, I understand. For those who are ok with the five-year commitment, I applaud you too and hope everything good comes your way because there is a possibility that it will. However, I am also a woman who believes that wisdom is a valuable personal treasure and would suggest to you to look around and assess your surroundings. If after you have thought about this for a while, you find that the pursuit is worth the sacrifice and you are willing to take that chance, then your next step will probably be a no brainer for you. Somebody's kid is going to make it; it may just be yours! My prayer is that your retrospective glance will echo that same resolve! But until then, let's look at a few scenarios and play the "What If" game.

# Dreams Deferred

What happens if after the "at any cost" pursuit for fame, the road ends and fame is not waiting to greet you with open arms? Has your child failed? Have you, as a parent, failed? How is his self-esteem? What now? The industry isn't welcoming to every kid. I know of a host of talented people, some young and some older. Many of them have been auditioning and studying their singing and acting craft for years, and some are now in their 20s, 30s and even 40s and still believe that it will happen. Some of them were focused on sports. They are now beyond discouraged because they invested time, energy and money into what they believed to be their path, and the path has led them to a dead end of sorts. They still love what they do and haven't given up, but they are becoming realistic about the next steps in their lives. They are redefining what "making it" looks like. The same thing has happened with some parents. They sacrificed their jobs, their kid's education, homes and some relationships for their child's dream and now their child is graduating high school with no future entertaining prospects, limited education and very few skills. The parents are disappointed and the child, now a young adult, is indifferent toward all things entertainment. Both the parent and child have lost their excitement and enthusiasm for what they thought their lives were going to be. There are emerging signs of hidden resentment and regret between parent and child.

I knew someone who had spent her 20s and 30s trying to land a career that would fulfill her and pay her bills. She was very frustrated and disappointed in coming to a realization that surprised even her. She said, "I have been focused on this for so long. I don't know how to do anything else. This is all I know how to do." It seemed as if she felt like she had cheated herself by not diversifying her skills and wasn't sure what to do next. She is not the only one who feels this way, but she had options that she had not considered until that moment.

## The Rollercoaster Ride

My family and I are rollercoaster nutcases! We love the excitement of these rides from start to finish and we never seem to get tired of them. The entertainment industry is like an amusement park full of exciting attractions. The rollercoaster, however, represents the true and sobering reality of show business. For some people, this high-speed show business ride seems to take off immediately and it is almost impossible to catch your breath or see clearly what is happening around you. Then all of a sudden the ride comes to a complete stop. It takes a minute to adjust to the motionless position that confirms that the ride has ended and it is time to get off. However, many people never get to ride on the rollercoaster of the entertainment industry. For those that do, a large portion of them just get a small window of opportunity to experience the industry and for some there are no second trips.

There have been many children who got their big break in a small role on a big movie or as a series regular on a successful television show. It felt like everything would last forever. However, overnight everything just stopped. The commercial stopped airing on television. The hype of the movie diminished and the television show ran its course. The money stopped coming, the interview requests ceased, the invitations ended, and the demand for appearances disappeared. Panic sets in. There is, for a moment, what seems like dead silence as the reality sinks in. For some, it only lasts for a while, because the phone rings again and another opportunity presents itself. But for most, the experience is over and it's time to leave the park.

## The Ride is Over

When the project is over, the parent and child have to decide how they will proceed. When the theatrical agent is not calling you for new auditions, or people no longer remember that you were in that famous print ad in every magazine for a year, what do you do? For some, that reality is devastating because they were not ready to get off of the ride. For others, the child and the parent had a good time but the production schedule had gotten in the way of other creative or educational activities. The silence from the industry became a blessing and gave them a reason to move on with their lives. This parent and child can move on with great memories, gather all of their pictures and put them in a scrapbook. From time to time, they pull out the scrapbook and talk about the years that they did that thing on that show. Their time in the industry becomes a part of childhood memories, like summer camp and holiday vacations. They move on with their lives, and all is well.

## Hard to Let Go

Some parents and kids will hang in there and wait for new auditions in the weeks and months to come. They pass on opportunities to travel or time with family for fear that while they are away, they'll miss out on an important audition. Some of the other parents and kids around them just give up hope after a few months, become bitter and reluctantly pursue other avenues. They'll never get what they had again. They make their peace with it and eventually move on. But not others; they are not going to give up even though it is stressful and no longer fun for them. They have negative things to say about the people that they worked with while they were in show business, and they feel as if someone owes their child another chance. They talk about their old experiences and time in the industry every chance they get. They have framed every picture, every work permit, and every time sheet so that people will know that they were in the industry once.

In situations like this, the parents have to put their emotions aside for a moment to address how the child may be processing the experience. It is okay to be disappointed, upset, embarrassed or hurt. However, it is more important that the parents convey to the children their identity is not wrapped up in the role that they want to play. It is the parents' job to make sure that their children have realistic closure with the experience, even if the children decide they want to try the auditioning process again later in life. In the mean time, there should be a plan B. Children need something else to look forward to.

Here is where the regret for many parents starts to kick in. They were so certain about their children's potential that they didn't prepare anything for them to fall back on. The ride is over, and so is the dream. How do you pick up the pieces, gather the memories, and use what you have learned in preparation for the next phase of life? It doesn't have to be the end. It can be the start of a new adventure. This is a chance to find another passion and explore a new opportunity that will renew your children's confidence and help them to discover what makes them uniquely irreplaceable.

## Drip-Drop

There are some parents and kids who know for a fact that this entertainment thing is what they are supposed to be a part of. Although they are rejected time and time again, they continue their pursuit. They have close calls for booking the role of a lifetime, but in the end it doesn't happen. They are hurt and confused but keep waiting and auditioning and hoping. They are optimistic and dedicated even though time seems to be passing them by. Then an audition finally comes in and although the child is prepared and did a good job in the audition, there are no callbacks for another six months. The agents and managers are also optimistic and will send the child out on future auditions as long as the parent and the child want to go. All of a sudden a small part comes up for a television show that would be perfect for the child. The parent gets a call a few days later. The child has booked the role that shoots for one day. They are very excited but understand that after the one day of shooting, there may not be another opportunity like this for another six months or a year. So they make their peace with that reality, cherish the moment and go on with their lives, until next time, if there is a next time.

# The "It" Factor!

The "it" factor, at times, is a term that the industry uses to describe an entertainer who has what it takes to make it big in the industry. This is what parents and kids want to hear from the industry. This means that they have the talent or the look that it takes to make the studios a lot of money. Most of the time the "it" factor is not a specific quality or something that can be easily described. Casting just knows "it" when they see "it." Some kids just have the qualities that are immediately recognized and embraced. They begin booking projects immediately. They go from one booking to the next with seemingly effortless energy. These kids are in high demand and work non-stop. As long as their "it" qualities are in demand, they will be too. If that is the case for your child, you have accomplished what you were hoping for!

These scenarios are realities for so many people, while rejection is real for others. Some people learn over time how to brush off disappointment, while other people internalize it. Some children begin to feel like they are not good enough or that they need to do something drastic to be accepted. Although the child may feel that way, neither of those resolutions are completely accurate. Many times, casting is looking for a look or a certain type of delivery for the lines. It may have nothing to do with the performance of that child specifically. Casting may not know what they are looking for at all until a child walks into the room with unique qualities that only they possess that sets them apart from any other child who is auditioning. For every child and parent, for the sake of financial security, sanity and emotional health, there should be another alternative. This moment in time does not define your child.

I have heard people say, "I will not have or create a plan 'B' because if I do, I am setting myself up to fail." I understand and respect that perspective, but I have also been around long enough to know that even people who are successful in this business have a plan B. If there is no plan B there is at least a plan to diversify their talent within this field. They have no intentions on focusing on just one area of their lives for the rest of their lives. They love working in entertainment but realize that it is not the only thing in life that defines them. Having a plan 'B' doesn't mean that you are preparing to fail. What it does mean is that there are other things that you are capable and qualified to accomplish. I see it as diversifying and being creatively flexible. It works with money management, and it will also work with creative careers. Not everyone in the industry agrees with me on this, so I believe that at some point the perspective you take has to be personal and perfect for you. It is so important to have regular conversations with your children about this, because they need to know they have options and that their opinions matter.

# 8

## Twenty Ways to Avoid a Mess

### 1. Don't be a Negative Stage Parent.

What is a stage parent? A stage parent is negatively defined as a guardian who is pushy, over bearing and watches too closely over his or her child. This type of parent talks too much, is excessively vocal and opinionated during a child's performance. This type of parent is annoying to those associated with the production. No one likes negative stage parents. Not even other negative stage parents. Parents, in general, are supposed to be involved, attentive, supportive and communicative. However, because adults run the entertainment industry, there is a certain level of maturity that the child actor should possess to be able to focus, function, and fulfill the responsibilities of a young working actor. In this case specifically, the child does not need a parent or caregiver to literally hold his or her hand, shout out words of support or validate acting choices.

That doesn't mean that the parent shouldn't be present and visible. However, it does mean that the parent should not be off stage whispering lines to them, or on set cheering his or her child on and making negative comments about the other cast members. That is not cool. Nor should the parent give their child creative directions on top of what they have already been directed to do. On almost every production, especially union productions, there are crewmembers, dialogue coaches and script supervisors who are hired to assist the child actor with all things production. They are the child's production support system. If by chance there is a problem, the child's parent should step in and address production via the studio teacher, the agent or manager. The parent should try to keep the child out of the middle of the situation so as not to create a potentially negative working environment. If all is well, the parent should stay in the parental lane and let the production team do its job. As a parent, it may take you awhile to get the hang of your role and that is understandable. However, just like the first day at a new school, in a short while, you start to get a handle on your new environment.

I had no desire to be a stage mother even before I knew what a negative one was or had met one. I understood the professional element of the industry, because I had worked in it, to some degree, most of my life. I knew there were measures of professionalism that children needed to have in order to do their job well, so I guess my sons were already somewhat prepared for that part.

When my oldest first started in the business I wanted everyone that mattered on set to know that he was qualified to be in the business and could handle himself professionally because he was mature for four years old. So I stayed at a distance so that everyone could see that I wasn't calling the shots or prompting him. I was so proud of him because he was focused, professional and ready without my affirmations. Being a "mother on set" whose child is working on stage is more rewarding than being a "stage mother." Some "stage parents" find it hard to simply stand back and watch their child grow and blossom into a performer right before their eyes and that is unfortunate. They don't realize that they can actually take a break from parenting so that they can watch someone else teach their children how to be creative. I found that the "mother on set" role was more fulfilling and less stressful than the other option.

Motherhood is one of my most important and cherished responsibilities. I love my sons, but I also like them as individuals. I love hanging out with them because we have fun together no matter where we are or what we are doing. Motherhood may be the most entangling, time consuming, selfless job on the planet. But it is the most rewarding. One of the main reasons why it took me 18 years to write this book is because I was living out and committing to the information *in* this book. By the time I finished doing everything I needed to do throughout the day, there was no time left to do anything but sleep. I had to live it before I could write about it. So, in essence, I was the trial experiment, along with my sons, so to speak, for this book. We were the guinea pigs. I knew the time would eventually come when my creative side would emerge again. I just didn't know when. I feel like that side of me had been tucked away in a drawer or hanging in a closet like my 28-year-old wedding dress. I am ok with that because I became more committed to being the best mother that I could be than being on the Best Seller's list. I was more concerned about preparing my sons to fulfill their purpose and to positively contribute to the world rather than focusing on anything else. Being the full time mother of three home schooled kids who are on the honor roll and work in the industry is a full-time job. Thank God for Leroy, my husband and truly the most supportive man on the planet. A retired NYPD Sergeant, he held down a full time job with good benefits and pension plan for more than 20 years so I could have the freedom to concentrate on everything else and so that his boys could pursue their purpose. We've been through many ups and downs together but the four men in my home are truly my closest friends.

I quickly realized as a new mother that my sons were given to me by God to nurture and to give them the necessary tools that would prepare them for life. This mothering thing requires prayer, unconditional love, laughter, patience, rules, discipline, courage, respect, high standards, saying no at times, consistency, laughter (I know I mentioned this twice), unlimited personal discussions, flexibility, field trips, uncomfortable conversations, support, remembering when I was their age, knowing each child's strengths and weaknesses, doctor's visits, celebrating each child, discovering each child's abilities and passions, learning how to wrestle like boys, run fast, jump off of high places and getting boy-dirty! I quickly and happily noticed that while my sons were on set taking directions and becoming young professionals in an adult environment, this was one of the rare moments when I didn't have to do all of my mother stuff! I embraced those moments and celebrated! I saw those moments as mini mommy-vacations and sat back and enjoyed someone else pouring into them while I read a book, had adult conversations with another parent, got familiar with cast and crew or sat in silence just to hear myself breathe. Don't knock it 'til you try it! Even though I had to be within ear and eyeshot of them, I still got to have some "me" time.

I must add that there have been times when the adult environment wasn't so productive, professional or respectful to my sons. It was during those times, that I would quickly and calmly emerge from my chair, trailer or dressing room. Without explanation or hesitation, just like a true New Yorker from the Bronx would do, I professionally but tersely handled the situation at hand. I became the mother of all Black Mother Bears; Google "Black Mother Bears" - they actually exist! When I walked over to the people in question to address the issue, they knew that Ms. Black Mother Bear was staring them in the face. By the time I walked away, they knew whatever had just happened, was unacceptable and was not going to happen again. I learned to do this without drawing much unnecessary attention to the environment, at least most of the time. Under no circumstances should your child have to endure disrespect on any set, platform, field, or stage, regardless of who is disrespecting them. So make sure you put more focus on being a parent of a child who is on stage, whatever the "platform" is, and focus less on being a stage parent – because you might miss something that you needed to be aware of. Once something negative happens and goes unchecked, it will be on your watch - and that is not a good place for you as a parent to be in.

## 2. Don't forget YOU are the Safest place in the world for Your Child.

While piggy-backing on the end of the last section, the advice that I am about to share may seem to be a no brainer to most of you but truthfully, some parents don't really understand what "safety" means on set from a child's perspective. I prefer to assume that you didn't know and include this section, than assume that you did know and leave it out.

- Safety, for a child, means knowing that my guardian knows what's wrong with me just by looking into my eyes or watching my body language. Sometimes I don't have the proper words to indicate what's wrong.
- Safety, for a child, means loving me enough to say "no" about something that I really want to do even though I know in my heart that I am not old enough, mature enough or ready for that experience.
- Safety, to a child, means giving me rules that I don't like sometimes because you are paying attention to my well-being.
- Safety, to a child, means if I tell you something that is really important, even if it seems unimportant, you will take the time to listen because I matter to you.
- Safety, to a child, means complimenting me about something good that I have done or highlighting something that I am good at to another person and saying it loud enough for me to hear. That makes me feel like I am valuable and important to you.
- Safety, to a child, means protecting my eyes, my space, my body and my small voice in the midst of other adults in front of me.

These statements are not all encompassing regarding what safety means, but it is a start in the right direction.

## 3. Don't compromise your Ethics.

I have some challenging questions for you to answer.

- What moral standards and principles do you follow in your household?
- How do you talk to your children?
- How do your children talk to you?

- Do you cheat on your taxes?
- Do you cheat on your partner?
- Are you a gossiper?
- Do you let people take advantage of you?
- What are your children allowed to watch on television?
- Do you take advantage of others for the sake of achievement?
- How do you feel about violence?
- Do you make it a habit of lying to get what you want?
- Do your children hear you doing it?
- Are you physically or verbally abusive?
- Are you chronically judgmental?
- Do you stand up for injustices?
- When someone disagrees with you or your choices do you tear them down?
- Are you disrespectful to others on purpose?
- Do you look the other way if you can benefit from unlawful or unethical conduct?
- Do you have a lifestyle of hypocrisy?
- Do you speak well of people in front of them but tear them down behind their backs?
- Are little white lies a part of your parenting style?

I ask these questions because it is important for you to know, understand and be able to articulate your ethical posture. No one knows the answers to these questions better than you do. In the entertainment industry you will be invited, suggested, encouraged, manipulated, threatened or even forced to participate in unethical behaviors. If you don't know what your ethical posture is, you will most likely succumb to pressures that you didn't realize were even an option. I liken it to a novice politician whose sole purpose it is to make a difference in his or her community. That politician read all of the books, studied and committed to becoming an agent for change. Then he or she is introduced to the realities of back door meetings, campaign secrets, dirty money and under the table deals. This novice politician quickly realizes that he or she will either have to surrender to the environment or walk away; compromise ethics or stand by them. The final choice will be his or hers to live with.

In most cases, everyone has a choice, even if they don't feel like they do. They may not like the choices that are available, but they do have choices. It is very important for you to know what your ethical posture is before your child enters the entertainment industry. It is equally important for you to have clear and candid conversations about what these ethics are with your children, family and representatives. Allow your children the chance to speak and ask questions. Discuss what goes against your way of life and how you are going to maintain that standard. Talk with your children about what you and they are comfortable doing. Every environment is different and every situation is different. Over time, even some of our own mindsets change as we evolve, grow and learn. That is understandable and expected. But even as we evolve, our ethical foundations rarely shift dramatically. A good habit to develop is to have regular conversations with your family and your child about where you all stand so that when an opportunity or situation arises, you will all be comfortable standing your ground and will be able to articulate it appropriately and effectively.

## 4. Choose to Walk Away – if Necessary.

I know this is a hard pill for some parents to swallow, but if you don't have a walk away limit, no matter what happens, you are setting your child up to be a disrespected and devalued object for the industry to use and throw away. As soon as the unethical powers that be realize that you will let your child work no matter the role, the time limit, the pay scale, or environment, you become a pimp and your child becomes an industry prostitute, as I mentioned before. There are many wonderful folks in the industry who love, respect and treat industry kids as if they were a creative extension of how they would treat their own children. But trust me, there will also be those who are ready to exploit your children, if you let them. You have to create a line that no one can cross, not even you, and if they cross that line you will walk away. That doesn't mean that you have to quit the business altogether. It just means that you may have to walk away from a role; a person or an unethical contract, provided you sought legal counsel to do so.

My son Tyler was in a situation years ago, as a minor, where he/we chose to walk away from an opportunity. He was up for a role that called for him to do something as the character he would portray that he wasn't allowed to do personally. The behavior did not make or break the plot of the script, nor was it necessary for the role. So he respectfully took a stand but auditioned for the role without compromising his ethics. At the end of his audition, after being called back several times, he was told in the casting room that they wanted him to read the lines the way they were on the script or he wouldn't be able to book the role. He still didn't do it and after a while, he got frustrated because casting kept asking him the same question.

Adults have never easily intimidated Tyler and that day was no different, even though the casting room was full of them. He walked out of the casting room and over to me and asked "Ma, why do they keep asking me to return for callbacks if I never do the lines the way they are on the script?" I told him, "Because they know talent when they see it." Casting even came out to ask me if my son could audition for the role as it was in the script. They told me that there was another boy who was just as good as my son but he was willing to do the lines the way they wanted him to. I politely told them that they should hire the other boy because they were getting exactly what they wanted with him. They asked me if I was sure and if I wanted to reconsider my answer because it would be a good opportunity for my son. I told them yes I was sure and no, I didn't want to reconsider. I also told them that if it was a good opportunity for him and my son was supposed to book this role he would. I thanked them for the opportunity for my son to audition then we left. Casting looked at me like I was crazy, then walked back into the casting room.

Tyler got in the car disappointed because he really wanted to book the role. He understood what was happening but did not like it one bit. He seemed almost offended because he had done his best and they told him that he was what they were looking for with the exception of the lines that he wouldn't say. I was disappointed for him and understood his confusion but I also knew that this was one of those teachable moments that would end in some type of life lesson. Nevertheless, I was very proud of him for standing up for himself in the casting room and although I could see that he was very disappointed he tried not to let them know. After we left, we decided to go to a cool restaurant to recap the experience. After a while his posture of disappointment turned to indifference then to a "Whatever... forget them!" type of attitude. We laughed and ordered everything we thought looked tasty on the menu and our waitress was so courteous and patient we decided to give her all of our *per diem* (spending allowance given to us to travel to the audition), as a tip.

She was in shock and began to tell us her story of how she had just come to town to be an actress and didn't know what was going to happen and the money confirmed to her that she was going to be ok. We even got to pray with her and left the restaurant feeling great and happy for the waitress. It felt good to shift the focus from what had happened to us onto what was happening to the waitress. A while later, we were on our way home, preparing to move on with our lives as we usually do after an audition. Suddenly, the phone rang. It was my son's manager calling to say that he had booked the role anyway, without compromising! The look of satisfaction and accomplishment on my son's face as he threw his arms in the air in relief and yelled out, "YESSSS!" was worth more than words could express. I gave him a huge High-Five as I nodded and smiled! Talk about a teachable moment! He was so proud of himself for not compromising! He was the best person for the role and that trumped everything!

I must close this section by saying that the end result is not always in our favor. My sons don't always book a job because they didn't compromise. However, we always get to walk away with peace of mind knowing that we did the right thing and that trumps booking the role of a lifetime any day of the week!

## 5. Don't tolerate Drama, Stress and Foolishness.

I am now in my 40s, and at this time in my life, I have zero tolerance for drama, stress, and foolishness. Maybe it comes with age or realizing what really matters in life. I can generally get along with just about anyone, but I find it a waste of time that I will never get back when it comes to foolishness. There is a minority of parents who thrive on foolishness. I have known of parents fighting in dressing rooms or parking lots, negative and hurtful comments on social media, and toxic attitudes on television sets and movie locations. Some of this behavior is directed to other parents, spouses and their children. It is not exclusive to just the television and movie industry; organized sports suffer from the same types of behavior as well. I understand that everyone is not always going to get along. People have their differences, and no two people will see eye to eye all the time. However, there is a way, for the sake of the project, production and game, for people to put their differences aside. There is a happy medium of sorts where everyone can find or agree to at least be cordial with one another. There are parents that I have met through the years who I did not prefer to associate with in casting rooms and studio sets. I am sure some of them didn't prefer to spend time with me either. However, I don't remember a time when the environment was so bad that we couldn't at least attempt to be respectful and say hi to one another. Sometimes that is easier said than done, but for the sake of the kids and the project, I believe that it is worth attempting because the kids have to work together.

There is something to be said about being cordial, nice and talkative. It makes for a more peaceful atmosphere. However, when people get so cordial that they start gossiping about other parents' and children's business, that's not so good. I know that there are times when parents need to vent and have to bring up certain topics. I am not talking about those discussions.

We all have those. However, I am talking about parents who always seem to have all of the information about everyone else. Just remember that if the parent is talking to you about someone else's business, chances are, that same parent is talking about you to another parent. A wise woman once told me, "A dog that will bring a bone, will also carry a bone." A good rule of thumb can be to respect all of the parents that you come across, and try to be friendly and respectful. However, when they start gossiping, walk away from the conversation, address it or find something to read no matter how intriguing it may sound. Word travels very fast and the industry is much smaller than some people may realize.

I have had many occasions when people would gossip to me about dear friends of mine, or their children, and they had no idea we even knew one another. Most of the time, the information they were sharing was false, misunderstood or fragmented. I rarely attempt to correct the person, the information or stand up for my friends or their children. I tend to let them dig a hole for themselves and soon they realize that I'm not responding as someone who normally gossips would. Sometimes they just get silent, sometimes they realize that they said too much and other times they are just so used to talking that way that they don't even realize they said anything offensive. I never make a big deal about it because I know people who find the need to talk about others that way will continue to do so. I just change the subject or ask, "Do they know how you feel or have you told them how you feel?" to give them a chance to make some adjustments or to hold them accountable for their comments. I generally just make a mental note of what they said as a reference of who to trust or not.

My mother had a saying: "Don't worry; let people keep talking or doing whatever they are doing that is negative. They will soon eliminate themselves." She was right!

## 6. Know "Who" you are.

Let me introduce myself. I am a passionate black woman who purposes to make the world a better place although I am a work in progress myself. I do this by being a functional wife, mother, minister, businesswoman, friend, mentor, life coach, teacher, student, speaker, and all of the other hats that I wear. Integrity, fruitfulness, regard, health, purpose, spiritual growth, ethics, benevolence, fun and laughter are very important to me. I attempt to practice them daily. I am passionate about prayer, mentorship, learning, teaching and hearing from God. I am flexible like a palm tree when it is necessary and as solid and flatfooted as an oak tree if the environment calls for it. I try to balance friendly and funny with focus and straightforwardness. I'm not a crowd pleaser, but I am a team player. I am not shy but can seem reserved. I like to spontaneously dance while walking down the street or sing aloud when the mood hits me. I am extroverted, conversational and pleasant most of the time, but if given a reason I can be feisty, fiery and brutally honest. I am sometimes quiet and will sit silently when listening for God's voice, which can seem distant, but catch me around people I love to be with and I can be the loudest person in the room. Although I am opinionated I respect everyone but only trust a small group. I have a problem with the word tolerance as it relates to putting up with others. I feel the word "tolerate" is more suited for rush hour traffic or a toothache, not people. Rather, I attempt to respect all people whether I agree with them or not.

I work on loving and giving people the benefit of the doubt unless they confirm the doubt, then I give them distance. The standards that are set for my family and me are high, but I do not expect perfection. We all tend to fall short of our own standards at times and that's what makes us all human. Anyone who knows me well enough, or has spent a sufficient amount of time with me, hopefully will confirm one or most of these traits that I have mentioned above because I purpose to take my identity with me everywhere I go. Whether I am in the pulpit, a board meeting, hanging out with family and friends, on a studio set, getting a mani-pedi, at an audition, meeting a stranger, in the grocery store, wrestling, on a date with my boys or my husband. This is who *I* am. Who are *you*?

## 7. Don't just Stand – Stand Up for Something.

The world systems that have their sights set on the bottom line - which is, inevitably, always money - have a way of asking and sometimes demanding that you bend or bow to its wishes for the sake of making as much money as possible. Sometimes compromise is necessary when trying to reach a unified goal, and sometimes compromise is *slavery*. I am not talking about ethical compromise. I am talking about the business or mutual compromise that leaves both sides getting some of what they asked for but not everything that they wanted. An example of this would be a television contract. The network may be offering an actor a smaller amount of money than he expected to receive. Because the network wants to hire this actor and the actor wants to be hired for this role they compromise. The lawyers go back and forth for a while, and the end result is met by a compromise from both parties. The network agrees to pay a little more and the actor agrees to receive a little less than requested. That would be a fair *compromise*. The compromise of slavery involves one entity that appears to be more powerful forcing the hand of the other. When the other entity surrenders to the power or pressure of the other, knowing that there are other options, he subjects himself to slavery because the one who appears to be more powerful knows he has the other under his control.

The system of entertainment is focused on money through entertainment. The drive is motivated by all things money: how to make it, how to make more of it, how to reinvest it, and who to hire to generate even more of it. If the bottom line is money, you, the entertainer, are dispensable and replaceable in the eyes of the system. So if you feel like your child is being disrespected or taken advantage of, stand up for them. The moment you compromise who you are, people will see you as a person without a backbone. They won't tell you this to your face, but this will become a part of your identity. Don't be afraid of the system. You have more power than you think. If you don't know how, reach out to your child's talent support system. They are a great resource. Let them help you. If you don't have a support system for your child's career, I have included resources and research information at the back of this book that will help you find and create your support system.

## 8. Know how to use Social Media.

What an interesting world we live in these days where everything that a person says or does can be either posted, uploaded, downloaded, streamed, leaked, recorded, snapped, liked, flipped, twisted and whatever else is to come from the evolution of social media in the future. There exist many wonderful benefits to this social electronic-movement from a business, long distance relationship, marketing, publicizing, outreach and community support, alert and promotional perspective. However, I see a measure of harm and pending personal regret in social media's future and those who abuse it. The future for many individuals who use it incorrectly is going to be an interesting one. I have seen many entertainers, as well as their parents, use it inappropriately, some by mistake, others due to ignorance. Nevertheless, just because you have a thought, idea, or something funny to say doesn't mean you should share it on social media. Just because you have an opinion doesn't mean you should share it with the world (because that is exactly what you are doing). Just because you have a picture you want people to see doesn't mean that you won't regret that you shared it five years from now when it is too late to remove it. For some there is no discretion, restraint, filter or wisdom when using these tools. The terms "less is more" and "silence is golden" seem to have little meaning for some who use social media. Mass-voyeurism and self-exploitation is now popular, but is it a good thing? Please be careful and I will try too.

## 9. Don't let your Child see you Surrender to Pressure.

Children learn more by watching what we do than by listening to what we say. This is a good thing if we are consistently practicing what we preach, but it is not a good thing if we are not. Again, none of us is perfect and none of us has it all figured out. However, there should be a consistent paralleled balance between what we say and how we act. This is very important as they watch how we conduct ourselves with other adults. If you don't teach your child to stand up for what he or she believes in, what will happen when a non-union producer attempts to pressure you again for a few more hours on set with your child when you know that it is not legal to do so? You have to show your child how to respectfully stand his ground without apology by doing it yourself.

## 10. Don't put your Child on a Pedestal because He will Fall.

Pedestals are made for plants, art and sculptures; not people. Your children are not perfect so don't set them up to fail because at some point they will confirm to you that they are not perfect. They are going to do or say something that you or others don't agree with. So, in the meantime, teach them how to make wise choices then give them permission to exercise what you have taught them. If you haven't taught them how to make wise choices, you should be a bit concerned. However, you don't have to feel hopeless. Life has a way of teaching us lessons of what not to do, or of what not to do again. But throw away the pedestal; it just creates unnecessary frustration for you, your children and your relationships in the future. It is great to have high hopes, standards and expectations. Keep those...just throw away the pedestal or get a pretty plant.

I have also seen situations where parents, producers and cast members told a child that they were so talented they were sure to work in the business forever. The child starts to believe and own this declaration and becomes very confident or over confident until the show that he or she is working on is cancelled. Years pass and that child, who can't seem to book another job, gravitates to comments about himself in the media to see what people are saying. The child becomes confused because of the conflicting comments and becomes introverted, reckless or disturbed. Something in that child changes, and it is not necessarily for the good of the child. So instead of the pedestal, how about giving your child a mirror – to take a glimpse at who he or she really is no matter what happens in the industry? And while you're at it, why not give them some solid life survival tools and a pair of open arms?

## 11. Don't force your children to be "The" best – rather "Their" best.

No matter where your children go or what they do or become in life, they will probably encounter someone who is going to be better at something than they are. They should not have to constantly hyper-focus their time and energy on how they measure up to someone else. Competition is great and comparing yourself to others in a competitive atmosphere is normal, natural and even expected. However, to take the unhealthy pressure off, they should be and set their own standard and set their sights on being their best. The alternative is exhausting. If that ranks them #1 in the world, fantastic! If it doesn't, fantastic! Hopefully it will next year!

## 12. The Truth doesn't eventually hurt as badly as a Lie.

I am a firm believer that in the game of a lie vs. the truth, the truth will win every time. The truth has one step and a lie has two. The truth says, save time and be honest now. A lie says, waste time now by telling a lie then clean up the lie when it is exposed. My husband and I didn't tell our kids stories as they were growing up about the tooth fairy, Santa Claus, and the rest of made up childhood characters. When their classmates and friends found out that these childhood characters didn't exist, some of them were confused and saw their parents as liars. Some kids didn't make a big deal out of it one way or another. They just grow out of believing in these childhood characters and move on with their lives. When my kids were little, they had conversations with their friends and innocently but bluntly told their friends that these characters were made up. Some of the kids were shocked and didn't believe them.

Parents have a right to tell kids whatever they want to tell them about Santa Claus and anything else, I suppose. However, I have heard parents purposefully lie to kids about where their money goes, how much they make and what they are going to get if they booked a role. I would ask them why they do that and they would say things like, "My kids are too young to understand the truth," or, "I am not ready to talk to them about it yet." I was not surprised to find out that when some of those kids did find out the truth about certain things (especially money), many of them severed relationships with their parents, sued them or even exposed the parents in public. I also believe that if you lie to your children when they are young, they may be more likely to lie to you later.

## 13. Magnify the little things – Minimize the big things.

In the entertainment industry people often make a big deal about the big events and occasions that take place like the awards shows, front page features, television ratings, weekend box office numbers and the like. These events are big deals, but only a few people get to experience the big moments. As a result, celebrating the little things in life helps to validate the child's essence where as just celebrating the big things may give your child a warped view of himself or herself. It may be difficult to do, but you will be glad you did if your child is not nominated, doesn't get the award or doesn't get the cover of the magazine. Your child is still valuable and needs to feel that way by people closest to him or her.

## 14. Take a Break (book out) every now and then.

Because there are so many ups and downs in this industry, it is very important to prioritize your life. When our schedules got really busy with the boys, I felt that we were running around too much and running out of steam. I would call my sons' agents or manager to "book them out," or take a break from auditioning. That means if an audition would come in, their agent or manager would not call us to tell us about it. We wanted to focus on other things instead of running around the city every week. We would go on a quick weekend vacation or stay in for the weekend and not answer the phones. At times we felt like industry rebels and it was a good way to recharge. Some parents dare not do this for fear that their child might miss an important audition. My sons appreciated the break because it gave them a time out where they could focus on video games or just hang around the house and watch television.

This kind of behavior is probably the reason why we are not the average or typical Hollywood family. I tell people all the time that we live *in* Hollywood; Hollywood is not *in* us. We are not big on the socialite or party scene. We aren't constantly seen at industry parties, and if we are there we are usually one of the first to leave. I'm sure in most cases we would seem boring to folks on the outside looking in. We do most of our socializing at charity events, with our friends and colleagues in the industry, at private homes, and philanthropic opportunities where there might not be a lot of cameras. We enjoy socializing and having a great time, but the industry can be a bit too much after a while. So we have learned how to take breaks, get out of town and disappear until we feel like it is time to reemerge. We love that. It helps to de-stress, reprioritize and assess what is most important at the time. When we return we are well rested, have created some great new memories, took awesome pictures and found several things to laugh about. Usually our new experience during our break taught each of us something that we didn't know before. In most cases the lesson could be applied later.

## 15. Use Good, Bad and Uncomfortable experiences as "Teachable Moments" – because there will be a "Test."

All of the experiences in the industry are not warm and fuzzy. Prejudice, jealousy, sabotage, and the like exist in the industry just like everywhere else. Even when the boys were young, I would point out certain situations so that they would know exactly what was going on. I would ask them questions like, "Now that you have seen this, how would you handle this if it happened to you?" The experiences gave them a reference and a confidence to know what to do in the future. There are many wonderful kids, teens and young adults in the industry. Many of them go unnoticed, unrecognized, and uncelebrated. They are generous, philanthropic and respectful to their parents. They are educated, socially fit and financially literate. They are not highlighted in articles and certainly not spotlighted in the media. That is a shame and this should change immediately! I would love to be a part of that movement! They are well rounded and grounded young people. They are focused, professional and well balanced. They have good parents and excellent support systems. They will be fine as they make their transitions, and it doesn't matter if they stay in the industry or not.

Then there are some self-absorbed, narcissistic, academically stunted, mean-spirited, greedy, indifferent to others, drama-filled, attention seeking, alcoholic, reckless, drug abusing kids who party entirely too much. This industry, as it relates to the young performers, is a lot like traditional school settings with regards to peer pressure, rivalry, gossip, cliques, betrayal, bullies, rumors and those who are trying to find themselves. Just imagine everything that goes on in school settings. The same things happen in the industry as well. These young people however, tend to have more money, freedom, access, power and influence. That is not necessarily beneficial.

Much like in everyday life, it becomes easy to see or learn which young entertainers belong in which category. The first sign is to check out whom they are hanging out with. What are those people doing? How are they conducting themselves? Over time one can pretty much determine what is happening. There are exceptions to every rule of course, but the rule is still in effect. Some production sets are child friendly and some are not. Some cast members respect kids and create an environment for the kids to grow up safely and others do not. There are great lessons to learn in these situations like:

- Just because everyone is going to be at the party doesn't mean you should be there. If you do go, it doesn't mean you should stay all night.
- Just because you have seen them on television doesn't mean you can trust them.
- Just because people will be impressed to see you hanging out with them, doesn't mean you should.
- Just because production treats you like an adult, doesn't mean that you are one.
- Just because the bouncer will let you in to the club even though you are a minor doesn't mean it is legal.
- Just because you can afford this car today doesn't mean you won't be behind on the payments in a year.
- Just because you see them living in a big lavish house doesn't mean it belongs to them or that they can even afford it. Stop trying to measure up to other people.

Here is one lesson that I spent a lot of time showing my kids when they were younger. I also tell other parents who ask for advice. *If smoking cigarettes and weed are gateway drugs that can lead to stronger, more harmful drugs; then overloading on candy, soda, chips, junk food and sweets on set to keep a small child's energy up can be the gateway to vices, strongholds, dependency, bad habits, poor health and dysfunctional behaviors in the future.* On set, these things are around in abundance all day, every day. There are many healthy, nutritious and beneficial foods and items to eat and drink throughout the day and parents who are mindful of what their children eat, take advantage of those healthy choices. However, I have seen kids show up on set at six o'clock in the morning and head straight to the craft food area and grab a donut with sprinkles, a can of soda and a hand full of candy – for breakfast. A couple hours later they will return and grab a caffeine-filled power drink, two bags of chips and more candy. If they seem sluggish later in the day they get more soda.

I have seen kids do this with or without parental supervision. The first few times I thought, "Maybe the parents are just letting them have a few treats for the extraordinary day they're having." But it happened just about every day they were on set. Some of the parents look at me as if I am crazy and keep their distance from me in the future when I comment or if they don't see the boys eating the way their kids are in the morning. This happened especially when the boys were really little. However, others are taken aback realizing that there may be unforeseen pathways or roads that lead to a negative place. Many of them noticed over time that they have seen addictive behaviors and signs in their children when on set and wished they had listened.

Simply put, the industry – much like life - is like a large classroom full of tremendous information, experiences, and teachers, both good and bad. At some point there will be a test to determine what you have or have not learned. Some people don't pass the tests and others don't realize that they are being tested. This is the hard part. In the midst of it all, parents have to be around but they also have to be aware.

## 16. Every Parent shouldn't Manage their child's career.

Let me start off by saying that there are some brilliant "momagers" and "popagers" out there in all forms of entertainment. They take their job and role as manager or agent very seriously. They commit their lives to it, and they have taken their children's careers to a place of success that no one or company would have been able to. These awesome individuals quit their day jobs, retired from companies or businesses just to jump in with both feet to assist their child's career full time. They postured themselves for a "failure is not an option" stance and learned as they proceeded. All of the hard work and dedication paid off for them and for their child. Some are well respected in the industry and some of them aren't. When I watch a couple of them I am thoroughly impressed. I salute them, their efforts, their accomplishments and their children!

But most parents are not qualified, capable and smart enough about the industry to manage their child's career. I have seen the lives and careers of some very talented kids crash and burn because their parents decided to manage their acting careers. It is true (in many cases), that no one will look out for and love a child better than his or her parent. But let's define love. It involves nurturing, protecting, communicating, sheltering, teaching and preparing. I know to some, this definition sounds a lot like managing. It does, but it doesn't. Some of the reasons why parents become managers are prideful; they don't want to pay commission to anyone else, they want to control their kids and their kids' careers, or think that they know what they are doing without any industry or business experience.

Many parents don't know much about the complexities of the casting, developing, grooming, growing, acting, marketing, scheduling, networking, promoting and branding process of a career. Most parents don't even know the scope and potential of the creative side of their child. In many cases, if you listen closely to a parent having a conversation about these things, you can tell what type of manager that parent is. I have found that it's better for most parents to leave it to the professionals to guide their child's careers. I am intelligent. I have college degrees. I am a personal manager and a savvy businesswoman. However, the idea of me spending all of my days on the phone talking, fighting with industry folks, making deals, scheduling with casting, setting up meetings, looking at resumes, reading scripts, trouble-shooting and the like is not something that I want to do with my life. It is a lot of work if done correctly. Granted, do I have much more on my plate than just being a "momager?" Yes, but I do it all on my terms!

I have seen situations where parents have arguments with casting directors, producers, and other department heads about issues irrelevant to their child.

They are making unrealistic demands or trying to make side deals with them, attempting to get their other children involved with projects. Many parents don't know how to separate the managerial responsibilities from the parental one, or they don't do either of them effectively. Their child loses a parent *and* a talent representative. Quite honestly, so many parents have no idea what they are doing. I have even seen parents act as their child's accountants and lawyers as well. Let me just say, like any other profession, all managers, agents, lawyers and accountants aren't good for all kids. There are some shady professionals out there that parents need to stay away from, but there are some great professionals who take their job seriously. It takes research, interviewing and discernment to determine which is right for your child.

Some parents think that because they have been around the acting environment (via auditions, reading scripts, reading call sheets, chatting with producers and directors, and making phone calls for logistical purposes) for a while, that they know enough about the industry, and it's many moving parts. They think they can do the same thing that agents, managers, lawyers, public relations and even accountants do. It is a very scary situation because at the beginning, of course, the children trust their parents when they are young. When they grow up and realize that the parents made a mess of their business affairs, money and their career choices, they are livid. Many of them either end up getting emancipated, firing or suing their parents for mismanagement. Some of the kids have no money left and the parents have done such a bad job handling the business side of things that they have burned too many bridges in the industry. No one wants to work with the children any more.

For these reasons, I decided early on not to become my sons' manager or agent. Although I am a businesswoman, performer, and former CEO/COO of a music and literary publishing company, I didn't want to take a chance and ruin my relationship with my sons. I have had a great deal of experience in the entertainment industry. I am creative and good at networking and handling businesses. But as I did my research early on, I read about too many severed and wounded parent/child relationships; I didn't want us to be on that list. Instead, I decided to become their professional, talent, business and personal *overseer.* I decided to oversee the team that we carefully selected to make sure that the strategy for each of the boys stayed on track so that the vision for them would be realized. It was a great decision for our family. This role is just as hard, time consuming and involved; however, I do this all from a mother's perspective. I get to be the momma bird that watches over everyone that watches over every aspect of my three sons' careers. There are no blurred lines; I still get to be the parent without the drama, creative arguments, regrets and resentment that would come with the potential "momager" role.

I am their mother, wise counsel, friend, confidant, business partner, and COO of their businesses. However, when we go into business meetings that extend beyond our family, they are the ones in charge of their careers. They have their lists of questions ready. They choose the auditions and roles that they do or do not want to do, at this point. I have raised them to be wise businessmen; professional, focused and articulate individuals. I don't speak for them nor do I speak with them in meetings; I only interject if necessary. We have discussions before and after meetings. I help to facilitate and work closely with their team, but they have a voice and they make the final business decision at the end of the day. They are presented with all of the information that they need, then they take it from there with me standing right there with them if they need me. They get tons of advice and if they need help deciding what to do, I am right there.

At home, however, they don't get to make the final decisions. We have family meetings and prayer that are similar to our business meetings. They get a vote and the chance to voice their opinions and points of view, but their mother and father will let them know what the final decision is. We are usually on the same page unless someone is out voted, which happens quite often. Whether or not we like the final decision, it stands - and we agree to comply with that decision. When they turn 18, their vote has a little more weight and they can start to branch out and spread their wings a bit, if they feel that they are ready to do so. Once they turn 18, as with my now

22 year old and 18 year old, they will be already equipped with everything needed to be independent. We purposed to teach and prepare them to fly so that when they become legal adults, they will have the choice to fly or take a little more time flapping and practicing. My oldest was given the opportunity to make some decisions for his own life because we knew that he was mature enough and ready to do so. He already knew about money management, how to manage a house, college responsibilities, how to cook, work ethic, respect for himself and others, how to wash clothes, pay bills, conduct himself as a professional and make wise decisions. Now that he is 22, he makes all of his decisions but he knows that his mama bird/overseer/ friend, his dad/friend, his brothers and the rest of his support system are all standing by if he needs us.

## 17. Consider Incorporating.

Incorporating is one option to establishing a business. It is legally forming a separate business entity to handle all of the financial and legal aspects of a company. It is a stand-alone entity that can afford the entertainer additional legal protection and some additional flexibility when it comes to deducting expenses and paying taxes. Because there are additional costs to keeping this type of company operational – including annual filing fees and additional accounting costs to prepare tax returns - it may not make financial sense to form this type of company until there is a decent amount of income to manage. A corporation should have a bank account and a separate set of books. Because children have no dependents and, in most cases, own no property, their paychecks are taxed pretty heavily.

One of the ways that their salaries, or income, can be protected from excessive taxes is if a corporation is established. A corporation (a.k.a. "Corp") is a legal business or operating structure that separates the child's personal monies from the business monies. A corporation is also a financial safeguard of protection from liabilities that may befall the person. It is also a great way to separate the child's business spending (car rentals, acting classes, out-of-town living expenses, etc.) from the personal spending (clothes, groceries, haircuts, etc.) It is very important to keep clean money trails in order to know exactly how your child's money is moving. Having separate personal and business accounts and activities is crucial. It prevents the risk of being audited in the future. It's best that your entertainment lawyer help you to set up a corporation for your child. Your lawyer will explain what your options are and help you learn about the legal and financial benefits.

## 18. Set up your child's Blocked/Trust/Coogan accounts.

Trust, blocked, Coogan or secure accounts are mandatory bank accounts that are set up in the child's name and blocked from anyone having access to it until the child turns at least 18 years old. This account holds 15% of the gross amount of the money that your child will make. The money is withdrawn from the child's gross checks and automatically deposited into this account. No one is allowed access to this account until the child is 18 to 21 years old. The parent or guardian is allowed to make deposits in the account, but no one is allowed to make withdrawals. These accounts must be set up and proven to exist with a letter from the banking institution, with the letterhead from the bank and it must state the account is a blocked account. If one of these accounts does not exist, according to the Coogan Law that protects child workers, that child cannot work. These accounts are mandatory, with no exceptions. The reason for this strict law is many parents in the past were notorious for spending the money that their child earned. There was nothing put away for them once they became adults. Many of the child stars were very successful and worked for many years only to find out once they became of age that they were completely broke.

## 19. If you have more than One Child in Entertainment, remember that each one is Unique.

I've briefly mentioned earlier ways to handle having multiple children who are in the spotlight. We are all aware of acting, singing, dancing, sports and music siblings. There are families that have multiple children in the family who are professionals in the same entertainment field. It happens quite often. These siblings can learn from one another, celebrate each other and serve as a solid support system for one another because they speak the same creative language. Granted a few of these sibling entertainers don't get along or even speak to one another once they become adults but many of them do. Nevertheless, if parents happen to have more than one entertainer or athlete in the family, here is some advice.

- Don't compare successes or failures.
- Don't support one more than the other.
- Don't talk about one child behind the other's back (yes, that happens).
- Consider taking all of the advice in this book and applying it to each child, separately.

Allow each sibling to be an individual. If one child wants to follow in the path of his or her sibling, find the best route for the entire family and help them to do so without putting pressure on either child. But also allow and help your child find his or her own unique path and celebrate them both equally. I understand the benefits of nepotism but that was never a go to strategy, option, or plan in our house. Each child had to earn their own opportunities or create their own open doors so that they could celebrate each other's opportunities without a hidden agenda. They each have separate careers, goals, strengths, gifts and approaches. Each has separate companies, accounts, networking contacts, circles of associates, friends and creative outlets. There has never been any jealousy or competition issues because each vision is different and they are 4 ½ years apart so they rarely auditioned for the same role. The great thing about where they are now is that their strengths and weaknesses are different. When one needs help in a creative area but doesn't have that creative quality, they will reach out to the other for assistance. The great part about that is, together they make a powerful self-contained force for particular projects.

## 20. Associate with People who are Smarter or Better than you are in some area and never take advice from a fool.

As in the real world, there are some smart people and there are some foolish ones. Because of this, surround yourself with people who are smarter than you or those you can learn from. Because there is something to learn from everyone, I prefer to hang out with different types of people, from different cultures, and different walks of life. Learning what not to do is just as beneficial as learning what to do. That doesn't mean that you need to hang out with experienced drug dealers to learn that that lifestyle is not the one for you. It is more about connecting with people who promote forward motion, regard for functionality, common interests and goals, and personal growth. This will keep you focused, positive, purposeful and productive.

# 9
## *Notes*

*I*n the industry, director's *notes* are given to actors during the genesis of a production, usually during rehearsals or throughout the production at times, to make sure that the wrinkles in the script, any blocking issues or the actors' performances are all ironed out. These notes are generally suggestions, ideas or advice from the director to an actor and given so that the end result of the performance can be as flawless as possible. Below I will be sharing with you notes of information that I have gathered, mentally filed and shared with parents throughout the years. I have mentioned some of these already in other chapters but have highlighted them here. These little lines of insight, wisdom, instruction, questions to ponder, and information have helped many parents, in different ways, to stay focused, even if they were just passing through the entertainment business on their way to something more suitable or important for their kids.

I must admit though, as with some actors I'm sure, these notes have made a few parents a bit upset with me, some even frustrated. I believe they felt that way because they wanted a formula or something more tangible that seemed to make more sense. I understood their positions and I would have appreciated that myself when we started, but there is no formula. Everybody's journey and how they perceive, respond and adapt to it is different.

I liken it to working out. Yes, the goal and desire is to be fit and fabulous. That's the goal and the desire, but who is going to realistically put in three days of cardio, two days of resistance training, eliminate fatty foods, commit to portion control and drink water all day to reach that goal or desire, for the rest of their life? A very small percentage of the people who initially said that they wanted to be fit and fabulous will make that commitment. That's why there is no formula to this industry. What may work for me, my sons and my family in the industry may not work for or even be realistic for another family. However, there are general pieces of insight that can be taken and applied to just about any situation. I love to share information if I feel I have something of importance to add to a conversation or situation. If I feel that I can help one person, my sharing will not be in vain. I have used, applied, learned, seen, and experienced all that I am sharing with you, and I know that it works because it worked for my family. Everything may not appear as palatable, helpful or doable for you as it was for me, but if you find something in this list, you have my permission to break a little piece of something off for yourself to use for later.

- You are a parent first. Nothing is more important than that.
- Your child might be a product to others, but should never be to you.
- Wear "Duck Feathers" often (look it up); they're a parent's most useful outfit.
- There is power in the word "No." Learn when, why and how to use it.
- Trust me...you don't know everything.
- Many childhood tragic stories start in the home.
- Hollywood: The Myth is everybody is happy.
- The Entertainment Industry is 90% Business and 10% Entertainment.
- Hollywood's Pie: 30% talent, 30% work, 8% fun, 5% illusion, 5% delusion, 2% who you know and 20% what you know. Some slices tend to change.
- Remember, the word "No" is not a negotiation tactic – it's a decision.
- If your family is not stable at the beginning you might not have one at the end.
- No one should love your child more than you do.
- Everyone deserves your respect; not everyone deserves your trust.

- Your child is neither *for* sale, nor *on* sale.
- Compromise can book a job, but it can also destroy your character.
- If the grass is greener on the other side consider the upkeep and the water bill.
- Integrity is far more powerful than fear!
- Intimidation is only effective if you don't know who *you* are.
- Some prostitution *is* legal; therein the parent becomes the pimp.
- Every parent is not "management" material so stay in your lane.
- Working with your child vs. living off of your child: there is a BIG difference.
- Finding ways to avoid paying taxes doesn't make you an accountant - it makes you a criminal.
- Money is like seeds…what are you growing?
- Your child's fame doesn't replace your discipline.
- Your child's big break doesn't mean he has a career.
- The spotlight is a momentary experience for most - not a life-long guarantee.
- Your child is working while on set - what are you doing while on set?
- You shouldn't be your child's only support system in this industry.
- Just because someone is a star doesn't mean they can be trusted alone with your child.
- Social Media can be used as a tool or time waster. How are you using it?
- Who do you think you are talking to on social media?
- Balancing life and the industry is like walking a tight rope: with focus, practice and discipline it can be done.
- The industry is wired for some kids, but some kids aren't wired for the industry.
- Don't burn professional, business and creative bridges if you can help it.
- Your reputation will follow you everywhere you go.
- Try to respect everyone, even if you don't prefer him or her.

- If you're having problems in your marriage before you enter the industry, you have a problem. Now is the time to get help.
- When putting together a creative team for your child, don't let one part of your team pick the rest of the entire team. There maybe a conflict of interest that is not beneficial for your child.
- Not every opened door is an opportunity for *your* child.
- Parents who explode and argue on set embarrass their children.
- Many parents are addicted to prescription drugs; will you be one of those parents?
- Some parents party and do drugs with their kids. Will you?
- Teach your child the difference between "wants" and "needs" and be their role model.
- Having access to your child's money does not give you the right to spend it all.
- Having regular meetings with your child about his or her money and business is a good idea.
- Myth: Everyone in Hollywood is Rich. Truth: Not even close.
- Myth: Everyone in Hollywood owns big houses or mansions. Truth: Many rent them.
- Myth: Everyone in Hollywood knows each other. Truth: Not so much.
- Be careful who you give power of attorney to sign checks on your behalf, they may take it.
- One of the best ways to navigate through this industry is to be a working entertainer who lives and moves about *under* the radar.
- Overexposure is overrated.
- Obtaining fame and riches DOES NOT and WILL NOT cause your problems or dysfunctions to go away. It usually magnifies them.
- Know with whom your child is associating.
- Know how they are using technology.
- Learn how to use technology.

# 10

## Reps: Your Child's Talent Team

There are many moving parts to this entertainment system, and this industry is not a place to attempt to be self-contained or a one-man-band. You will be creatively swallowed alive or burnt out in months trying to be all things for your own child's career. That mentality may work in a circus (although some people think this business is a circus), but it won't work in the entertainment industry. As a result, in order to successfully exist and maintain a career within this system, there are key players that must come on board at some point in time in your child's career. Sure, there are people who have been discovered at a grocery store, the mall, or a coffee house then were put in a blockbuster movie. Yes, a few have been hand picked out of a crowd one day, then were found seated on a national platform the next. However, after that exciting moment, these people will need a support system in place. Agents, managers, lawyers, business managers, accountants, Public Relations firms, security, body guards, personal managers, and the like will probably become a part of your team at some point if that person wants to achieve or maintain a measure of success. You may not need some of these as much as you need others, but you will need some type of support. Yes, they all get paid at different times, in different ways, for different reasons. Some of the team members are on retainer; others are on an hourly rate, while others may work by percentages.

## *Lawyers*

An entertainment lawyer is no different from any other type of lawyer, except that he or she serves as the legal ambassador for the rights, regulations, enforcement, collection, distribution, agreement and execution of all things entertainment and its complex relationships with other entities. An entertainment lawyer specializes in entertainment realities and outcomes relating to everything from sports, music, setting up corporations, record companies, tax advice, television contracts, trademarks, licensing, movies, animation, and book deals to drawing up contracts, negotiating contracts, royalties, producers, agents, managers and copyright issues. *Note: Child entertainers need good legal representation. They all need entertainment lawyers when dealing with contracts. Trying to cut corners or avoiding this reality is a bad idea.*

Because of this there should never be a short cut to getting legal counsel, no matter how much money you want to save or how badly or quickly you want to make or sign the deal that is on the table. NEVER sign anything without first having a lawyer review it and advise you on how to proceed. Just like it would not be wise to have a real estate agent handle your divorce, or a dentist perform heart surgery, don't substitute any other type of lawyer for an entertainment attorney. Lawyer's generally charge a percentage based fee of 5-10% of the contract negotiated or an hourly rate approximately around $300 to $500. These percentages and hourly rates are sometimes adjusted depending on the situation, gravity or amount of work the situation entails.

## *Talent Managers*

Managers handle the day-to-day operations for their clients' careers. They tend to have a more personal, one-on-one type of relationship with their clients. They are like the extensions of the talents' hands and are proactive in anticipating, planning, foreseeing and dealing with public relations issues that the talent may be able to handle but shouldn't be handling personally. A good manager is a visionary or the driving force behind the talent's vision, a teacher of the industry, a cheerleader, a troubleshooter and a logistical organizer. Many of them become extended family members and assist clients with personal and emotional situations that come up. Managers may be hands on wherever and however the client needs them that is directly connected or associated to the client's career.

Some managers create or set up auditions. They typically handle everything from confirming auditions, promoting and refining talent, and reminding clients of future or pending appointments. They also update resumes, demo reels, websites and IMDB statuses. Talent managers address problems that may arise on set or at an audition, set up meetings with networks, agents, lawyers or other industry related realities. They assist in creating the strategy that will take the client to the next stage of their career. Managers set up gifting suite appointments, interviews and appearances; make travel arrangements; help to choose photographers; and make sure all is well while the talent is on location. If acting were a vehicle, the talent manager would be the steering wheel. Not every performer has a manager, but they can be essential to the movement of the performer's career. Their commission is typically 10%-20% of their client's gross income depending on the agreement between talent and manager.

## *Talent Agents*

Agents are the engines that keep the talent's *career* moving forward. They submit headshots and resumes to casting directors to see if their client is right for certain roles. Agents should have good reputations and be respected in the industry. They are the ones who are setting up meetings and getting the word out about their client. They are proactive in landing potential jobs for their clients and are actively opening the doors for them so that they can audition for the roles in the future. If or once the client books a role, the agents, along with the entertainment lawyer and talent, will discuss and negotiate the contracts that will determine how much the talent will get paid and other particulars. Every successful actor that I know has an agent. The agent establishes relationships with the most important people in the industry in order to give their client the opportunity to be seen for certain roles. The agent sets up the opportunity for the client to have the role of a lifetime. The agent's commission is typically 10%-15% of the client's gross income for the work that the agent gets for the client, after payment for the job has been received. The percentage is determined by the agreement between the talent and agent.

## *Personal Managers*

Personal managers are very similar to talent managers in that they handle the day-to-day operations of their client's *personal* life. They assist with everything from setting up their personal checking and savings bank accounts, to paying their bills, helping them find a safe place to live or a good school for the children, and sometimes establishing ways for them to purchase their groceries, if the talent is very well known and can't go out to shop without a hassle. Many well-known stars can't just walk into the bank, or pick up their own dry cleaning without getting mobbed by fans. So a personal manager makes life much easier for his or her client. The personal manager's commission is typically 5%-10% of their client's gross salary.

## *Business Managers*

Business managers are very similar to talent or personal managers in that they handle the day-to-day operations of their client's *business affairs*. They assist with everything from setting up corporations, corporate accounts, finding out what the tax laws are in other states and countries and how it affects the client regarding paying taxes, allocating and paying commissions to the agents, managers, lawyers, accountants, paying their bills, helping them purchase and rent business vehicles, helping them find a place to live, and helping to make solid business investments. Many successful stars need business managers to help them manage the business side of the entertainment industry. The business manager's commission is typically 3%-5% of their client's gross salary.

## Financial Advisors

Financial advisors are quite beneficial if you have substantial assets. They will be helpful with showing you how, who, when, and where to invest your money. A good financial advisor is financially savvy and can create a financial and investment portfolio that will be beneficial to a client from the first day that they start making money in the industry to the day that they retire and beyond. Financial advisors typically charge a monthly fee of about 1%-5% of the value of the investment portfolio that they manage for you. This varies of course depending on the agreement between client/advisor.

## Accountants

A working child entertainer absolutely needs an accountant. There are many benefits and tax shelters that an accountant can educate the child and the parent about. An accountant is trained and educated to address, process and help the parent and child. Parents are not accountants, unless a parent is an actual accountant. Unless that is the case, parents should not be handling and working on their child's tax business. Many entertainers are not familiar with what is and is not tax deductible, and children's taxes are even more complicated. In addition, some of the tax filings and parts of the tax return that are relevant to an entertainer are out of the norm for most people, and they find it extremely difficult to prepare such filings or returns on their own. Simply put, a good and ethical accountant knows more than you do about money and tax matters and how it applies to your child's money. It is extremely important for taxes to be paid, and tax returns filed on a timely basis. The IRS and state tax authorities do not care how old or young you are when it comes to paying taxes. Unpaid taxes and un-filed tax returns never go away. It is also imperative that quarterly estimated tax payments (if applicable) be paid to avoid penalties. The accountant will walk you through this. Ask lots of questions so you can learn as much as possible.

## Publicists

There is a right time and wrong time to get a publicist. If your child is not working on a project or starring in anything that will give him exposure, you may be able to wait a while for a publicist. The good ones are very expensive so wait until you really need one, or can afford to hire one. Publicists usually work on a retainer and will charge about $1,500-$3,500 a month. Some may charge more and some may charge less. A publicist is usually on retainer for a few months while they are publicizing a new project for you, which involves booking you on talk shows, special events, parties, red carpet affairs and the like.

## Acting/Dialogue Coaches

For the sake of growth and development, acting coaches are quite necessary. Typically for young children, coaches are not necessary because there is a natural, organic quality that all kids have that is evident and attractive to casting. However, over time a child may develop habits, may become conscious or aware that they are "acting" and need to redefine or redevelop their God given talents in order to transition into another phase of their career development. Some kids never get coached and lead successful careers because their instincts are fresh and discerning of their environment and they know how to grow as they adapt. Some kids are fortunate to be auditioning at a certain casting agency, for the right role at the right time; while others are constantly coached from the first day that they embark on their acting journey. To determine if your child needs to be coached, ask his or her talent representation. If they don't have a rep yet research good acting coaches in your area and ask them. Make friends and ask other parents if they know of a good acting coach that could assess your child's acting ability. Acting coaches typically charge from $75-$250 per session. Many of them have reasonable weekly, monthly or annual deals.

## *Studio Teachers*

Studio teachers are not necessarily a part of your child's creative team, but they are a very important part of your child's academic success and productive time spent on set while they are working on a project. Studio teachers have dual roles. They serve as your child's on site educator and your child's welfare worker. The studio teacher is hired by the production company and chosen from a pool of industry teachers who only work with industry kids. There are some wonderful teachers in the system, but a few of them serve as irresponsible substitute teachers (all though they don't last long). If you come across a good one, your child will be able to make the transition from grade school to higher education easily and effectively.

# 11

## The Assassins

I must start this section off by laying a foundation. If you stick with me for the next four paragraphs you will understand its purpose. Ok…here we go. Everyone, kids and adults alike, has different strengths and weaknesses, measures of disciplines, obstacles, various flaws and challenges, evident strongholds and lucid resolutions. From traumatic childhood experiences to a single event that served to change the course of a person's life forever, we all have moments in time or situations in our life that prompt, trigger or evoke certain behaviors, habits, mindsets or attitudes. I must also add that no one has reached the destination of perfection, although we would like to believe we have at times. Life is a journey that can lead to many amazing, dark, bright, enlightening, depressing, celebratory or thought provoking places. We are all works in progress and no one has it all figured out. We all have areas that we need to work on during every stage of our lives. Each of these areas can serve to assist us and assist others to become better or worse individuals.

There are seen and unseen forces (good and bad), personal choices, behaviors and actions that contribute to many of the situations and realities that manifest in our lives every day. Some of these realities are self-inflicted or embraced, some could have been avoided and others have been thrust upon us. The realities that are seen, and even the ones unseen, present us with moments that will shake, break, or make us. They can create dark junctures of no return, lead us to enlightened roads that change the course of our lives for the better or present us with those "life will never be the same again" situations that alter the way we view ourselves, others and our futures. I am one of those people who believe that very few things in life just occur by happenstance. Most often, there are circumstances, chains of events, actions, or seeds (negative or positive) that were watered and nurtured. There exist personal choices, mindsets, contributing reactions to a situation, or a chain of events that can affect a person, with a rippling effect on, to, or for something or someone else or many others. I'm talking about everything from obesity, Obsessive Compulsive Disorders and stealing candy at a grocery store, to gambling, car accidents, random acts of violence, terrorist attacks, lack of motivation, a smile that can brighten someone's day, a negative attitude, a kind word that can bring someone to tears, hoarding and anything else imaginable.

Before my sons were born, I spent years in daily prayer (and still do) regarding all areas of my family's life. I wanted to know how to proactively eliminate negative and dysfunctional behaviors and outcomes that were evident in my immediate and extended family's history and social environments. I desired to do this because I realized that these negative or dysfunctional attributes, mindsets, behaviors, and generational predispositions were the main reasons why certain people didn't reach their potential in life, fulfill their purpose, died early, or negatively altered the lives of others around them. I realized, of course, that most people come from dysfunctional families, but I did not believe that anyone had to live and die in that dysfunction. I didn't want to pass these negative realities onto the next generations if I had the power to prevent it. I wanted my sons to do more, be more, learn more, help more, be better and even make different types of mistakes (because we all make them) than generations before them had. I didn't want them to be perfect or better than anyone else. Rather, I wanted them to make better life choices. I knew, as most parents do, that my sons had a great purpose. I didn't want anything that my husband and I had the power to control, seen or unseen, to stand in the way of them reaching their full potential and accomplishing everything that they were created to fulfill - even though I didn't know what that purpose was at the time.

I knew that I could only teach them what I knew. So I committed my life to becoming an eternal student, forever learning and constantly growing. Before I became a minister and even in my teens, I had a desire to live a fasting/consecrating lifestyle. Fasting is a biblical principle that I researched often. Fasting/consecrating is simply abstaining from food or other desires for a certain period of time. I didn't develop this lifestyle for religious reasons or pressure from church experiences, but in essence, to live a vice-less, disciplined, purposeful and focused lifestyle. I was convinced that this would be the variable that could eliminate many negative and dysfunctional behaviors and mindsets in my life. I believed it was the key to open some of the doors to my purpose. I didn't want to live a scattered life, and I didn't want anything, or anyone, controlling me or having control over me, except God. I didn't want to be controlled by food, manipulation, family, chocolate, church doctrine, peer pressure, culture, social circles, religion, society, drugs, alcohol, money, attention, my pride or anything else that could serve as a vice or gateway to dysfunctional behaviors, mindsets or attitudes.

Over these many years, I have experimented and abstained from meats, fast food, television, dairy, texting, phone calls, talking to negative people, desserts, entertainment, shopping, sugar, junk food, traveling, attending public events, listening to music, drinking my favorite beverages, gossip, and just about anything else imaginable. Not all at the same time, of course. Nevertheless, fasting doesn't serve as a punishment in my life; it is not a diet, nor is it the seed or beginnings of anorexia or bulimia. Rather, it is a proactive, lucid, and purposeful lifestyle choice for me. It is a practice that is useful in detecting, alerting, and preventing any addictive or destructive behaviors that might be lurking in my future. It also serves as internal or spiritual radar, of sorts, that recognizes anything that I might be predisposed to, but that I may not logically be aware of.

Fasting helps me to shift my focus from things that I may want to do for a certain period of time, so that I can focus on things that I really need to or must do. It doesn't mean that I never get to do the things I want to. Actually, it's quite the opposite. I get to grow, develop and expand my knowledge, experiences and perspective of life and the world as I shift my focus from one thing to another. In essence, fasting doesn't change you or your environment. It changes your mindset and strengthens your level of discipline. I wanted to live my life in a way that I could live without or walk away from anything negative or toxic without having withdrawal symptoms or struggles to do so. Let me give you an example.

There was a time when my sons were little that my family loved eating pork bacon and a specific type of canned meat. Yes, meat…in the can. Please don't judge me! Anyway, we loved eating it like no one else we knew! As I studied, researched and learned about the unhealthy ingredients it had, I became more health conscious, and we began to slowly eliminate it and other foods from our diet. Because I have been fasting since I was much younger, my sons began a fasting lifestyle in my womb. While I was pregnant with each of them I would talk to them and tell them things like, "Ok, baby, we are not going to have chips for the whole month, ok?" Or, "Ok, baby, we are not going to watch anymore videos until after Christmas. We can do it, right?" During that time of fasting, pregnant or not, we would spend time discussing, laughing, in prayer, playing, or on a family trip and finding other things to do instead of what we were fasting from at the time. We would find ways to shift our focus onto something else whenever we were tempted by what we were abstaining from. We'd discover some new adventures or new things about ourselves, which was a great distraction. Before we knew it, time had passed and we had completed that fast and were on to another one. Over time, it became more of a training exercise than a fast, much like a body builder, except we were training the muscles of the mind and our will power. In actuality, we were all unwittingly being trained for life. Fasting for us is not a Hollywood fad; it's a healthy, disciplined lifestyle. Much like a family of fitness trainers or a family of athletes, it takes daily focus and discipline for all three.

The goal of fasting, coupled with daily prayer, was always to achieve a greater level of insight. This daily prayer time gives me clarity; understanding and helps to fine tune many areas of discernment and allows me to be sensitive to everything and everyone around me or connected to me. It has always been the key to life changing answers, direction, business and personal strategies and situations. I learned when to say yes, when to say no, when to wait, when to go forward, how to close a door, who to work with, who to trust, and other strategic movements. So that became my foundation as I began soul searching and making sobering assessments of my own life and behaviors to get to the root of many potential, unfortunate and unseen realities that were lurking in my future and my family's future.

As I mentioned before, every family has dysfunctional family members, behavioral traits or negative behavioral consistencies or tendencies. With some families, there exist predispositions to alcoholism, sickness, physical abuse or drug abuse. With other families, it could be white or blue-collar crime, dead-beat dads, obesity or anorexia. Every family has some type of issues to address, recover from or deal with. Yes, every family, large or small, black or white, rich or poor, American or Indian...well, you get the point.

During my prayer time, God began to speak to me about reasons why certain things happened in our lives. For those who would need clarity regarding my last sentence, yes, I do believe God speaks and that truth is not up for debate.

He speaks in ways we can all recognize and discern. We can pay attention to His inaudible voice if we discipline and posture ourselves to do so. I am a researcher at heart, and in doing so I found that biblical scriptures along with social and psychological research all confirm what I am about to say to you regarding the cause and effect of certain situations. God began to reveal certain things to me through prayer, assessing my environment, and a cognitive behavioral approach of evaluating my life and environment. I discovered some profound facts about people. Our behaviors, our lives, how we live them and how we handle occurrences within them create variables that can serve to help us along the way. I learned during this time that for everything in life there is a reality of opposites that many people may not notice. Let me explain. Many of us have learned Sir Isaac Newton's Third Law of Motion that states, "For every action there is an equal and opposite reaction." The notion states that for every positive there is a negative. Everything has an opposite. There are even two sides to every coin and story, and this is apparent throughout our daily lives. Some examples of these realities could be 'good and bad,' 'hot and cold,' 'push and pull,' 'love and hate,' 'left and right,' and so on.

From this same perspective, God began to reveal to me, in many ways, that for every positive personality trait or behavior, there is a potential for the negative or opposite personality trait or behavior to manifest or emerge. For example: for every wise choice there is also a foolish one. We have within us the capability of expressing either wise or foolish behavior, depending on the types of variables that are embraced, that are adapted, that are presented, or that are forced upon us. In most cases, we all have the power to choose, but within that power to choose, we have been influenced one way or another by our past or current experiences that attempt to pull us in one direction or another. Based on the variables I just mentioned, our strengths and weaknesses battle with each other, and many other realities serve as the instigating crowd behind us as if these opposing realities were in an after school playground fight.

As a result, I have come to learn that we all have "Fork in the Road" moments, almost daily. In these "fork in the road" moments, there are, what

# The Assassins

I call "Destiny Thieves," "Demonic Spirits," "Demons to wrestle with" or "Assassins to our purpose." For this chapter, I am going to use the word "assassins" to define all of the above. An assassin, by definition, simply put is - a murderer. Some of these assassins are external persons or realities, and some of them are spiritual or internal struggles or realities. We have all had to contend with assassins at one point in our lives, and so will our children. I believe that the sole purpose of these assassins is to make sure that we live and die *without* ever accomplishing everything that we were meant to accomplish. Some of the assassins achieve their goal and some of them do not. I assume by now, some of you are scratching your head in confusion or questioning my sanity. If you are, fantastic! I hope you finish reading the rest of this chapter preparing to confirm your suspicions of my mental stability (or lack thereof). I am up for the challenge. I am sharing this information with you because if I can say anything that can help one person fulfill his or her purpose in life, whether it is in entertainment or not, this book is a success! As I mentioned in my introduction, I will be talking to you as if we were out having lunch and I was sharing as candidly as I possibly could with you.

Some people may not want or feel they need this information because it doesn't have a formula to riches and fame. The truth is there is no formula to riches and fame. It's an illusion filled with drama and trouble. Just ask most "rich" people who were not prepared for it, or "famous" individuals who didn't understand the gravity of it. However, there is a breadcrumb trail that I can share with you that may help you find your measure of wealth and success to accomplish your purpose. I will share the breadcrumbs after we get past this section of the book. For those who are reading thus far and feel that you don't want or need this information because you are either well aware or well equipped for fame or riches, I applaud you! For everyone else, the assassins, as I mentioned earlier, tend to manifest in several forms that may not seem obvious, until now. Let me add for the sake of the obvious that life happens to all of us and some things are out of our control. However, if people don't focus or recognize some of the characteristics, movements or personalities of these assassins, they may find themselves helping their own personal assassin reach its goal. I will be sharing some (but not all) of these assassins with you. As you read further, I am sure you will be able to notice how some of these assassins were successful in reaching their goals with individuals that you may know, or even yourself. Anyone can fall prey to them. They are not just isolated to the entertainment industry, although these assassins seem right at home in the show business arena. However, the problem with being rich and famous while dealing with these assassins is much worse because it puts you on the front line of disaster in many other ways that I will explain later.

Unfortunately fame and riches don't necessarily make life better. They tend to magnify the truth of what a person's life really is because it affords them access, opportunity, and availability to the good and the bad without the usual consequences – that is, at least, at first. If a person is violent, the power behind riches and fame magnifies the violence. If he or she struggles with drug abuse, it magnifies and gives a person access to feed, fund and fuel the abuse. If a person is stingy, manipulative or greedy, fame and riches will magnify that as well with unethical business practices, deceptive ways to get what they want, and smoke screened opportunities to steal. Nevertheless, these assassins show up and attempt to affect and infect people from all walks of life, in all fields of employment, in every area of the world, no matter what the address or income is, or if you are young or old, rich or poor. Some of these assassins have been hanging around out in the open for years, but fame or money just exposed them to a greater degree. These culprits were successful in the lives of some of the past, present and future rich and famous people, your family members, co-workers, neighbors, and in some cases, even you. These assassins are equal opportunity goons and will attempt to show up, invited or uninvited. Some of these assassins overlap one another or have characteristics or traits found in others on the list because they are all inter-connected to a degree. Fortunately, there are ways to outsmart the assassin's agenda if you are paying attention and are willing to be honest with yourself, do what it takes, are disciplined enough, and are ready to lay a foundation of alertness, discernment, prevention and preparation for your child, yourself and your family.

# ASSASSIN #1

## *Poor Money Management*

*Poor* is defined as deprived. We all know *money* is cash and *management* is defined as skilled in handling something successfully. The definition of *fortune* is a position in life that is determined by wealth or riches. Wisdom is knowledge obtained that enables one to make sound decisions for the future. There are people who have experienced tremendous amounts of fame in a short period of time and as a result, the quick trip to the house of abundance gives them a warped perception of themselves, their amount of talent and their future. They begin to believe that their current reality will last forever. They fail to take into consideration that poor money management, poor business deals, inflation, taxes, life, kids, family, failed relationships, wasteful spending, divorces, alimony (for men and women), child support, and the like, will empty a bank account as if it was water going down a drain. There are those who struggled to pay their dues and eventually began to benefit from all of their hard work. Unfortunately, they somehow forgot, or chose not to remember, that they were once struggling financially. They begin to live life as if money was no longer an issue. Somehow the vehicle that drove them to the door that gave them access to money came back for a return trip back to the land of poverty. They are left in shock, devastated, regretful and embarrassed. They lived every day to the fullest, never thinking about what could happen in the future. They never considered what would happen if the next album didn't sell, the next string of movies flopped, the television show got cancelled, the 15 minutes of fame dissolved, the "sure thing" investment fell through, the marriages didn't work out, the break up was vicious or their reckless spending lifestyle caught up with them.

These scenarios are played out in the entertainment industry, as well as other industries, daily. The first scenario is overwhelming for the person who wasn't ready and able to adjust to the advantages and disadvantages of their fortune. It's pretty much like a person who has been playing the lottery for several years and dreams of one day winning millions of dollars. They believe that if they ever win big all of their troubles will go away. This person visualizes that once they win, they will walk into their place of employment and tell his or her boss how they really feel about them, then quit and live happily ever after with their big house and lavish lifestyle. However, dreams and reality are two separate things. If a person has the opportunity to win a large jackpot, their lives will never be the same. Before they are able to spend a dime they will find out quickly, who their friends really are, who their enemies really are and how many people want a portion of their money. From taxes, to lawsuits, to bankers, to leeches and business consultants, everyone will try to get a portion of their money. All of a sudden, the jackpot winner is popular…he or she is now rich! Another factor that is rarely considered during the dream phase is money management. It is so important to understand what the purpose of money really is. If you don't know its purpose for your life you will misuse it and quickly lose it. These scenarios leave people wondering, "What did I do with all of that money?"

Many folks can't remember where all of their money went and are frustrated to realize how fast it disappeared. Some people shop it away. There is nothing wrong with having nice or expensive cars, clothes and houses. However, if these tangible things are used to define you or they allow you to attempt to impress others or help you to make yourself feel more important, then you are headed in the wrong direction. Some people drink it away. Some people party it away and sadly some people just throw it away with their foolish dysfunctional behaviors. For most people, you don't get a second chance to be rich! I am sure that many former sports, rap, television and movie stars would agree with that.

I tell people all the time, "If a person doesn't know how to manage $100 they will not know how to manage $1,000,000." I say this because there are general or foundational principles found in money management. It is applicable to all and for all. The first thing to know is that every dime that you have in your possession has an assignment or destination. Every dime that you make, receive, and spend has a purpose. If you don't know what the purpose of the money that you have is, you will most likely mismanage it. Learning how to be good overseers of money is key, and a great indicator of how much you will possess. Let me give you an example. Let's say, David makes $2,000 after taxes (net income). He does not have a savings account but he does have a checking account. His check is directly deposited into his account every month. Let's say that $1,600 of his paycheck goes to living expenses every month (car note, car insurance, rent, groceries, gas, cable, utilities, and the like). After his monthly expenses are paid, he has $400 left for the month. He routinely goes out to dinner a couple nights a month (25 x 2 = $50), orders takeout a few nights a month ($20 x 3 = $60), goes to the movies twice a month (30 x 2 = $60), has a cup of Starbucks coffee every morning on the way to work (4 x 20 = $80), gets a haircut every two weeks ($40), and tends to buy a little something for himself (jeans, a hat, a jacket, etc) just because ($50). By the time he gets to the end of the month he only has $60 left. He hasn't used his money wisely, and now he is uncomfortable, unhappy and low on cash because his next paycheck will not be deposited into his checking account for a few more days.

Every person should have a financial goal. This goal can be to save a certain amount of money by the end of the year, to buy a house, to start saving money for college, to put away for emergencies, to create a savings account solely for vacations, and the like. Doing this is so important because it causes people to become financially disciplined. I have found that there should be at least five components to managing money every month. The components are *Saving, Giving, Helping, Investing and Planning*. Everyone knows how to spend money, but not everyone knows how to save, give, help, invest and plan. I have found that money is meant to move. It should be a verb instead of a noun because it should always be in motion and affecting its environment. Even when money is "sitting in the bank," it is moving. The money that we literally and physically deposit in the bank is rarely just sitting in the bank, unless it is placed in a safe deposit box. We have heard enough stories in the news about how banks use monies deposited in personal savings/checking accounts to loan to other people or institutions. That's one of the reasons why you get interest on your money in your savings accounts, because the money that you have deposited is being loaned to someone else, for something else.

If a multi-millionaire were to walk into a local bank in a small city and ask to withdraw, in cash, four million dollars of the money that she has been depositing over the years, this wealthy person will probably see the bank tellers and managers, making phone calls, whispering at each other and scrambling like crazy, trying not to look panicked or like they are in over their heads. They will probably begin having private little conversations over at the manager's desk before coming back to the teller's window with some type of interesting information to give them. The millionaire may or may not get her money, in cash, right away because, although the money is figuratively in her account, all of it may not literally be sitting in the bank waiting for her. This millionaire will eventually get her money of course, but it will most likely not be in cash or on the same day because the bank probably doesn't have it all sitting around waiting for her to come get it.

### *Save, Give, Help, Invest, Plan*

I have found that saving, giving, helping, investing and planning are the key components to becoming financially healthy and wealthy.

- Each month, no matter how much a person makes, putting a percentage of that money away for *savings* is key. This money can be put in an account or somewhere in your house or somewhere else safe.
- Each month, no matter how much a person makes, putting a percentage of that money away for *giving* is key. I believe in the biblical principles of tithing (giving 10% of my earnings to a church, charity, outreach, or the like). I have found that giving a portion of money

away is like planting seeds in the soil. As with a plant, I may not see a harvest on it right away, but at the right time I will.

- Each month, no matter how much a person makes, putting a percentage of that money away for *helping* is key. Help people who "need" help. Helping family, friends, strangers and organizations is a great way to become philanthropic. Helping others allows one to take the focus off of him or herself. This also keeps them from being stingy or greedy.

- Each month, no matter how much a person makes, putting a percentage of that money away for *investing* is key. There are so many ways to invest. One can invest in the stock market, someone's *sensible* start up business, someone's life or education, investing time for community service, and the like. Of course, you have to use wisdom regarding what you are investing in and seek advice from someone (preferably a professional) who knows more about investing than you do. I am not talking about investing in your uncle's tire patching business because he learned to patch his pants well as a child or a friend who wants to start a record company because she knows the titles and lyrics to a lot of songs.

- Each month, no matter how much a person makes, putting a percentage of that money away for *planning* is key. Planning for a retirement, purchasing property, going back to school, a future event, and the like are some ways to use money to plan. No matter how much money a person makes or has saved, we can all work toward this goal.

Now let's talk about *spending*. Some people just don't know how they should be spending their money when they get large amounts of it. Many people realize that the money may go away as quickly as they get it and become very frugal with it. That is not an entirely bad perspective to have. Others, on the other hand, take the "life is short" approach or the "money will be flowing like this forever" approach and will spend their money as soon as they get it. This may not be such a great idea. I have seen very unfortunate situations where as soon as a person acquired a considerable amount of money, they bought very expensive cars, homes, and clothes, went on trips, made very bad investments, gave money away to their friends, hosted big parties and took an entourage of people with them to clubs and spent thousands of dollars a night.

They spend large amounts of money on the sexual services from women (or men) and once that door is open, it becomes part of the spending frenzy that never seems to end. It is very sad to see those same people just a few years later broke, empty, friendless, regretful and sometimes homeless. When a person acquires a large amount of money, it is very important for them to get sound advice from someone who has been successful in their field to teach them how to manage their money. Contrary to popular belief, people who are in similar situations are willing to help by giving advice on either what to do or what not to do because they have been through it. Oftentimes, the person who is hearing the advice is not always "listening" to the advice, nor are they planning to follow it. Unfortunately, some folks are determined to learn the hard way. One final note to mention in this area is that there is a difference between *"Wants"* and *"Needs."* Just because you want something, does not mean you need it or that it is beneficial for you now or in the future. Many people don't know the difference between the two words. As a result, they end up with a life full of "stuff" that they never needed in the first place: the "new" jet, two sports cars, 18 bedroom houses, statues in the home, gold plated toilets, elaborate but dated state of the art electronics, and the like. I have heard many people say, "It seemed to make sense at the time," but now they realize that it was an unwise purchase. As a result, they try but can't get all or any of their money back from these extravagances.

On another note, when many people hear that a celebrity "bought" a multi-million dollar home or a mansion, in most cases they immediately think that this celebrity purchased the house with cash. Often times, the house is mortgaged just like the average person's house is but with tremendously high and ridiculous monthly payments. Once the money stops flowing and the taxes on the house quickly mount up, many celebrities are swallowed up in debt and lose their "dream house." A great lesson to learn before making many of the financial mistakes that tend to plague certain celebrities is you don't need to have the newest, biggest, brightest, shiniest, tallest, loudest, fastest, flashiest, most elaborate, most fun, toys, parties and attention grabbing trinkets, people and experiences to be valuable, important or relevant.

If you *know* your value, you won't have to *prove* your worth.

If these things are a must for you, the assassin of poor management might just succeed in taking you out. One of the best ways to use your money is to live a lifestyle that is beneath what you can actually afford to pay with cash. That doesn't mean that you have to live like a pauper. With this mindset you can still live, enjoy, be adventurous, have fun, travel, buy nice things, celebrate and live to the fullest and make a difference in the lives of others. The biggest difference is you will be doing it from a financially disciplined place.

## ASSIGNMENT CHALLENGE: TO OUTSMART THE ASSASSIN OF POOR MONEY MANAGEMENT

If you feel like this may be the assassin that has targeted you, I have an exercise for you. Try a 12 month fast. For an entire year, don't buy ANYTHING for yourself (yes this fast includes birthdays and all holidays for one year). No shoes, clothes, perfume, no eating out, no take out, no asking anyone to buy something for you, no hats, shirts, chips, candy, gum, pillowcases, make up, magazines, and the like. The only things you can buy for yourself are the essentials like personal items and toiletries (tissue, soap, dental floss, lotion, feminine products, etc). You can teach your child to do it too. Before you say, "I can't do that!," let me tell you that that statement is not the truth. What you probably mean is, "I don't want to do it." If you don't want to do it, that is your choice. If you take on this fast, it will help discipline you and help you make sure that the assassin of poor money management does not take you out. Truth be told, most of us already have the essentials of what we really *need* any way. The rest of it is "stuff" that we *want*. Anybody can do this! No matter how much or how little you have or you make. This will free you up and allow you to look at your behavior and assess the difference between "wants" and "needs" in a new way. Whenever you feel tempted to buy something, "DO" something for someone else or help someone else in some way - from a kind word to buying someone a scarf if the weather is cold.

*If you choose to take this 12-month challenge on, let me know on my website www.angelajwilliams.com or tweet me @my3tjwsons and let me know which fast assignment you have chosen and when you are going to start. At the end of every month send me an update. If you choose not to attempt this fast, that is fine too. However, you are without excuse and you can no longer say that you didn't know about this assassin or you don't know what to do about poor money management issues.*

# ASSASSIN #2

## *Business Ignorance*

Business ignorance, or lack of knowledge, has been the demise of a great deal of entertainers who were once successful but are no longer as relevant in the realm of entertainment as they used to be. This is the area that they will tell you that they failed in the most. Many of them would start by saying, "If I only knew then, what I know now, I would have done things differently." The business of entertainment, no matter what sphere it is in, is called "Show Business" for a reason. It encompasses everything from sports, music and art to television and film. Nevertheless; the truth is, "Show Business" is 10% show and 90% business. If you don't know the business and political side of entertainment, you can be swallowed up before you even know what happened to you. Knowledge is powerful. No one should know more about your child's business than you do. No one should have more authority over your business than you. With that being said, I would suggest that you do not give someone authority to sign checks on your behalf or the behalf of your child. There are many ways that entertainers set up the payment system stream with their team or representatives. If it's just a two-team structure or a ten-team structure, you can still sign your own checks so that you will always know what you are signing and what you are paying for. If your child's accountant or business manager has a problem with that, then maybe you need to reconsider having them on your team. You *will* however, need an accountant and an entertainment lawyer in this business. You can talk with them and ask questions about the check signing issue. Most ethical lawyers and accountants will give you the same or similar sound advice.

While you are interviewing or considering working with them is the time to ask questions about the legal aspects and the accounting side of your child's business. Once you find the ones you are comfortable with, just know that you will be paying your lawyers and accountants to work on your behalf. Ask questions. Ask lots and lots of questions, especially of your accountant. If you don't understand something, ask again and take notes. Don't ever go along with what they say if you don't understand. If you find yourself saying things like "Oh, ok" more than twice while they are talking to you, stop them and ask more questions to get further clarity. There is no such thing as a dumb question if you really don't know the answer. Don't call your lawyer or accountant every day with random questions though; they don't have time to waste talking on the phone with you all day. Be professional. Have a clear, well thought out list of questions ready for them to address when you call them. Pretend that you are your child in this case and you don't completely understand what they are talking about (because you probably don't and that's ok).

Have them explain it to you until you understand. Again, don't forget to take notes so that you can share the information with your child. If you have to go back and ask the question again, another way, that's ok too. A good lawyer and accountant won't mind if you do that. Then go home and research the information that they gave you. Always conduct your child's business affairs as if you may not be able to trust the person working for you. I didn't say, however, that you shouldn't trust them or you should be suspicious of them. Just don't take a vulnerable stance of silence or ignorance with them. There is no greater feeling than doing your research to find that your accountant or lawyer was completely straightforward and honest with you. Let your child go to the meetings and let your child ask questions too, even if the questions seem silly. Eventually, if your children are successful in the future, they will be the ones in the room or on the phone talking to their representation about their contracts or money matters. You may not be around in the future, so you want to make sure that your children know how to handle themselves and handle their business. They can learn by watching you conduct their business now. However, if you do your own research and stay up on the information that your accountants give you, and your team knows that you are doing that, you are less likely to be taken advantage of if by chance you have an unethical person on your team.

The same goes for agents, managers, business managers, PR and everyone else on your child's team. You need to know as much about what they do and how they do it as you can - at least in terms of the general responsibilities. Relaying that information to your child is a good thing too, taking the child's age into consideration, of course. Don't be annoying and disrespectful with your approach when asking questions though. This especially applies to the SAG/AFTRA laws and rules, Coogan accounts, school and home schooling laws and rules. Get to know the SAG/AFTRA folks in all departments. They are pretty cool. Reach out to them and acquire a contact person so that they will know you when you call with a question. Don't be shy, but again, don't be annoying and overbearing. Conduct yourself professionally and respectfully when you ask questions. Also, remember that you, the parent, are representing your child. I have several people, parents and young adult actors tell me that they don't have time to do all of that. They just want to entertain or watch their children entertain. I understand that, but that is not a good position to take. There are people who have lost everything because they were not paying attention to their own business. You and your child should mind your own creative and money business while working on your craft. You may have wonderful business associates who are ethical and integral, and because of that they would never betray you. But suppose they are not as ethical as you thought? No one loses out as badly as your child. As a mentor, life coach/consultant, I tell people quite often, "I prefer you not trust what I say and conduct research for yourself and find out that I am right, than to trust me blindly and realize that I am leading you the wrong way." Some of them look at me like I am crazy for saying it, but it is true. That keeps me on my ethical toes too. Knowledge, on all levels, is powerful.

## ASSIGNMENT CHALLENGE: TO OUTSMART THE ASSASSIN OF BUSINESS IGNORANCE

If you feel like this may be the assassin that has targeted you, I have an exercise for you. *Try a one-hour a week fast, for 12 months.* Every week abstain from watching one of your 1-hour-long favorite televisions shows, listening to your favorite music or abstain from something that you know that you spend more than an hour a day doing leisurely. Instead of doing those things, research information that is relevant to your child's career. While gathering information, keep a journal of what you learned that week and share it with your child. Don't get distracted by links or pop-up messages while doing so. The goal is to discipline yourself, and learn something new about all areas of your child's career. Do this for an entire year. By the end of the year you should have learned 52 new things that you didn't know about incorporating, taxes, child labor laws, pension funds, how residuals work, work hours, and the like. Remember, you will not be doing me a favor. This is for the sake and the success of your children. You can teach them what you have learned so that they will be well informed. When you feel tempted to watch your favorite show, stop and instead research "celebrities who lost it all" in a search engine to get you back on track. Or go back to your journal and read what you have learned thus far.

*If you choose to take this once a week/12-month challenge on, let me know on my website www.angelajwilliams.com or tweet me @my3tjwsons and let me know which fast assignment you have chosen and when you are going to start. At the end of every month send me an update. If you choose not to attempt this fast, you are without excuse and you can no longer say that you didn't know about this assassin or you don't know what to do about business ignorance issues.*

# ASSASSIN #3

## *Lack of Accountability*

If entertainers are only surrounded by people who are on their payroll, and there is no one around them, on a daily basis, to hold them accountable for their actions, those entertainers have become, what I call *"Celebrity Pimps."* There is no easier or nicer way to say it! A *pimp* is someone who solicits for prostitution. A *prostitute* is someone who degrades talent for money. A "celebrity pimp" is someone who solicits others to degrade themselves for money, favors, perks, drugs, sex, a nice house, an alibi, to lie for them, to excuse reckless behavior, to handle "messy" or "suspect" situations, to get into parties, to be a part of an entourage, or to be used as a scapegoat. Those entertainers, even as talented, successful and powerful as they may be, are paying everyone around them to do whatever they want them to do. Whether it is legal, ethical, moral, civil, lawful, and respectful or not, for the right benefits, these celebrity prostitutes will do it. Over time, rich, famous or privileged folks who are used to getting their way, have a tendency to become masters of manipulating others. When this happens, these artists develop a warped and self-absorbed perception of life and a tunneled view of the environment they live in. The real world and its boundaries take a back seat to skewed perspectives and realities. From high to low profile celebrities, investment bankers, doctors, lawyers, pastors, parents, teachers, kids, presidents and the like, everyone needs someone to hold them accountable for their actions.

The moment we no longer have the accountability component in place, no matter how successful we are, no matter how much money we make, and no matter how powerful we think we are, that is the moment when the lines get blurry and the rules change. The disregard emerges, self-indulgence is justified, and wheels to the slow motion train wreck begin to roll. One of the scary things about the entertainment industry, in all areas, is that the amount of money and fortune that come along with the title is not average or normal. I hear many people say that an entertainer's life is "not real." There is no other field of employment that pays as well to be as creative and allows one to do what one loves to do while people pay to watch you do it. Professionals like teachers; cops, firemen, nurses, security guards and store managers may never experience the luxury and financial freedom of some entertainers. As a result, it is very easy for an entertainer to become spoiled, delusional, ungrateful, unrealistic and greedy. These types of attitudes need to be checked. Everyone, and I mean everyone, needs someone in their life that will pull them to the side or call them out and let them know when they are out of line, they have gone too far, they need to go home, they need to shut up, they have crossed the line, or they need to go away for a while to reevaluate all of the moving parts in their life. I have found that if a person's accountability people are also on payroll or are reaping some of the benefits of success, these people are less likely to address the entertainer's negative, sensitive or personal issues because they may fear losing their job, missing out on perks or becoming less valuable to the entertainer.

One of the main reasons why I chose not to be a talent "momager"/manager/agent for my sons is because my role as a mother has always been more important to me than anything else in the world. I didn't want anything to interfere with that. I love my sons to life, and they are awesome young men. My sons are now 22, 18 and 13 (at the time of finishing this book). They have always known, understood and respected what is most important to our family and our home. They also understand what is unacceptable in our family and our home. We purpose to create a "no disrespect, everyone matters, and everyone has responsibilities in our family" type of environment. I, of course, had to add in another little nugget into the mix that they can now probably recite word for word: "If you'll lie – you'll steal, if you'll steal - you'll kill, so don't let me catch you lying." With that being said, I have dedicated my life to raising them to be assets to the world and not liabilities. Unconditional love, communication, laughter, adventure, knowledge, applying the book of Proverbs, prayer, fasting, family time, discipline and respect has always been the foundation to the way that I mothered my children, even when they were in my womb. If I became their talent "momager"/agent/manager, my success or failure would directly be linked to or dependent upon their success or failure. What is worse than that reality is there may come a time when I would have to overlook or dismantle some of my parenting or our family's foundational structure or value system just to appease them, to make them happy or to make sure I kept my job. Just the thought of that makes my eye twitch.

There are two scriptures that I studied before my oldest son was conceived which serve as the nucleus of everything that I do as a mother. Proverbs 13:24 states, "Whoever spares the rod hates their children, but the one who loves their children is careful to discipline them." Proverbs 22:6 states, "Train up a child in the way he should go, and when he is old he will not depart from it." Once I read and understood these two scriptures I embraced them as if my entire parenting legacy depended on it. I purpose to apply them to every moment of our lives together. The funny thing is, in all of these years, each of them have only really been spanked once. They may have gotten little taps on their hands or pampers when they were toddlers for touching something dangerous, but that is about the extent of it. I found out quickly that if I focus on the second half of that scripture – "but the one who loves their children is careful to discipline them" - teaching them right from wrong (for example), while talking with and to them, I wouldn't have to focus on the first half of that scripture ("Whoever spares the rod hates their children"). The second scripture is self-explanatory and applicable to any situation, be it sports, entertainment, cleaning a room, public speaking or community service. This scripture requires every day application and teaching, but over time, I found that the process becomes second nature, fun, rewarding and beneficial for parent and child because we are all learning together.

These scriptures helped me explain life lessons, comedy routines (when the boys made me the brunt of jokes) and insightful or useful "Do you see why me and daddy didn't let you get away with stuff like that when you were younger?" teaching moments. Especially while watching movies, the news and dysfunctional television shows. I would often make many of the following types of statements while we watched the news, a movie or a show about kids who were disrespectful toward their parents or just acting inappropriately. "Don't let me find out that you were somewhere you were not supposed to be like *his* mother did" or, "Let me find out that you are acting like you have no common sense. You won't ever have to worry about the cops. If-you-see-me-coming-you-will-know-that-this-moment-is-not -going-to-end-well-for-you! I will call the 911 myself after I am finished with you!"

The boys would look at me, as they still do, and say something casual, and non-affected like, "Mom, relax, breathe, we are sitting right here," or, "Mom, it's ok…it's just a movie," or, "Yeah we know, if we tried to hit you like that 'actor' who is playing a 'role' in this movie, you would hunt us down and kill us…we get it."

My husband, who is a retired NYPD sergeant, would often tell them through the years, "I discipline because I love you now, so that the cops, who don't love you, won't have to discipline you later."

Through the years our sons learned to understand the gravity of comments like these and, in time, via experiences in the industry, saw what it looks like when that accountability is not present in a child's life. They would often have to calm me down after watching the news and hearing about one of the kids in the industry who didn't have the proper accountability component in his or her life that they needed around them. They would say, "Mom, remember, all of the kids in the industry are not like that and you can't save them all." They are absolutely right.

While learning to understand what these comments of correction meant to them when the boys were little, there were times when my husband or I had to discipline my sons. I am not the type of parent to yell or scream at them, unless we are wrestling, playing a board game or on a rollercoaster. I never felt the need to scold them because I inherited an awesome quality from my mother that was more potent. I have… "The Look." Yes, "the look" is an innate facial expression that many old-school African American women are known to possess. Many of these awesome women automatically and instinctively passed this down to their young daughters (and some of their sons). For those who know what "the look" is, there is no need to elaborate. For those that don't know, "the look" is more powerful and effective than spanking, yelling, time outs, or punishments! "The look" is a non-verbal and non-physical way of disciplining a child from a distance. All one needs is eye contact, the ability to zero in on a child's face, a few seconds to focus until you get the child's attention, and enough eye control not to break eye contact until you are confident your silent message has reached the intended target. The look is a stern and matter of fact expression on a mother's face that she gives to a child who is being disrespectful or acting as if they have forgotten how to conduct themselves respectfully, especially in public. This look is a hierarchical posture that the parent reveals and the child learns, or is conditioned to recognize very early in childhood. In essence, any behavior that is unacceptable or that embarrasses the parent gets this look. This look says, *"Don't-Let-Me-Have-To-Walk-Over-There-And-Deal-With-You-In-Pub lic-Because-If-I-Do-I-Will-Shut-Your-World-Down!"* For each parent/child, "the look" is generally a threat or a warning of impending and negative repercussions resulting from the child's negative behavior but the general or universal language of the look translates, "STOP-IT!" This is a fantastic accountability tool if used early enough in the child's developmental years. If the parent waits too late to exercise it, roughly after the child learns to talk or walk, the look is generally ineffective!

I paint this picture for a purpose. The other reason why I didn't want to manage my sons' careers from a talent point of view is because I didn't want to eventually have a "manager moment" that needed a mother's input or discipline. I didn't want one of my sons to have to figure out which side of me they were talking to. Just the thought that I could be saying something to discipline them, while in business mode, and they might disregard me or respond to me as if I were their representative instead of their mom invokes images of an old school, 1970s, World Wide Wrestling Federation (WWF) match. Yes, I did watch it as a kid; don't judge me. I can see myself now, first giving them "the look," from across the ring (I mean, across the room), then I'd take a page out of Jimmy "Superfly" Snuka's handbook and stand on top of the ropes, pointing in my son's direction preparing to do a flying leap in the air only to land on which ever son it was at the time. So the "momager" title and position was never a consideration or desire for me. I prefer to be the overseer of all of their business and the team instead. Needless to say, I have no tolerance for disrespectful kids, especially my own. My sons learned that very early on in their childhood. In my opinion, a child disrespecting a parent is unacceptable, in private or public. My sons and I play together all the time and they can get away with sayings certain things to me when we both know that we are in "play-mode." We wrestle, debate and disagree with each other too. But we all know where the line that should never be crossed is. There was no such thing as the stressful "terrible-twos" or the dreaded teenage phase in our house.

When I was growing up, talking back, raising voices at parents, temper tantrums, throwing objects across the room, walking or stomping away while arguing or while parents are talking, and slamming doors are things that my parents let me watch on television. It was never allowed in our home. I wasn't allowed to exercise it as a child and my sons' were/are not either. They learned this so early in life in private that by the time those "phases" arrived they already knew what was generally not acceptable in public. So instead, my sons learned how to communicate instead of just lashing out, even if we don't always agree. Thank God they still do and want to communicate. This is important because kids have voices that need to be heard and respected too (no matter how old or young they are). That doesn't mean that my sons are going to get what they want all the time, but it does mean that they will always be heard if they have something to say. It is a matter of balance. We have a non-verbal parent/child line that we don't cross. I am friendly with them, and I refer to them as my best buddies. However, we are not friends in the sense that we are on the same parental relationship level. Through the years, we have found a balance of communication that include mother/son dates, family meetings and chat sessions. During these times, we cover everything: entertainment industry experiences, family issues, politics, social issues, spiritual teachings, sex, drugs, parties, biblical discussions and moments of hilarious observations. At times, these discussions get pretty passionate, heated and loud (I admit we are loud people by nature). The foundation of our relationship is that I am the mother and they are the sons. This foundation has many moving parts that emerge from it and grow out of it, but the mother/son relationship is the core of it all.

As a result, I work *with* my kids in the industry, not *for* them. As a mom, I can speak freely, honestly and openly with them about anything (good or bad) because they are not my source of income, identity, shelter or stability. If we all decided to leave the entertainment industry completely, we would just simply move back to our home in New York and go on with our lives with great memories and many lessons learned but our family will be without fracture or dysfunction. For that I am grateful! So there is no pressure on them or me, no threats from this industry or concerns about the quality of our personal relationships with each other. I am grateful that I had a full, creative, emotionally healthy life before they were born, and I will have one after they all grow up and move out, although I will miss our times hanging out together on a daily basis. That's how our life is with Tyler who no longer lives with us, but we are as connected as we were when he did. Tyrel will be graduating high school this year (at the time of writing this book) and Tylen will be a freshman this fall. So my many years of home schooling all of them will be over soon, thank God! When that happens, it will be time for a great and necessary transition for all of us. As with Tyler a few years ago, I expect Tyrel and Tylen's to be a smooth and healthy transition as well.

Tyler has his own life and lives it well and can now apply and live out what he was nurtured in, his way. He no longer needs a mommy because I spent 18 years of his life doing that with him. I have graduated to mom or mother, or another one of his special names for me when he is coming to me with a certain type of question or a request for something that he wants me to make for our special family dinners! Once they all move out, I expect that we will just create new memories as they all walk into their "adult" phases. However, I will never cease from being their mother, accountability, wise counsel, support system, cheerleader, spiritual intercessor and the like. That is pretty cool! If they choose not to (or no longer) have me serve as overseer of their businesses and careers, I am completely fine with that because ultimately this is their life and career path. They know that I purpose to be an integral and ethical person, and that is how I posture to handle their business. I oversee, rather than rule or control, their creative, business careers and talent teams the same way. In that sense, they are accountable to me. However, how I oversee has to be open, honest and transparent. They have to know everything that I know, and no decision is made without a family meeting. I may call the meeting to order, but everyone votes and every vote counts.

Their behavior in public and private will be checked if I deem it necessary whether they want it or not. That of course is much different with 22 year-old Tyler, even though the accountability and overseeing piece is still a factor. He is now an adult, living on his own and making all of his own decisions. He is open about his decisions and usually run them by me, but he knows that he doesn't have to or need to if he doesn't want to. Although we see each other all of the time, his life is his own. I say this with a big smile on my face because when he moved out, even though we were all sad and looking quite pitiful for a few days, my husband and I knew that he was ready, able and prepared to do so. He had all the life tools that he needed to survive and thrive - even though we were not living too far away from him.

If there was ever an issue that needed to be addressed, the plan was to address it, along with others that we trust, long before it got out of hand. If the boys choose to work with someone else later in their career, I will celebrate them, give them advice as a mom and a current overseer, then step aside and probably go on a very long, adventurous vacation with my husband or sister-friends. We talk about this often so I expect and trust that the transition will happen when/if/how it should. Nevertheless, I know they love me because they honor and respect me. As they get older, I still give them sound advice. It comes from a place of respect for their age and freedom to make their own choices, whether I like or agree with them or not. I believe they take a lot of my advice, because they know that I care more about who they are than what they do for a living. Also, I have a good track record of not trying to manipulate them or disrespect them. Nevertheless, they have the choice and free will to either take my advice and the advice of wise people around them or not, with no pressure. Either way, they know that they will deal with the consequences that come, which may or may not be a good thing for them.

The good news is I don't plan to retire from motherhood. I will never stop being their mom. I will always be there for them if they need or want wisdom, the truth, correction, and the like. We have spent so much quality time together that even after I am gone, they will still be able to hear my words of wisdom in their ears and in their memory. That to me is an honor in itself and worth every moment spent with them. Their relationships with God and their parents are at the top tier and in the foundation of their accountability structure without question. They have other wonderful, ethical, professional, spiritual, family and close personal people who love, respect and care about the young men they are becoming, not about how much money, power, celebrity, popularity or access they have or will have. My sons know this, and they can rest assured that all of this serves as accountability and a support system that doesn't expect anything else from them should they want, need, or require it. If at some point, my sons remove themselves from their support system, they will have to deal or live with the consequences of their actions without the proper covering around them. However, they will never be able to say that they didn't have the support around them. Some of the tragic industry stories that we hear about in the news are about young kids who did not have the support that they needed. Many of the parents were absent, dysfunctional, trying to be entertainers themselves, or did not lay a foundation that was necessary to handle this industry.

There are too many industry stories that have made the news regarding events that could have been avoided. If only those celebrities had an accountability component that they trusted, respected and responded to, laying in the foundation of their career strategy, maybe things would have been different. We all need accountability components, especially if we don't think we need it. In this industry, my family and I have seen this particular assassin take out more people, families, morals, bank accounts and careers than we care to know about. I don't know everything about all things and my purposed path in life is not necessarily my sons' purposed path. I respect that because I know that they have been given all of the foundational tools that they will ever need to survive and thrive - and that brings me great joy. I am grateful. If it weren't for God instructing, guiding and disciplining me, I would have been a hot mess of a parent! My prayer is that the unfortunate circumstances of others that we see firsthand, and that others see on the news, will be the reality checks that keep my sons and all of those who read this book from falling prey to this assassin in the future.

It is an unfortunate reality to state but some of the young entertainers who fall prey to this assassin do so because their caregivers, mother, father (or both) condone, teach or allow unacceptable behavior to happen around them. Or in the case of many entertainers, the parents themselves, who are supposed to be the accountability, are participating in the unacceptable behavior with them. The first few times I saw this happening, I thought, "Ok, maybe the person I think is the parent is really an uncle, older sibling, a body guard or someone like that." I did not want to believe it. There are parents who party, drink, do drugs, fight, are sexually promiscuous, and do it non-discretely, along with and just as much as their kids do. I wish this reality wasn't true because when I hear about a child or young adult's social misconduct, in some cases, I already know what it is about. In a few of those cases, the news report isn't even scratching the surface of what is really happening. Hopefully it is not too late. I am cheering for them, because no matter how effective this assassin has been to date, the celebrity has the power to make the necessary changes.

## ASSIGNMENT CHALLENGE: TO OUTSMART THE ASSASSIN OF LACK OF ACCOUNTABILITY

If you feel like this may be the assassin that has targeted you, I have an exercise for you. *Try a once a week fast, for 12 months.* Abstain from keeping parts of your daily routine to yourself by sharing it with someone ethical that you trust and feel safe with. Let this person know that you have chosen them to hold you accountable to share this information with them. This is not a game or a joke, but it doesn't have to be a deep, dark secret either. Rather it can be something as simple as telling them about every website you have visited within the last week, without leaving one of the websites out; that means you have to make a mental or physical note of them. You could also disclose all of the people you have spoken to or texted throughout the week. You don't have to necessarily tell them what you spoke about, or maybe you do. Just let them know whom you talked to throughout the week and how often. This exercise will help you be more aware of who you speak with and how often. It will also help you to be transparent to your accountability person; you will discipline yourself to make a note of or recall the information, and help you to be consistent with sharing it. The person that you are sharing with doesn't have to do anything but listen. You can teach your child to do this, using homework, play dates, bad words they have used, or websites, for example, with you or someone trustworthy. Do this for an entire year. By the end of the year you should have shared information with someone you trust 52 times that has held you accountable.

*If you choose to take this once a week/12-month challenge on, let me know on my website www.angelajwilliams.com or tweet me @my3tjwsons and let me know which fast assignment you have chosen and when you are going to start. At the end of each month send me an update. If you choose not to attempt this fast, you are without excuse and you can no longer say that you didn't know about this assassin or you don't know what to do about lack of accountability issues.*

# ASSASSIN #4

## *Self-Destruction*

This assassin has several components, and I will attempt to cover just a few. Think about the growing list of entertainers and average folks alike who appear to become the conductors of their personal train wreck that is represented by their own life choices. Think about the many self-destructive behaviors, attitudes and lifestyles that we see played out in the lives of the rich and famous on the news, websites, and social media every day. Many people will quickly respond as they read or watch the news, "Why is he doing this to himself? He should know better. He is a mess. What a waste of talent. This is a shame, why in the world is he acting like this? He has everything, fame and money, and he's just throwing his life away? I wish I had his life. I would trade places with him in a minute." The truth is, entertainers are just ordinary people with extraordinary abilities, talents, access and opportunities. They have struggles, issues, and unfortunate situations happening in their lives just like the average person. In most cases, the struggles that do exist in their lives most likely would still exist if they were not entertainers. The difference is they use their talents to entertain small or large portions of the world while their lives are made public. Many of them are paid very well to do so. Unfortunately, they also have to live out their lives - as functional, destructive or dysfunctional as they may be - on a very public stage. Just think about the private dysfunctions or potentially self-destructive behaviors you have that no one, or just a few people, know about. What would happen if you had the financial means to fund, buy, feed, breed, endorse, hide or cover up those issues, for a while at least?

## *Addiction and Abuse*

Addiction and abuse can manifest in many forms: drugs (illegal, prescription, liquid, solid, or over the counter), food, plastic surgery, attention, sex, work, exercising, binging, sweets, shopping, tanning, tattooing, watching the news, TV shows, electronic games on your phone, all forms of social media, gambling, driving too fast or recklessly in fast cars, hoarding, etc. *Addiction* can be defined as any negative or destructive behavior that one cannot stop doing at will. *Abuse* can be defined as mistreatment or inappropriate use of a person, substance or situation. It seems that our society has become desensitized to addictive or abusive behavior. At times, even apparent struggles, in some circles, are embraced, condoned or excused by people. Others may justify that the behavior of some people are the norm, like taking sleeping pills every night to get to sleep, until something tragic happens. People have learned to use these two terms loosely and carelessly like they are, at times, socially embraced mindsets. I am sure we have all heard people mention their addiction to shopping, social media, food, or television. An addiction is typically anything that you can't walk away from on your own. It seems that people will admit to abusive behaviors easier these days because many of them know someone else who is abusing something or someone else in the same way. The good news is that some people will commit to getting the help that they need and eventually live addiction and abuse-free lives.

However, there are those who live volatile lifestyles in secret, and they go on living that way for years without getting real help. Some of these people are those that we live, work, or socialize with. Others are the very people we watch on television, whose music we listen to or whose products we purchase. They are wreaking havoc on their bodies, homes, or families. I have heard interviews on television or radio shows where certain entertainers talked about their addiction and how they overcame it. Some of them were really trying to deal with their issue and others were absolutely lying. A few of them were high or drunk during the interview and had no desire to get clean. While I'm on the subject of people getting the help that they need, I would not feel comfortable without mentioning that there are different types of facilities that appear to help those who really need it. For some facilities (not all), the words "Rehab," "Detox" and "Program" are just covert names for "Resort," "Get Away" "Hide-Away" and "Vacation."

Some people will not get the help that they need because of these crutches or co-dependent facilities that cater to the celebrity rather than proactively treating the disease or chronic condition. These facilities do this because the entertainer pays top dollar for non-therapeutic services and to keep the individual's whereabouts a secret. The entertainer's support system, or lack thereof, goes along with this façade, and a few months later the celebrity emerges back on the scene, supposedly "clean" but truthfully unchanged. Unfortunately, the individual is another tragedy just waiting to happen.

---

*Note: If you are not sure if you are addicted or abusive, try this exercise on for size.*

*Think about something that you love to do, something that you do constantly, or something that other people say that you do or say all the time. Now imagine at this very moment that you are no longer able to ever have or do that very thing, ever again. Does the thought of you abstaining from it make you anxious, upset, or uneasy? If you find yourself relating to any of these responses, you may have an addiction. If that is the case, you may want to seek help to better understand what is going on with you or which direction you might be headed in. Please seek help by a mental health professional. **Please don't wait until you are the topic of a "Breaking News" story on a popular news channel. I'm rooting for you!***

---

I hear people say all the time, "I just have an addictive or abusive personality." If that is the case, the last place you probably want to be is in the entertainment industry.

• Please check for these abusive or destructive traits in your children as well. If you find that they have certain negative traits or behaviors, or have been affected by someone who exhibits these behaviors, you may want to address these behaviors with them and with a professional sooner, rather than later.

- Please be honest with yourself – for yourself. Lies and denial will do nothing but prolong the situation. I have had the misfortune of knowing people who clearly had substance abuse problems. Industry insiders knew about it and sometimes some of these people would end up on the news. It grieved me to see them out in public thinking that they were hiding their problem. I would often see some of them on television talking about how many days, months or even years they were sober or drug free. I was shocked because I knew that wasn't true. But then, I remembered that they were performers. They knew how to act like they were telling the truth.

The biggest problem for me is the reality that these awesome but troubled people are adults. They were all 18 or older. No one can force an adult to do something they don't want to do. We can beg, cry, use tough love, stage an intervention, scream and even fight with them. But the bottom line for most is, unless they want to change, they won't change. It's a painful reality because by the time some people make the decision to do so, they have caused so much damage to their minds, bodies and spirits that their situation has a "too little, too late" outcome.

Imagine if you had the same opportunities that the entertainers you read about had. Would you be any better or worse off than they are? Think about those areas in your life that you know are counter-productive, but you do them anyway. Now just imagine if you had the money, notoriety, opportunity, clout, guarded hedge of secrecy, hired co-dependants/enablers or lack of accountability around you to do whatever you wanted, whenever you wanted, however you wanted without taking a step back to assess your behaviors and their consequences. Would you be in the same situation that many celebrities find themselves in? Or would you be able to rise above your challenge and overcome your destructive behaviors? Most of us will never know the outcome of a situation like this unless we have lived or survived it. Many people never reach their potential in life because they fall prey to self-destruction. I owe it to myself and you owe it to yourself and your life's purpose to look for self-destructive traits in your life, on a regular basis, and strive to uproot them before they become a habit. We must be transparent with someone we trust about these traits and allow ourselves to be accountable to them and ourselves, and then deal with those behaviors so we won't fall prey to the assassin of self-destruction.

This is very important because cemeteries are full of gifted, talented, trailblazing geniuses that never fulfilled their purposes in life because of their self-inflicted demise. I know too many people that are dead now because of this assassin. I hope that I've influenced you to assess the stability of your child and ask the hard questions about your child. Here are just some that you can begin with.

1. *Do I see seeds of self-destructive behavior in my child?*
2. *Is he the type of child that can handle the stresses of this fast paced industry with its ups and downs, good times and bad times?*
3. *How can I help him now so that destructive behavior won't be a factor for him in the future?*
4. *What does she reach for when she is happy?*
5. *What does he reach for when he is sad?*
6. *What routine does she have when she is bored?*
7. *Is she a leader or a follower?*
8. *What type of people does he gravitate to?*
9. *Is she a validation seeker?*
10. *When he loses does he become depressed?*
11. *Is she an attention seeker?*
12. *Is he a loner?*
13. *Is she introverted or extroverted?*
14. *Does he keep the doors to his bedroom closed? Why?*

Ask yourself these same questions as well. Learn what destructive behavior looks like and teach this to your children so that they can learn how to spot it for themselves. Don't wait until you think they need help to tell them about this. They may already need help, and this will be a defining moment for both of you. Don't wait and do this later. That day may never come or even worse, if it does, it may be too late to tell them.

## *Self-Sabotage*

Have you ever met a person who seemed to have his or her mind made up to make a mess of their own lives no matter how much support they receive or how many chances he or she gets? They live hard, fast and recklessly. They drink excessively, party hard and abuse drugs regularly. Many times, they surround themselves with people who act out the same type of negative behavior as they do. They tend to take on a lawless type of posture and don't seem to understand or care about repercussions. Of course, many of these people are also dealing with chemical, emotional, abandonment, anger, unresolved, or mental issues. However, some of them are aware enough to know that they are making a mess of their lives. Nevertheless, just because they know it doesn't mean that they are willing to do something about it. For many reasons, they sabotaged their own careers, relationships and finances. Some of them end up homeless, roaming the street, living in shelters or nursing homes, sleeping in their cars, or living with the lifelong debilitating effects that their lifestyles have rendered them. Many of them end up living with relatives or end up in prison. Some of them remain a shell of who they used to be. They are not dead…but they are not functionally alive, either. I often think this reality could not have been the plan for their lives when they were dreaming as children or at the top of their careers.

## *Pride/Narcissism*

*Pride* is defined as feeling superior to others or feeling a skewed level of self-importance. *Narcissism* is defined as vanity, self-absorption and conceit. This is a dangerous assassin because it is a warped internal and validating mindset that tends to disregard others. Pride or the notion of being prideful eventually causes people, if not checked, to implode and make public spectacles of themselves at the worst possible time. I am not talking about self-confidence and self-assurance. I am not even talking about having faith in oneself or being fearless in the face of competition. I am specifically talking about people who are condescending to others. Prideful people demand the spotlight, special attention or privileges in the midst of others because they may have had a level of success that seems superior to those around them. Prideful people only associate with certain types of people and will not entertain conversations with people they don't know or feel are important enough. These types of people may be disrespectful to their associates and representatives. They have a tendency to burn personal and professional bridges and sever relationships, not realizing that every action has an opposite reaction. Overtime, because of their success, they become mean spirited and indifferent people with little regard for others.

One of the problems with pride is it will convince you that you are indispensible, invincible, and irreplaceable. If people listen to the voice of pride, they will believe that they are above failure and will always be on top of all things successful. None of these realities are true for most people. Time has a way of teaching us all lessons that we need to learn. Time and life has a way of showing us things about ourselves that we have never noticed before. Pride plus time will present a few failed career choices, public outbursts, and help some prideful people make changes in their perspective, although some people never make the necessary adjustments. There are celebrities who were once successful and confident but didn't really appreciate their fans, the opportunities or the attention, unless they wanted it. However, because of a series of unfortunate events, the phone stops ringing, the meetings and bookings dry up, they are no longer as important or as interesting as they once were. They now feel insulted, disregarded and rejected. Rejection is a tough pill to swallow for people who are prideful. However, rejection, in many ways, can be helpful for some because it can teach a person, over time, to consider other people and not take success, talent, opportunities, or people's feelings for granted. It will serve as a tool to assist them in dealing with their personal issues while dealing with parts of the industry that cause them to think more highly of themselves than they should.

Years ago, I had a candid conversation with a wise woman who is also a living legend in the music business. She said something to me that I never forgot. After a studio session in Manhattan one afternoon, she began to share some of her good and bad experiences in the industry. She gave me some sobering advice that she had given to her own daughter, who was a successful singer at the time. She referred to the entertainment industry as perfume. Her advice was, "Smell the perfume baby – don't drink it." That statement resonated with me and served as a cold drink of water during a heat wave. It was a short but stinging statement that immediately got my attention and allowed me to respect her even more. I heard her words but I will never forget the look of urgency in her eyes as she said them. I somehow understood exactly what she meant. Fame, like perfume, is toxic, if used inappropriately. She meant don't believe the hype. Accept the environment for what it really is. It is a job. Fame and riches, no matter what forum you achieve it in, has its advantages and its disadvantages and one must know the difference between the two.

There is a scripture that warns, "Pride comes before destruction and haughty eyes before a fall," Proverbs 16:18. If gone unchecked, pride will silently but callously chip away at a person's heart and mindsets and end a career in no time. The higher you are when your prideful reign begins to descend, the more painful the landing is going to be when you hit the ground.

There is a fantastic movie that I use as a teaching tool for some of the people that I mentor, along with my husband. The movie is called "The

Devil's Advocate," starring Al Pacino and Keanu Reeves. It is a wonderful teaching tool for people who want to "make it big" in life or have a "fame at all costs" mentality. It teaches that every choice has a price and every person has a weakness. The biggest lessons in the movie for me are: When chasing after fame (1) keep your focus on what is most important; (2) be careful what you wish for, because you just might get it; and (3) check your pride at the door. The entertainment industry tends to be a self-absorbed and self-driven type of industry anyway, so there is no more productive room for pride. My mom's saying would apply here too when addressing selfish, prideful or rebellious people who conducted themselves in ways they knew would eventually and negatively affect others. She'd say, "Don't worry about it, baby. In time, they will eliminate themselves." So, proceed with caution.

## *Mental Health Related Issues*
*(Anxiety, Paranoia, Bi-Polar disorder, Isolation, Depression, Anorexia, and Bulimia)*

Most mental health issues can be as complex, complicated and layered, as they are simple, depending on the severity of the symptoms and conditions, root of the problem and length of time. Some of these issues emerge once in a person's life or it can be a life long struggle.

* *Anxiety:* in essence, is a condition that can evoke dread, nervousness, fear, and discomfort (increased heartbeat, crying, sweating, and the like), when confronted by certain situations or certain objects.
* *Paranoia:* simply put, can be defined as an over-exaggerated, delusional or irrational perception of other people's perception of oneself. This condition can present patterns of distrust, assumptions and suspicions of other people, which may not have any proof or validity. A paranoid person may posture themselves to gauge most situations from this perception. They may commit to assessing and internalizing

conversations, their surrounding environment and their relationships through this filter.

- *Bi-Polar Disorder:* can be a complicated condition that may involve varied fluctuating types of mood swings from extreme highs and depressing lows, and colorful happiness or dark sadness.
- *Isolation:* emotional or social, can be defined as a voluntary behavior that separates a person from others. The person sometimes chooses not to socialize, engage or participate in outside activities, events, or even appear in public. In many cases, this is natural, necessary, healthy and a normal thing to do, especially in this industry. However, there is an extreme and a dark side to this behavior that can become dysfunctional, unhealthy and abnormal.
- *Depression:* can be defined as a feeling of extreme hopelessness, sadness and despair that goes beyond the moments of just having a bad day or feeling down. Some liken it to walking around through life in slow motion or feeling as if the sounds of life are muted. Some may feel totally alone and even helpless.
- *Anorexia Nervosa* (a fear of gaining weight) and *Bulimia* (binging on food then purging it): can be dangerous and many times fatal eating disorders that can present a hyper focus or obsession on all things relating to weight loss or weight gain. These two disorders affect the emotions, mindsets and behaviors of individuals regarding food and controlling the consumption or elimination of it.

There are many people in the entertainment industry, as well as passing us by on the street, who struggle with degrees of mental health issues. Because there still seems to be stigmas attached to them, some people have not been properly diagnosed or treated. As a result, some will refuse treatment or just ignore the issues, symptoms or signs altogether. There are emotional and mental pressures, stressors, and demands that the entertainment industry will present, just like many other types of work environments. These variables can cause the average person to feel overwhelmed, especially if the person is not or struggles to be emotionally grounded. These stressors, pressures and demands can involve hyper focusing on image, intense rehearsal, performance or travel schedules, preoccupation with weight gain, quick success, public moments of failure, media over-exposure, strained or distant relationships, financial struggles, lack of work opportunities, cancellation of a show, poor box office sales or low television ratings. If a person feels like his or her identity is defined by or wrapped up in these situations, his or her perceptions can become skewed. If mental challenges exist along with these other situations, the person may not be able to cope properly or effectively. Some people in the industry simply don't cope well. Some of the reasons are because they feel suffocated by people reaching for or pulling on/at them, watching them, fans wanting to take pictures with them, photographers taking pictures of them, and agents, managers, lawyers and family members wanting to meet with or require something from them. Some people feel uneasy or uncomfortable attempting everyday activities like shopping and walking the streets, especially alone.

Sometimes all of the attention and movement causes people to withdraw to a place of uncertainty and lack of trust, not feeling safe around anyone. They begin to feel obligated to be perfect, smile, be courteous, perform, engage, and interview, even when they are not feeling well or just need a break. Over time, all they want to do is find a quiet place to retreat and hide. Eventually they isolate themselves from friends, family, and associates in the industry and only come outdoors occasionally. Some resort to finding alternative ways to deal with the issues. Contrary to popular belief, some entertainers aren't extroverted and outgoing. They can be wonderful at their craft, confident and friendly, but as I mentioned before, entertaining is what they do, not who they are. Some of them are introverts and would prefer to stay home or out of the public eye unless there is a special occasion or event. I must add that many entertainers embrace all things entertainment and have no problem, whatsoever, with the celebrity life. Some people just push past what they don't like and maintain a normal lifestyle of going out in public and living a normal life in spite of what is going on around them. They take control of their environment and determine how and when they will engage and how much they are going to share with others. They are the functioning entertainers. However, some people are not wired that way and internalize each experience – which is not a good thing.

*Tragedy*
**Premature Death**
*Suicide*

How many times have we all turned on the television to watch the news, got a message or an alert on our phones to learn that someone passed away quickly, tragically, accidentally, or due to sudden illness? These tragedies seem to be happening more often these days, not just in the entertainment industry, but around the world as well. Some of these occurrences happen because of poor judgment, foolish mistakes, untreated mental health issues, chronic sickness, drinking while driving, freak accidents that seem to be no one's fault, falling asleep at the wheel of a car due to lack of sleep, drive by shootings, deliberate assaults, hate crimes, texting/talking on the phone while driving, product malfunctions, speed racing, self-inflicted wounds, natural disasters and so many other life threatening situations. At times, some of the people who were hurt or killed were sadly in the wrong place at the wrong time. I heard a story of a person who was headed out to a party. He turned around to go back home because, for some reason, he didn't feel comfortable about going. He quickly changed his mind again and headed out to the party anyway because he didn't want anyone giving him a hard time about not going. Unfortunately, soon after he arrived, he was shot and killed at that party.

Some people may have instigated a volatile situation or have been victimized. Some were involved in freak accidents that caused their untimely deaths. Some were involved in cover-ups or plane accidents. Others may not have been as aware as they could or should have been regarding their surroundings. Some died accidentally. Those who have been snatched away die so instantly, without warning or preparation. They are literally here today and gone today. Life is so precious and so short. We must learn to cherish every day and do what we need or can do to stay as safe and as healthy as possible. Some of the ways we can proactively do this is by: (1) being more aware of our surroundings; (2) knowing whom we associate with, and make changes if necessary; and by (3) trusting what we are sensing (in other words trusting our gut feelings).

However, there are unspoken and secret realities about fame and fortune that are brutally unsettling for some people to think or talk about. There are also unspoken, unexplained, painful, fragile and secret realities about a person's life that are brutally unsettling as well. At times, those two unspoken and secret realities collide. As in the real world, some people are stronger, or better equipped to deal with stressors than others in certain areas. Some people have different types of coping mechanisms than others. As a result of a mixture of many other variables, certain people may slip into a dark hole of despair and find it difficult or near impossible to climb out. For some, they find themselves in situations where they see no way out or no other option but to take their own lives. Every experience is different, the reasoning behind the choice to end one's own life is complicated and sometimes mind boggling to the outside world and family members. However, there are so many things that can distort a person's reality and/or their response to it. These include unresolved issues in the past, struggling with drug abuse, secret mental illness, untreated or mistreated mental illness, the pressure to perform or stay relevant, dealing with rejection, making an overwhelming mistake, feeling underappreciated, sadness, emptiness, loneliness, painful experiences, financial problems, tax or investment disasters, coping with failure, undiagnosed, long-term or untreated depression or trauma, the weight and demands of the day to day pressures of life, and of course, the reality of being a celebrity itself.

Some people may be dealing with what I call "industry emptiness" or "industry depression." I am sure many everyday people deal with emptiness and depression, and it is just as devastating. However, for those who experience it in the entertainment industry, it is a bit more skewed, because they appear to have "everything." Some people who are tremendously talented and in demand find themselves at a very interesting and surprisingly lonely place. Some have self-esteem problems coupled with emotional disappointments. Although they are popular and loved by their fans, the entertainer experiences feelings of sadness and darkness and wears it like an invisible cloak.

Some have sacrificed relationships, including marriages and children, early in their careers only to find that they achieved a measure of fame but have no one to share it with. They get to a place where they don't know whom they can trust because people know they have achieved a measure of notoriety and often times can't see past that reality. When they are working and entertaining their fans, entertainers are motivated and grateful for the chance to do so. There is no greater joy and fulfillment for them. However, although they like the attention while they are performing, they don't care for it every time they step outside of their front door. They don't always like it when the cameras and telephones are flashing in their faces.

Some would say, "Oh please, they can have big parties at their big homes and invite whomever they want to party with them. Celebrities don't ever have to be lonely because the average person would kill to hang out with them. Stop complaining, what is the big deal?" My response is always the same. "Yes, you are correct. However, when you want to spend quality time at home with people who you can trust with your vulnerable side, who are closest to you and know you better than anyone else, would you call a casual acquaintance, a co-worker or someone you hang out with in the club? I didn't think so." At the expense of their own celebrity, some entertainers feel as if they have little freedom to live normally. For the sake of full disclosure, some of them create their own "glittered trap" and eventually regret doing so. Nevertheless, they feel as if they are living in an inescapable bubble. Although they would like to go out to public events and meet new people and maybe go on blind dates, the people that they meet can't seem to see past their celebrity.

If that's not enough, imagine that all of the people who are in your close circle of associates are those who are being paid to surround you. Imagine if everything you have ever said and done in public had been scrutinized, judged, or placed under a microscope. Consider being misquoted and having your interview dissected and assessed by harsh public opinions on social media. These perfect strangers don't know you, but they get to chime in on your situation without really knowing much about you, what hurts you or what really matters in your life. On top of that, imagine that comedians and talk show hosts are writing skits and joking about you. The media is casually speaking your name and discussing your situation without all of the facts. They don't know the whole story, but even if you tried to explain it, they may make light of that too. Once these social media forums are typing your name and your situation, there is nowhere to escape. In this industry, as in life, you have to learn to take the good with the bad. You have to develop thick, waterproof duck feathers and let what people say about you roll off of your back. But that's easier said than done. Some people feel wounded, betrayed and misunderstood. For whatever reason, they can't shake the dark place that they are in and want out by any means necessary. Some feel safest at home but also feel alone there and the "loud" sound of silence can be deafening. So they choose to escape, at home, within the walls of some type of private destructive behavior.

At times, people can have a caved view of their situation and they perceive that there is no way out. Some feel like they are riding on a never ending rollercoaster of highs and lows and the ride is no longer fun or exciting. They just want to get off of the ride or have everything to stop for a moment but don't know how to accomplish it. They may feel like a failure, because they should be enjoying the ride. That reality causes them to slip deeper in despair. Some feel they no longer have control over their lives so they take control over their deaths. Some of them may be dealing with a secret or private situation that is about to be exposed and they cannot, or will not, deal with the repercussions that may follow. Some used drugs and alcohol for so long that their organs and bodies collapsed from the constant ambush of unnatural chemicals. I feel so sad for them and what could have become of their lives and the lives of those who loved them. Others, on the other hand, didn't even realize that death was imminent. They may have mistakenly mixed drugs and alcohol, overdosed on medication or attempted to ease physical, mental, emotional or social pain too aggressively. Death was the farthest thing from their minds. Many of them just drifted off to sleep not knowing they would never wake up again.

I believe that there is a minority of people whom in the midst of all of the loud noises, chatter and voices around them, just want to hear silence for a while. So they take a break from it all by attempting to just sleep "for a few hours" for the sake of rest, but used a lethal combination of drugs or alcohol that sadly turned their temporary stillness into permanent silence. The goal may not have necessarily been to die but to make life just stop or stand still for just a few minutes. Unfortunately some people take drastic, fatal and long-term approaches to short-term problems. This grieves me a great deal, and every time I hear of another person dying by his/her own hands it shakes me to the core because the reality is always the same. They-did-not-have-to-die! I can somehow envision their last moments alone feeling conflicted but resolute, contemplative but somehow reassured about their final decision, afraid but empty, regretful but settled by their permanent choice, overwhelmed but hopeful that their impending state of eternal peace will be the perfect remedy. Sadly, they had other options even if they didn't realize they did. Whatever the burden, there is always a way of escape and always a reason to live another day.

## Suicide Is Not The Only Viable Option

Even though it doesn't seem that way, there are other ways to deal with difficult situations. Everyone needs someone they can trust and reach out to. We all need to feel like we have someone's ear to freely speak into. This is one of the reasons why I began mentoring, counseling and life coaching individuals and couples in the entertainment industry. Everyone needs a safe place to share and be transparent without people knowing, sharing or selling their business to outside sources. They need a place where they can be vulnerable.

**If you are reading this section and you are looking for a safe place, please *don't hesitate to log onto* http://www.suicidepreventionlifeline.org/**

I convey to people who find themselves in some of the situations that I just mentioned in this section that life is worth living. There is a plan for your tomorrow and this moment in your life will not last forever, even though it feels that way right now. I tell them all the time there is only one you. **There is a purpose and a plan for your life that does not involve suicide. The world will never be the same without you! You are the very reason for staying alive because you matter!**

## ASSIGNMENT CHALLENGE: TO OUTSMART THE ASSASSIN OF SELF-DESTRUCTION

If you feel like this may be the assassin that has targeted you, I have an exercise for you. Every time you are tempted to participate in destructive behavior, abstain from being silent about it and tell someone you can trust immediately what you are thinking about doing. Then ask them to help you get the help that you need. Every time you are tempted to embrace the behavior, say out loud, *"I am stronger than I think, and I am worth the change I am making!"* Also, abstain from isolating yourself and let someone know immediately that you want to isolate yourself and why. Ask them to help you get the help that you need. Every time you are tempted to embrace the behavior, say out loud, *"My purpose in life extends beyond this moment. My purpose in life extends beyond this moment. There is so much more to my life beyond this moment."* This assignment will take more self-discipline than the other assignments, but you have it in you to do this. Mark on your calendar the day that you choose to start this fast and make a note on that same day a year from now. Give yourself permission to be vulnerable. I am rooting for you! **PARENTS:** Have this conversation with your children and give them the opportunity to be transparent with you, even (or especially) if you think you know what they are going to say.

*If you choose to take on this challenge, fantastic! I am so proud of you! If you would like to share updates, you can on my website www.angelajwilliams. com or tweet me @my3tjwsons. If you choose not to attempt this fast, please call and make an appointment with a mental health professional near you as soon as possible. I have information on the Resources and Research page in the back of this book. I am rooting for you!*

# 12

## Riches and Fame vs. Wealth and Success

$\mathcal{I}$ find myself telling parents quite often, "If all you want is for your children to be rich or famous, make an about face now and unpack your bags." The last thing parents really need to desire for their child is to simply be "rich and famous." Many parents think that's what they want because it sounds good and with riches and fame all of their financial problems will simply go away. However, in actuality, these individuals have no idea what riches and fame really mean or require. Whenever I make these types of comments, some parents look at me as if I am crazy, until I explain. Typically, I have found that if parents want their children to be rich and famous they will allow their children to do just about anything in order to achieve it. When the doors of compromise, clearance, freedom, and lack of boundaries are opened, it is nearly impossible to close them. Few things in life are free and there are costly personal and financial price tags on almost everything else. Often times, folks who make comments like these have already and unknowingly made a decision to accomplish the "rich and famous" goal by any means necessary.

Again, there is nothing wrong with being rich; in fact, there are many wonderful benefits to having access to a great deal of money. There is nothing wrong with being famous, because there are doors that are available to those who are famous that will lead to opportunities for many others. But if becoming rich and famous is the primary and ultimate goal before anything else, most people will become a slave to the grasp of it and sacrifice anyone

171

and everything to obtain and maintain it. When I say a slave I mean that instead of the person being driven by the passion of their gifts and talents, or motivated by the ability that allows them to get rich and famous, the focus may shift to a money making quest above EVERYTHING else. The quest for riches and fame can take precedence over everything else: family, friends, ethics, legal boundaries and the like. This usually leaves a person, assuming they accomplish his/her goal, lonely, bitter, self-absorbed, addicted, and empty, to list just a few consequences. Let me make some things clear for the sake of the "outside looking in" critiques.

MONEY is not evil, damaging, bad or corrupt. Rather, the unhealthy LOVE of it, or the fear of losing it, over all else, is what will slowly creep up on a person and warp his or her life. Someone may say, "Well, if that is the sacrifice I have to make to reach my goal, I will just have to do it, because I want to be rich!" That sounds like a determined and relentless comment to make but saying it and living it are two different things. I have seen the end results of that comment while watching others. Trust me when I say that the quest for fame and riches *only* is not a pretty view. I know of many people who had financial challenges growing up because their families didn't have much money or many opportunities. Although they became rich by working hard and staying focused on their goal to live better than they did when they were younger, they remembered the struggle and learned how to live below their financial means. They paced themselves, kept a realistic focus, stayed grounded and allowed their memories of the past to keep them balanced in the future. They did this because they never wanted to be broke, depleted and financially empty again. That is a great approach.

They realized something early on that others have to find out the hard way. Riches are fleeting for many who have it and don't know how to manage it, and fame comes at a price for most who abuse it. Again, I liken it to people who win a large state jackpot. They are diligent to purchase tickets every week because they *dream* of one day becoming rich. However, they don't actually *plan* on that day actually arriving. There is no tangible action plan in place for the slim chance that it might happen. Before the surprised winner of the jackpot realizes that he or she has actually purchased the winning ticket; that person might be working at an average job, making average money, with an average balance of money sitting in a savings account, but hoping to strike it rich one day. All of a sudden, overnight, this "average person" is now rich! Amazing! Awesome! Unbelievable! My worries are over! But wait...what's next? What does one do with all of that money? How does one count it? How does one pay taxes on it? Where does a person store it? Who does one trust with it? Who looks after it? Who manages it? How does one spend it? How does one save it? How does one share it? Who does one talk to about it? How does one keep oneself, family and home safe after everyone knows? Who protects it? Who benefits from it?

With instant riches, bogus lawsuits, mismanaged money, foolish spending, leeches, betrayal, poor financial advice, feuding family members, thieves, accumulating taxes, greedy associates and the like may soon follow and make their way into your pocket, bank account, living situation, lifestyle and more importantly, your peace of mind. With fame, especially for entertainers, social media overload, paparazzi, invasion of privacy, tabloids, paranoia, suspicion, loneliness, and the like, may follow as well. So if you are presented with tremendous riches and fame, just consider the combined and never-ending challenges for you, your child and your lives. I try to explain my version or the difference between being "*rich* and *famous*" versus "*wealthy* and *successful*" to people so that they can better articulate what it is that they really want, need or desire. Once they know the difference they can learn to do what is necessary to achieve their goal, manage the outcome and posture to expect the unexpected with the least amount of stress and drama as necessary or humanly possible.

*Wealth*, according to the dictionary, is a large amount of money and an abundance of something. *Success*, according to the dictionary, is an achievement of intention, attainment of fame, wealth and power, or something that turns out well. With more than 30 years in the entertainment industry and in many areas, I have come to realize that there is a distinct difference between the terms "riches and fame" and "wealth and success," although the two seem very similar. What I have discovered is when people are wealthy, they have a substantial measure or balance of financial, emotional, relational, mental and physical health, well-being or are actively proceeding forward to obtain it. When people are successful, they have a substantial measure or balance of professional, financial, creative, social, and emotional consciousness, and are intelligent and stable or proceeding forward to obtain it. Of course, it is quite obvious that wealth also involves having money so there is no need to highlight that.

However, what good is having money but no people around you that you can trust or a solid support system to experience wealth with? *Success* is walking in the front door of your home, no matter how big or small, hearing and smelling the sounds and smells of functional family life and knowing that your house is a home for you and for the other people who live or experience life with you. *Success* is being able to financially care for yourself and others without having to look over your shoulders because of shady or unethical business dealings or the IRS. A *successful* person knows that if and when challenges arise in life that there exist people, resources and options surrounding them that he or she can draw, learn and grow from. *Wealth and success* is financial, emotional, personal, and professional peace even in the midst of uncertainty, challenges, loss, disappointment, ups, downs, highs, and lows. I am not saying that wealthy and successful people don't have disadvantages and negative realities to deal with. But what I am saying is their posture in dodging some of it or how they address or handle the negativity is more productive or resolvable.

*Wealth and success* is choosing not to live, embrace, condone or validate a drama-filled and stress-filled life in any of the areas that I mentioned above. If/when difficult times come in a wealthy/successful person's life, he or she will most likely search for a long-term solution rather than create a platform to fuel the problem. There are many rich and famous folks who are drama/ trouble/struggle magnets for their own lives. *Wealthy and successful* people don't have time to promote, feed or embrace drama, trouble or problematic issues because their lifestyles are purposeful. Suggestion: anything or anyone in your life that promotes or attracts toxic situations, people or behaviors will not posture you for wealth and success because you will be spending your life putting out proverbial fires, refereeing fights and cleaning up messes. That is exhausting, fruitless and a complete waste of time (I know because I have had my share of it). But notice the operative word in that sentence is *had*. Lets be completely honest with each other. Life happens to all of us. No one is perfect, and we all have situations to address, but your life or lifestyle should not be a breeding ground for dysfunction. This is draining and unnecessary. This type of lifestyle should be unacceptable and left for television shows only. That's just my terse opinion.

However, obtaining *wealth and success* as opposed to riches and fame is harder to accomplish and maintain. It is more difficult to accomplish because one has to be mindful, on a daily basis, to make the right personal, professional, ethical, emotional, financial, and business decisions. One has to be lucid and aware on a daily bases that the choices one makes today will affect one's life in the future. *Wealthy and successful* people tend to make wise long-term choices. If a person's goal is to be rich, they will typically take the option that will lead them to the payday with the most zeros attached to it. A *wealthy* person may choose to make less money today, in order to build on what they have, to make a more lucrative and strategic business decision later. When dealing with a child's pending entertainment career, pace yourself. I have found that it is better to develop as you go and create a long-term plan that will promote a life-long experience than to focus on a more immediate experience and expect an overnight opportunity of a lifetime. This industry is unpredictable. Business deals fall through, television shows get cancelled and movies flop at the box office. You can't buy a million dollar house or a brand new car or go on a carefree shopping spree banking on money you don't have in your possession or that you haven't paid taxes on yet. If you do, that behavior is an unwise and "rich/fame" type of mindset. I have seen it happen more times than I care to mention, and the end result is ALWAYS an absolute mess.

Interestingly enough, I would venture to say that there exists more "rich and famous" people than there are "wealthy and successful" ones. Some rich and famous people have more money, things and access but they are not necessarily happier or at peace in their mansions. It is quite clear, believe it or not, that riches and fame are easier to obtain because the opportunities, ethical or unethical, are endless. However, the realities of maintaining them are fleeting. That is not to say that there is not a sizable percentage of rich and famous people who are successful and wealthy. To achieve that is a great fete but doable. *Success and wealth* take longer to achieve, but they last longer. There are many people on the Internet, television shows, and the news for that matter, who have become famous at one point in time. If I were to mention a few words or catch phrases of theirs, everyone would automatically know whom I am talking about, no matter how long ago it has been since their moment of fame existed. This is the case because fame is temporary for most.

*Wealth and success* is not a momentary achievement because they don't require, demand or need attention, validation or a certain amount of money in the bank. I pray that this book has given you a tremendous amount of information and several points of view to help you make sound decisions for your children, their purpose and your family. I pray that you and your family will trade in your quest for Riches and Fame for Wealth and Success. My final piece of advice to you is, please consider the pursuit of *Wealth and Success*. You may be so glad that you did. Now, as promised, it's time to hear from the industry.

# Insight from the Industry

Contrary to popular belief, the *entertain*ment industry is not a cesspool full of twisted, ruthless, greedy, narcissistic media whores who are leading talented newcomers, spectators and consumers down a road of no return; although, those folks do exist. The world that is the entertainment industry is made up of extremely gifted and talented minds with creativity and storytelling abilities that go beyond the realm of imagination and expectation. These expressive and passionate people wear their creative hearts on their sleeves, without apology, for all to see and experience simply because they love what they do. The core or the essence of the average entertainer's drive is that they love entertaining people and blessing people with his or her gifts. There is another population who do it for other reasons, but we are not going to focus on them with this book. The true entertainers are passionate and committed. I so enjoy watching artists do what they were born to do with so much seemingly effortless energy.

Make no mistake, when you are watching the end result of performances, movies, plays, television shows, and commercials, the level of creativity, time and ability it took to accomplish such a fete is absolutely awe inspiring. And to watch these professionals up close and personal prepare behind the scenes, behind the camera and behind closed doors, in their natural element is fascinating. It is a privilege to witness comedians, thespians, dancers, singers, directors, actors, choreographers, showrunners, script supervisors, story editors, wardrobe departments, hair and makeup artists, line producers, casting directors, grips, set dressers, assistant directors, writers, lawyers, managers, agents, publicists, personal-assistants, designers, stunt coordinators, background actors, art departments, camera crews and video departments, construction departments, craft services, security, sound mixers, stand-ins, studio teachers, transportation departments, and the like use their abilities to entertain or help others entertain the world. It's simply amazing, and it never seems to get old for me.

With that being said, it is my honor to introduce to you just a few of my friends, family members, colleagues, partners and associates who have offered to provide their keen industry insight – presented in no particular order. To my delight, they didn't hesitate to volunteer to be interviewed in person, via phone or by email, because they wanted to help me help you. They took time out of their busy schedules to join me in this conversation with you in order to give you an accurate and inside view of what to expect, what to do, how to act, what to look out for, how to stay grounded, and how to survive in this industry.

# Cindy Osbrink
*The Osbrink Agency – Owner*

### Why did you become an agent?

I became an agent 20 years ago. I started as a stage mom, so I know your side of it. My kids were discovered in a parking lot when they were nine months old and three years old. I literally knew nothing about this business, but my three year old went on his first audition and booked it. The other one went on a Johnson & Johnson audition and booked the campaign for the whole year. My kid's agent was Mary Grady. I will take care of her until the day she dies. I love that woman. So I'm thinking, because they began booking right away, "This is a piece of cake!" Not knowing that it doesn't normally happen this way. So my kids continued to audition, but when they became school age I noticed that they were being ripped out of birthday parties and baseball games to go on auditions and I thought, "This was never their choice." So, I called Mary Grady that morning to say, "Can we just book them out, I want to see if they even ask to start auditioning again. They didn't know any different; they just live in the car driving from one audition to another." But when I called, she didn't answer the phone. When I called back that afternoon, she told me that she was retiring and selling the agency and no one showed up for work that morning. So I told her, "I can help you while the kids are in school in the morning." I started going in every morning to help her and loved the experience. I went back to UCLA to take an Entertainment Law, Business Affairs class and Agency class.

In my Agency class, my professor, told me, "Go find your niche and start with your niche, by yourself." He calls that class his prodigy class because five studio execs and I came out of that class.

So, I opened a one-room office, 20 years ago and it just kind of morphed. I love it, because I believe that kids need to be protected in this business. Not just from the business but from their parents as well. Because nobody trains you to be famous and until you become famous you don't even know how to experience something like that. In the beginning, I used to keep these kids (clients), thinking that I was protecting them. But after going through divorces (of the parents) of my clients who were fighting against their parents, I had made up my mind that I will never do that again. The one thing that I learned from these experiences is that a parent cannot manage their own child. Your child is not a commodity and your child is not your business. The way I learned that is, at the end of the trial for all four children, each one said, "I just want my mom back or I just want my dad back." From that moment, we haven't taken on one child that is managed by his or her parent. It is just not healthy.

*So you became an agent out of necessity and because an opportunity was staring you right in the face?*

I was never afraid. It's funny because when I started, everybody said, "Who's going to call you? You are so nice." That almost gave me my strength to say, "Watch me." I honestly think being nice and friendly has been our power as a company and treating casting directors like friends, because guess what, they do call us! They like us. They have fun with us and they know we are honest. If we don't have a client that they are looking for, I'll say, "I don't have that type but call so and so." It's about building those relationships, and we have all grown up together in this business.

Cindy Osbrink

*How does it feel to know that you are one of the most respected child talent agencies in the Entertainment Industry?*

First of all thank you for saying that. I am proud of my guys. I am proud of every last one of my clients. I am proud of my families, and I am proud of the parents. The parents give up a lot to provide a path for their child's dreams. It would be the same if they played tennis or soccer but the biggest difference is that there is more money involved in this business. That's the only difference. Fame comes with tennis, soccer or whatever, but not like it does in this business especially with children within the last five years or so.

*What does a child need to become successful in this industry?*

They need to have an awareness of who they are. They have to have self-confidence when they walk in the room. That is the number one thing, whether or not they say the right or the wrong words or lines. If they say it from their heart, then it is believable. They have to have a great family base at home to be successful. They truly do. Otherwise it's a train wreck. Their parents have to be in it for the right reason. The child has to have that foundation to come home to and just be a normal kid again. If that is the case, then that's a good thing. There really hasn't been a child in this industry that I haven't been able to read and nail down, and say, "This is what they can do." I can tell in their eyes, I can tell in their soul and just by asking a few questions. You can tell if they are real or not. I look for the real them in the midst of everything else. There are six billion people out in the world and each one of them has a separate fingerprint and there is a reason for that. Everybody is different. I want to see what is different about every child I interview. When the child taps into what makes them who they are, they can be successful.

*Do you think it's possible for a single parent, who is trying to keep his or her house afloat and make sure their kids are ok, to have a child who is successful in this business?*

I think it's possible. It's really, really hard. I think that a parent has to be so secure in who that parent is and the path that they want their child to grow up in to be a healthy adult - not as an actor, but as an adult. They have to stay strong and not be swayed by this business. People will try to sway them one way or another. Don't listen to people in this business; only those who they have hired and those that they trust in this business. There are too many varying opinions and too many different sources. After a while of listening to too many people, none of it will make sense. This business isn't complicated. People in the business make it complicated. It's really simple. When you make it complicated, it doesn't work.

*If you had to give an accurate overview of what the entertainment industry is, what would it be?*

Yikes. The entertainment industry to me is about telling stories. Hopefully these stories have a meaning. Hopefully they are teaching people a lesson. Hopefully there is a lesson or message behind each story. Unfortunately, there are a lot of stories out there that are now looking for the shock value and not so much the entertainment. The goal is to outdo the last shock you created. But the entertainment business is about finding those actors who have gotten that gift from God and watching them tell that story. There can be negative sides to the story and a positive side. There can be negative ways to tell a story or positive ways. The bottom line is everyone involved has to have a base to go back to keep them grounded and focused on telling the story.

*What is your definition of a stage parent?*

Who better to be with their child than a parent? Who better knows that child? My *positive* definition of a stage parent is a parent who is present and with the child like they would be if they were getting their child ready for school or getting them ready for a soccer game. They are there to support their child. Do they unfortunately have to be around all day on set with their child? Yes they do, but what a gift for that parent. They get to see their child perform and use their talent. That reality makes the child *"stage happy."* The child is growing and learning right before their eyes. Stage parents should be seen and not heard. They need to have their own lives, and they can't put all of the pressure of this business on their child. They can't take on the idea that this is now their life. I get it that this is your child performing, and you are with them so the parent feels like this is their experience too. Children are only with you for a short amount of time. They need to have those cherished moments with their child as a family and they have to have their own things, separate things to do as a parent. It's not fair to your child if you don't. To me that is child abuse. If there is a problem on set, there are always people to reach out to. The first things a parent should do if there is an issue on set is to call the agent. The stage parent should never vocally say anything, unless it is something endangering their child, or the issue needs to be handled immediately. But then still get your agent and your manager involved. However, there is also a teacher on set at all times as well. The teachers, who are also the welfare workers, are there for the child's protection. A parent has to have a good relationship with the teacher as well. Let the teacher go and complain to the producer.

The *negative* side of a stage parent would be one that doesn't trust their representation and keeps calling every day to read us the *breakdowns*. We know how to read, thank you very much. A negative stage parent is one who is nothing but problems during the auditioning process. All casting directors have their own spies in the waiting room. They know who the parents are and they will not hire a child if the parent is a nightmare. They don't need to hire the child, no matter how good that child is. It's not worth dealing with. It slows up everybody, it is a negative experience and it becomes a cancer on the set. We've gotten a few of those phone calls. The parent who shows up on the set who is directing the child is not good. There is a director for that. There are parents who try to run the production show. No, you are the parent. Enjoy your child and be the parent.

***What is the most frustrating thing about having a child as a client who is talented but has a crazy parent?***

Unfortunately, those have been some of our most talented children. They live this crazy, stressful, adult life while not knowing what's going to hit them next because they are dealing with their crazy parents. It is an emotional rollercoaster for these kids because they have felt every emotion possible while they are living this life experience that most children don't have. Do most of them make it past 18 in this business? Absolutely not, they run as far away as they can get from this business because they have been controlled to do it. It may have been their dream at first, but they were forced to do things that they didn't want to do and lost the passion for it. A lot of them don't have that gift but they have life experience of living certain situations that prepares them for the business. So it's about knowing the difference and being able to pick that up when a child walks into a room. I've got pretty good radar now. You have to know if a child is damaged goods and is *that* the reason why they are brilliant at acting, or is this truly their gift.

***What if a child came in to interview and you saw that they had potential but you knew that the parent was going to be a nightmare. What do you do with that?***

We had this happen. This little boy came in and he was wonderful. We asked him, "Do you want to do this?"

He said, "No." He said, "I want to do theater, but I don't want to go on auditions. I want to do theater with my friends."

We said, "No problem."

He said to us, "No, my dad will get mad." His dad was the one that brought him to the interview.

Dads are by far the worst type of negative stage parent because they have that testosterone thing going and they walk in with this attitude that says, "My kid is the best." They can outdo any negative stage mom out there.

So after the interview we walked out with him to his dad and told his dad, "Thank you so much but we are not looking for his type right now," trying to graciously get him out of having to go on any more interviews.

*What do you do when you know that some type of abuse is taking place in your client's home? You can't prove it, but you know something is wrong.*

I try to be their other mama, I really do. When I am able to they come back and give me the biggest hugs. I try to be a mother figure to my kids if I can. I truly believe that is one of the reasons that I am supposed to be in this business. I have raised four children who are completely from different planets and each one of them has taught me so much about how to deal with different types of children.

*How does it feel to know that your clients feel safe around you? They respect and prefer you as an agent and a person.*

Ok, I am about 14 ft. from the ground right now. My heart just filled up, and now it's over flowing in my soul. To me this is a gift. I wanted to do this every day. I truly love my guys. I love my kids, I just love them and nobody better mess with them. Watch out for "Mama Bear."

*What do you do with a child actor who has gotten older and gone astray? They somehow lost sight of what was important or just lost focus.*

As long as that young person is doing what they are supposed to and I can see it in their eyes, I will try to keep them forever. The talent doesn't go away. That is a God-given gift. Something may have happened along the way in life. Tween-agers, for some reason every time they hit that eleven to twelve mark; it's like something happens. They have to make it to fourteen. We have kept them and a lot of time they will leave when they are fourteen because someone is telling them that they are amazing and they should be working but there aren't any projects out there at that age. But we will not give up on them. Whether they give up on us, well that's another story. I can't tell you of how many teenagers leave, how many of them want to come back. I don't usually let them come back. I have only let two of my guys come back once they left. One came walking in on his knees and said, "I'm sorry." Because he got caught up in the teenage "Hollywood Partying Thing," and that is not acceptable. The other one left through a manager that we had never worked with. He had gotten some bad information but he quickly figured it out for himself. I have a really hard time when we give 1000% and they leave, to me it's almost like tasting blood. For them to have come back I would never be able to give them 1000% again, and I can't work that way. I can't sleep at night knowing that. It's hard.

To do it the right way and come into the office and talk to us, that is fine. We just did it with two of our most successful girls, but we planned it for a year. We discussed the what, the where, the how, and I am still in their lives every day, but I am part of that transition. I want them to be happy and healthy and if this is what they want then they need to go for it. The ones that haven't done the transition where they jump from us to a big agency...I pray for those children every day and they still come in for hugs. They reek of alcohol, they reek of smoke and I am like, "What are you doing?" I will call them on it. They usually laugh and give me a hug, but it's not ok.

Cindy Osbrink

*When you see a slow moving train-wreck in front of your face, what do you do?*

I talk to the parents but 99% of the time the parents are right there on the track with them. I did my thing and I used to be devastated, but now it's like, I back off. I don't want to be a part of that train wreck anymore. I have been pulled into train wrecks thinking that I was going to help them, but you can't help them at that point. Unfortunately, they need to figure it out for themselves because they are not listening to anybody else. And it's always about ego, every time, every time, which is edging God out. Ego, it turns your brain off, I swear, because it is all about you all of a sudden.

*What advice would you give to a parent who is clueless about the industry but desperately wants their child to be rich and famous?*

Ugh. First of all, if you want your child to be rich and famous, run the other way. The minute a child walks into our office and says that they are doing this for college money, I tell them this is not the place to be. This is so not the place to be. Go get a scholarship, because this is so not the place to be. Being famous is a pain in the butt. The only reason to be famous is to be a voice to help others. That is the only reason to be famous. That is the only reason. You want to get in to the business to be rich? Most people don't get rich in this business. Very few children get "rich" in this business. At what cost, what do you give up to be rich? Your friends, your school, there is a lot to sacrifice in this business.

*I know you touched on it a little bit earlier, but after all of these years, expe-riencing the ups and the downs, why are you still an agent?*

It's funny because all of the big agencies tried to buy us out about four or five years ago. All of a sudden, kids became the hottest things out there. Nobody could care about kids before, then, all of a sudden they saw dollar signs on their foreheads. Then, everybody wanted to be in the *kid business.*

I set up meetings with a few of them to interview. It was so flattering and it was such an honor. I decided on one agency, but when I went into the office, I couldn't see kids running up and down the hall, I couldn't see kids hiding underneath my desk, I couldn't even see kids allowed in the building. The only way you are going to get the best out of anybody is to allow them to be themselves, and I didn't see that happening with this agency. Also, they just wanted me to come over with my chosen few and walk away from everybody else. How do I do that? So I thought, and I told them this, "You guys are cutting off the pipeline." Let me do what I do best. Let me find them, nurture them, get them to that point, then you can do what you think you do best after that. I can still run their careers, but you've got the big name and the big connections. If this is what you want to do, we can do it together; as far as turning down scripts and maintaining the child's career and making sure that they continue to go to the next level. The folks that I was meeting with got it but the board didn't get it because the bottom line was about dollars and cents. I'm sorry, when you are dealing with kids, it should never be about money. The money will come when they are successful, in its own form. It may be in hugs or big smiles on their faces when they walk into the door. That is success, too. As long as the kid calls me and says, "Yes, I did it," that's all they can do. We can call directors and producers and nag and tell everybody how wonderful our kids all are but they have to walk into the casting room and walk out feeling good about themselves. That's my goal.

*Well, you are succeeding because your clients, for the most part, trust you and feel safe with you knowing that you are looking out for their best interest.*

I don't believe that every kid should go out for every audition and every kid is right for every role. I love how when you guys came in to meet with us about eight years ago, for the first time you didn't interview us; 12-year-old Tyler did. You were in the room but he did most of the talking and asking most of the questions. You have always trusted us and felt that everything that your sons were right for or should be out on, they were out on. You can't burn kids out like that because they are no longer special when you do that. I believe that there is a role out there for everybody meant to be in this industry, but not every role is for everybody. My most successful families are the ones who don't know a lot of folks in this industry. This is not a team sport for all parents and kids. My successful families focus on their kids and their careers and are not focusing on what everybody else is doing. Their child is prepared when they walk into the casting room and they feel comfortable versus what everybody else in town is doing. It is a waste of energy for the child being aware of everyone else's movements in the industry. When one of my clients doesn't book a role, there are times when the parent will call and ask who got the role. I don't care about who got the role. My client didn't get the role and that is all I care about.

***Many agents and managers are frustrated and bitter by certain experiences of backstabbing, gossip, agencies stealing clients and clients leaving them to go to other agencies in the industry. Why aren't you frustrated or bitter?***

There is a lot of that, for sure. We have lost departments and we have lost agents that have taken departments. It's funny; we sent someone in for an audition the other day. We sent five girls in and after awhile every one of them started calling me. Come to find out, it wasn't an "audition," it was a management company trying to steal them from us. I have learned that if you yell and scream and jump up and down, which is what they expect you to do, you drop down to their level. When I call them, and I am calm, they don't know how to handle that. I just told them, as a matter of fact, what I was going to do about it and I did it. I got them shut down, their breakdowns were removed, and I got SAG to remove their signatory and you know what? It is what it is. The next day I got roses from the manager apologizing. I had to get to a point where I had to say, with my actions, that I am not playing anymore. Folks who do things like this are so creative. They do things like this all the time. I ask myself every day, how do they come up with this type of stuff? I had to learn to roll with it. I know that I am doing the right thing, I know that my kids are doing the right thing and hopefully casting and everybody is too. If they are not, I will call them on it. Am I going to scream and yell? No. But I am going to say that there is a problem, and ask, "How can we fix this?" Hopefully it becomes a win/win situation but you can't lose your class, you can't lose your grace. You can't lose your character and integrity.

Are there days when I am just ready to rip everybody's head off? Absolutely. But those are the days that I know that I am tired and I need to postpone this until tomorrow. I need to pray on it and the next day it's like bang, bang, bang all of these ideas start coming. I have been screamed at by the best of them on the phone. Producers and directors still scream at me when they want my clients to do what they want them to do. Some things never change. This business never gets boring, and that is what I love about it. That's why I am still in it. You never know what the next phone call is going to be. It's a stop, drop and go business and you have to be a gypsy to keep up. If you need a planned schedule, this is not the business for you.

**What bothers you most about what is happening in the industry these days?**

The shock value bothers me most. We had a call the other day for two 10-year-old girls to pretend they were lesbians...absolutely not! I had a parent call me and ask why their daughter wasn't going in on the audition. I told her what it was for and the parent still wanted her daughter to go in on the audition. I told her, "I am not doing a nudity contract for a 10-year-old girl, I refuse." I said, "You can leave, but I can't do it." So the parent left, but you know what, there was no reason for it. It was completely for shock value and it had nothing to do with the story. You know what, God bless that parent. The same thing goes for language, if there is a reason for it, that's one thing. But I negotiate every word and go through every word. If they want your child bad enough, guess what, they will fix it, they will change. If they don't then they didn't want your kid bad enough. If that word means more than your child performing in that movie, then you don't want to be in that movie. There has to be a line that you don't cross. If not, then what are you teaching your children? The reason why parents cross the line is because many of them think that that is their key to becoming rich and famous. Nobody's ever going to know who your child is from that one scene, I'm sorry. The scary thing is lately, because of the ultra low budgets of certain shows and modified low budget productions, is that everybody and their brother is in this business and nobody knows the child labor laws or will try to educate themselves about it. They get these jobs very quickly and they get on these sets and they have no idea what to do with these kids and how to schedule them properly. The kids are lacking in education because of it, and there are not enough people to look after them or know what to do with them.

I find that most of my time is going to policing and just educating people lately on how to deal with kids on sets. I educate producers, directors, line producers and tell them what they can and can't do. They really don't understand. In the state of California the kids are pretty protected. But in other states they are working kids all night and they are breaking every rule and every law out there. SAG laws and rules are a little more lenient than the state of California. Parents need to educate themselves once they get that work permit because every rule is on there. Instead of reading them, parents are framing the work permits.

***What brings you the greatest amount of joy as a talent agent?***

To see my guys fulfill their dreams. That to me is icing on the cake of being an agent. Walking down that red carpet with them and looking at that halo over their heads. I just look and say, "Wow, we did it...we did it!"

*If you can share, what has been one of the highlights of the last twenty years?*

The hardest but most amazing day of my life was the morning we had to go to one of our kid's funerals. She played a gang-banger on a series and art came true to life and she was killed in a drive-by shooting. That morning, talking about shifting gears, we went to her funeral but a couple hours later I had to leave because another client was being honored by Barbara Walters as one of the 10 most interesting people in the world. To walk in the room where Barbara Walters was sitting, and watch her interview my client was amazing. After a while Barbara turned and asked, "Cindy, what else should I be asking her?" She whispered and asked me, "Does she still believe in Santa?"

I whispered, "Yes!" My proudest moment was realizing that, after coming from a funeral of one of my kids, that I was able to keep this child safe and in a bubble to the point where she was able to still have that innocence of being a child at the age of 11. I think I am very proud of that. We did everything we could do to protect the one that was killed as well. I called one of my in house agents, her warden. She would go on the set with her, and go to her house and pick her up to make sure that she finished out the season because we knew she was in trouble. Her mom was a single mom, she was a sweet woman but things were out of control.

*Where do you file that in your mind and in your heart?*

Wow...Um...I just hand that one over to God. I know we did everything possible. I know my in house agent was such a good influence on her. She didn't go to work for weeks because she was taking care of or trying to take care of her. I know we added positivity to her life at the end. We allowed her to share her talent with the world. She wasn't talented because she was a damaged child and she used her hard life as a talent. I don't believe that with her; she had a gift. She was with us for several years.

*Do you have any final words for kids?*

It's ok to be yourself. It's so ok to be you. When you walk into the casting room, don't think when you talk. I know nobody tells you not to think. Talk from your heart. There is nothing more genuine.

*Do you have any final words for the parents?*

Parents, this is the most incredible business on the face of the earth. But you have to see it for what it is. It is not about you. It's about your child. Paving the way for your child takes responsibility. You can take them to that audition, I can get them that audition but ultimately they are the ones that have to do it in the room and they are the ones who have to do it when they book it. So they give up a lot for this business. Just make sure they are doing it for the right reasons. The only reason to be in this business is because they love to act. It's that simple.

# Mary McCusker
## Acting Coach for Television & Film

***Give me a little background on your career in the industry.***

I was an actress working in LA when Joel Schumacher asked me to coach an unknown 11-year-old boy who was set to star in a movie called THE CLIENT. With that film, I switched careers and have been a coach in the LA area for the last 20 years. In addition to set coaching I am a professor at Loyola Marymount College.

***What is the sign of a good coach?***

I think the sign of good coaching is that the children are completely themselves in the role. They don't appear to be coached. They have made the material their own. His/her personality is completely natural and free. When working with a client, I will approach the role a number of different ways (always staying close to the intention of the script). When we have come up with a way that feels good and comfortable, I often will tape it and look at it with the child or his/her parent. Then I suggest - be prepared to do it any number of ways. Why? Because often casting directors who have been looking for a role, will know what the director or producers are looking for and may want to give direction when the child goes in the room. LISTENING is key at that point and being FLEXIBLE is critical. Sometimes, a casting director will test the actor just to see if they can take direction. That is so important because auditions are very different from the actual shoot, so listening and taking direction is key. If an actor has memorized a role with a certain rhythm and is inflexible, they will have a very difficult time when they change the lines on the set. And in sitcoms, that is a major part of the job.

*How do you teach a child, who has no experience, how to be an actor?*

I recently met with a child who had that aspiration. I explained to the parents on the phone that I would send them a script for their son to memorize before coming to see me. He came unprepared. No lines memorized. Not a good sign. I worked with him on the material. I took him through all the stages of rehearsal, working on all the moments that happen. Identifying - "Who, what, and where". Then we did the scene as if it was a real audition, and I put him on tape. This was really hard work for him. I think he was a little shocked, which leads me to this point: child actors are doing adult work. The hours are long and the child must keep up with his/her schoolwork. The work of an actor takes a combination of a highly motivated child and PARENTS who can help these kids fulfill this dream. I never want to discourage kids from exploring this business. But it is very important to realize that: A. It is hard work. B. It is a little like Vegas. You can be very talented, work hard and still not get a job. So it takes enormous commitment and love to go the distance.

I truly believe a child can explore this work and gain many valuable life skills. Acting can teach children to find their own voice, to stand up in front of a group of people and be themselves. These life skills will reverberate whether the child continues in this business or not. Studying acting is very important. Learning the language and acting terms, how to act for auditions and how to do the work once you get the job are all aspects of learning the craft of an actor.

Mary McCusker

*Have you ever found a kid who was not cut out for the business but his/her parent was pressuring them?*

Yes, I have. I remember sitting with a child once and I could see how hard this was for him. And I said, "You don't really want to do this, do you?" and the child said "No." It was so hard to see. Make no mistake – casting sees and can feel that. It really has to come from them. It just doesn't work otherwise. I remember having a young woman who was taking dance lessons, ice skating lessons and doing gymnastics while going out on auditions. And she was never getting callbacks. I eventually said to the mother that I thought it was too much; she was being pulled in too many directions. She stopped coming to me, but I just could feel how stressed this girl was. Sometimes I have parents who were actors or always wished they had acted and are now living through their kids. I was on a show once where the child was not interested in acting anymore. He was told to get coaching but neither the parents nor the child wanted to do that. So, production and the writers kept his part to a minimum. He got fewer and fewer lines.

*What advice would you give to a parent who believes that his/her child is talented enough for the entertainment industry?*

Initially, I would encourage them to act in school plays, take a few acting classes. Be careful in choosing the class. Make sure it is a small class so the child can get individual attention. Afterward, ask them what they learned in the class. Check out the reputation of the teacher and classes. Going to a coach privately is extremely helpful in the auditioning process. The coach can give you feedback on their ability to focus. Being able to take direction is critical and to listen and try the role with different adjustments is important.

I have agents and managers who send me clients regularly. If they can focus, memorize lines, take direction and repeat what is asked of them, then that is a big part of getting the job. I often put them on tape, send the tape to the agent and manager and I give them feedback. As a team, we will decide if this is a client worth signing. It saves everybody a lot of time – does this child have the potential and the personality for this work?

# Kelly Park
## Industry Mom/Acting Coach

*Imagine that I am a mother of a five year old. I want my child in the industry but she has no experience. I come from the corporate world with no knowledge about the industry. What advice would you give me?*

Woo, there is so much to say. The first thing I would have to do is, I would have to ask a question. Does your daughter want to do this? Is this something that she sincerely has a passion for? Does she awake and breathe this? Is this part of her make-up? For my daughter, this was a part of her being. I had always coached Sydney because I am from an acting background. It was always just she and I doing improvisations together. Her background and experience was just comedy clubs. Then I would let you know that it is a journey. And a lot of times, it is not glamorous. There are a lot of "nos." Having strength, having a solid foundation, in terms of family, friends and people around you that care about you and are sincere is extremely important. Being honest with yourself about what you can and cannot do for yourself and identifying what the strengths are and what they are not is so important. DO AS MUCH RESEARCH AS POSSIBLE! EDUCATION IS KEY! If you don't know what a show runner is, you better find out! If you don't know what a producer does, you better find out! The more education that you have about this industry the better equipped you are about this industry. If you get those emails from your agent and they come in and you see who the producer is, you better know everything about them and your daughter better know everything they have done as well. Children have no excuse either. They have to know. We have no excuse. We have iPhones and iPads. We have all of this information at our fingertips. Arm yourself, that's your armor. I cannot stress it enough, education is everything.

Every time someone comes in and coaches with me, I tell him or her, "The reason why we are as successful as we are, and I am still learning, is because we educate ourselves". I am not relying on someone else to educate me; I am doing it for myself. I am asking the right questions. I am doing the research. I am calling people. I am inquiring. I am looking at the film that directors have directed. I am doing all that stuff because you have to know. You don't want to walk into a casting room and wonder what this person is casting for. You don't want to be in that situation where you are uneducated. People will take advantage of you every step of the way.

*I tell this very thing to hopeful parents all the time but when I do they assume that I am trying to prevent them from getting started.*

You're not. It is so real. There is so much you need to know to get in this business, become successful and to stay relevant. I even have to know who Sydney's competition is. I must know that. I need to know what her competition is doing right now, what projects they are booking and how the projects are doing. Sydney has competition that looks just like her and in her age range. What is her competition doing right now? I need to know who their representation is just in case I am in a situation and Sydney needs new representation. I have to make sure that I don't go to them.

*What if I said to you, "This is a lot of information. My daughter never really expressed interest, but she has the gift. This is where she is supposed to be because I can just see her on TV."*

Woo! That comment is two-fold. It worries me at one point, and at another point, I understand because I was kind of in that same frame of mind with Sydney. The only advantage I had was that I was already in the business and kind of knew my way around. I was already aware of talent and what that meant. It wasn't about me wanting her to be on television though. It was more about me knowing that she had what I knew it would take to be successful in this industry. I teach a class, and I have a five year old and she is cute and she looks like she could be on television. Her mother thinks that she is extraordinary. Her mother thinks that she is outrageous. I am coaching her and I am playing games and things with her and can see that she is cute and good and she understands, but it is not an innate talent for her. There are a couple of avenues people can take. I would tell you and other parents to test it. The first step of the test is, go to classes, hang around other children who are in the industry, take them to a coach, and take them to people that you trust that you think can see the talent in your child. Learn some improvisational games and acting exercises with your daughter yourself to see if they have the ability to take direction. You are looking to see if they have an understanding of what it is that they are reading and if they can comprehend. All of that comes into play. It's not just about how cute they are. Just because your child is funny and she can hold her hands up like this, doesn't mean that she has what it takes to be in the industry. This is a job and people have to understand that. It's work. I always invite people down to production sets so they can see it for what it really is. This usually dispels a lot of preconceived notions for people, which is deep. Yes, there are elements of fun and it's glamorous and glitzy, exciting and it's great…but it is a job. It's not just fun and games.

***As a mom, what type of sacrifices did you have to make in order for Sydney to get where she is today?***

I had to put myself on hold. I had to stop dreaming for myself and I had to put my dream energy into her dream energy. Now here is the deep part about it. Here is the blessing in that. Because I stopped pursuing my dream, I found another dream. Because I let go of myself, I allowed God to show me my true self, who is even bigger than that original dream. I sacrificed everything. We've lived in one-bedroom apartments because I couldn't work. Then I had to become a server and I served for about five or six years at the Hollywood Improv at nights and never saw my daughter during the day because I was trying to work at night while John, my husband, would try to take her to auditions during the day. It was a mess. We sometimes slept in our car so that we would make the auditions for the next day. Sometimes the auditions were too far and we didn't have enough money to go to a hotel room or back and forth so we slept in the car. We gave up cable because we couldn't afford it. I will never forget I had a pair of sandals that almost looked like boots (because they were closed in on the sides) but they had an open toe in the front of the sandal. I shoe polished them to make them brown for the wintertime and wore them with socks. That's deep.

There is a heartache that comes with this industry because most of the time the parent is wondering, "When is this going to happen, why isn't this happening, what am I doing, and why are we doing this"? Every time I was confronted with these questions, God turned Sydney around and reminded me why I was doing this. He had me look at the talent this person has. He let me see that, then develop an understanding that I have to struggle. I wouldn't change it for the world. I wouldn't change eating rice for four months for the world. I almost sacrificed my marriage, not having time with my husband. Having him question, "What are we doing this for? Nobody believes in this kid, nobody sees it like we see it." But something kept us going, and this child, every step of the way, kept telling us, "Mom, it's going to happen, I know it's going to happen because this is my life". This journey has been wild. Watching this life from a distance or imagining what this life of fame is and actually living the experience is something totally different. Once you live it, you find that you have a whole other host of problems and issues.

*Tell me a little bit about relationships with other parents in the industry and what that could look like.*

Hmmm. There is a terminology that is used readily in this industry called "Stage Parents, Stage Moms or Stage Dads". I have come across those types of people and it is not necessarily a positive thing when the term "stage parent" is used because of the smothering component, because of the harsh words used by the parents to their children or towards other parents on production sets. Some of the daggers in the backs, and the coldness in the eyes, and so forth, are some of the behaviors associated with stage parents. I have had really great relationships with some parents that got it and understood that I have a life. We all have lives outside of our children and we are supportive of our children and this is just a part of this journey that we are all taking. I have had these relationships and I still have some and they are great. I have had those relationships that were competitive in a negative way. They are very unhealthy and it is easy to get caught up in those. It's very easy because you think your child is the best too. I thought my daughter was the best too! I would say, "Wait a minute, how did I get caught up in this? I used to get hyped too! Wait a minute, why are you looking at me like that? I'm gonna look at you like that too!"

You have to go in grounded knowing that that is the type of energy that you bring into a room. There is a lot of money at stake, there's fame, and a lot of incredible possibilities at stake and these possibilities are life changing. You get on a show, that opportunity changes your life, period, for all time. So other parents are looking at that and they don't want anybody else to have all that. I've had to grow into knowing that, when you have that, I have that. I've had to grow into that, it doesn't happen overnight. It takes a lot of prayer, a lot of reality checks, and a lot of kicks to get you to the point where you say, "I need to be happy for this woman because she's me." A lot of parents don't get that. I don't get that a lot.

*Do you think that that type of negative or selfish attitude can affect the out-come of that parent's child?*

Yes. I have seen it happen. I am actually going through it right now with someone I know who has a child that is very successful in film and tele-vision. So he has the best of both worlds. He's had it all. But from his mom's perspective, "It's not enough. He could have done better. He didn't do his best in the room and I know he didn't." She says these things and portrays him as this incompetent person to his face, which she thinks is strengthening him.

*What are the highlights of having a child in the entertainment industry?*

The first highlight is to see this growing confidence in this person that you helped to create and to see the blossoming of this individual. It's interesting because Sydney was always this mature kid but she still had her little kid stuff. I find that when she is successful in this industry, when she is doing things that are working out for her, she separates herself from me in a way that tells me that she is showing me that I gave her the tools to do so. That is the most rewarding feeling I have ever had! It is over-whelming. It makes me feel like God is going to give me a gold star when I get up there. Having people say the most incredible things about your child, and it is no longer in your head, it is no longer hidden any more, and they get it, those are the rewards, those are the highlights for me. Seeing our family as a success, for us, is a big deal. Every time we come home from the set we look at each other and say, "We did that! Did we just do that? We struggled and did that and it will get better from here!" This industry brought my family back in an interesting way. It brought my mother closer to us. She was an actress years ago and was not able to fully achieve the things that she wanted to achieve because she was raising two young kids on her own. I always felt guilty for that. So, this was my gift to her, to share our acting and entertainment experiences with her and it has brought my mother and me closer together. We talk about the industry together in a way we should have been talking about it all along. We are discussing things that are important to us. So those are the highlights.

*Now that you see this beautiful young woman blossoming into who she was always meant to be and becoming a young, independent woman; what happens to Kelly, her mom?*

That is a really deep question and I had to ask myself this question when she was about 10 years old. What's going to happen to me and to us when she breaks off on her own? As I am trying to understand who I am from the silliest thing to what movies do I like, what color do I really like, really reconnecting with myself, asking what do I know about my husband, what types of things do I want to do? I want to travel. So, I force myself to acknowledge that I am here. I make myself do that now.

*Is it because, you jumped in with both feet to make sure that your daughter was all that she could be so much, and for so long, that you have been fused together with her and you now have to make that separation?*

Yes, exactly. It's like peeling away a banana peel because I am in there somewhere I just have to figure it out. I'm not going to rush myself, I am going to take my time, I am going to be patient with myself and I am going to forgive myself. That is the first thing; then hug myself, because everything is really all right. I am now starting to realize that I am not that much older than Sydney, in a lot of ways. I am still silly, I love to do silly things and there are so many things that I still want to do, and I now have time to do them. I am fearful but in a great way. This fear is going to motivate me because I taught that to Sydney.

***Can you celebrate where she's going and celebrate where you're going at the
same time?***

Yes. I see that and I feel that and she celebrates it too. I am starting a class
in January, it's going to be an improvisational, sketch comedy and stand up
class. It's going to be everything. I am doing the marketing now and Sydney
is celebrating with me. Eventually I want to take it around the country and
especially to my hometown in Philly to those kids who may not have any
hope. There is such hopelessness there. I got out, so I have to show them
that it is real. It can happen. That is my goal. I have been preparing my mind
and my body because I believe that God is saying that I have to be ready.
I am preparing and it feels great. I am not sad in a traditional sense. I am
sad because most of the work that I had to do with her is done. Of course
she will still have the questions, she will make the mistakes and she will
do all that. But a lot of what needs to be done has already been completed.
So here I am again. I never went away. Even though I will always be there
for her and she will never have to struggle alone. Many kids can't say that.
It's fun though. I love the moments that I have now.

# Michelle Rene Cole
*Costume Designer*

### What is a costume designer?

From my experience, a costume designer is a person who collaborates with the Executive Producer to bring to life the executive producer's wardrobe vision of the production. The costume designer is also trained to sketch, sew, select fabric, work on creating sketch designs - in pencil first, then in color - for the vision that the executive producer wants to see. The sketch artist and the costume designer work to make any preliminary changes that the executive producer wants before they move on to the designing phase. They then consult with the director of photography, props and the set decorator to make sure the lighting and the production set is suitable and working cohesively with the desired wardrobe, style and colors. The costume designer is essential in making the vision come true. The costume designer is like a conductor in an orchestra. He or she has a strong team like supervisors and costumers working to help make the vision happen. Tailors shop for clothes at department stores and other outlets, design clothes, and the costumer executes what the costume designer is looking for. The construction person, who is called the special effects tailor, builds the special design for walk around costumes (wardrobe that is bigger and more elaborate than regular clothes worn by actors), like someone dressed as the Statue of Liberty. That happens a lot in comedies. The dyer dyes the fabric used to make the wardrobe for movies like *Gladiator* or *Glory*. All of that material was dyed and aged. There are people who are hired solely to dye and age material.

*What do you love most about being a costume designer?*

I love training my assistants to become costume designers, dressing characters and meeting the variety of talented people in all areas of entertainment. I love when I get a letter or phone call from former production assistants who have landed a show or a movie that they are now the costume designers for. I am really proud to have instilled training in them that they can go on to do what they really love or what they really wanted to do themselves.

*What would you compare the entertainment industry to?*

The industry is like a blue, calm storm, in that you don't know what to expect; sometimes it's quiet and sometimes it's not. It's almost like football team tryouts too. When guys are trying out for a team, nobody knows if he is going to get picked or not. If you are out there, you are just trying your best to make the team. You have to be on top of your game. That is a mental game. This industry is a mental game to me as well. It doesn't mean that you are better because you make it in this industry. There is just a certain breed of people that this industry attracts. When I first started I was so naïve about what the industry was because I wasn't exposed to all of these different types of personalities. There are many ups and downs on this journey because you are dealing with so many types of people. You have to be on the top of your mental game. Each job is so different from the other, even if the executive producers or other key players are the same on every job. His or her personality will be different on every job because the atmosphere is different on every job.

*What has your experience been like working with kids in this industry?*

I have worked with a lot of kids. I love working with kids because they are so honest. While they are in wardrobe fittings they say things like, "I'm tired.

How many more changes are we going to have to do?" They are so easy. In all of these years I don't think that I have ever had one bad experience with a kid actor. They are sometimes cranky but they are entitled to that because of the schedules, school and they have long workdays. They have so much on them to do. In college my minor was psychology so I think that has helped me in my career and dealing with the kids. I have been in dressing rooms where kids are having meltdowns because of so much pressure from the parents or Vice Presidents of production studios. It becomes a lot for the kids. I've often thought, "If I had kids, would I have put them in the business?" I think I would say no, because you really have to be rooted and grounded to make it in this industry, and you have to have good parents. I heard a mother once say about her child, "When he is no longer having fun and it is damaging him, I am going to take him out of the business." I have had some of the best times with the kids but some of those kids have fighting parents. I don't think I have ever seen two kids on set fight, but I have seen two parents fighting on set. I have heard of other shows where they have that too.

**What has been your experience with the parents?**

Oh boy. Oh boy…parents can sometimes be brutal because they want "it" so badly. They want it for the kids and for themselves. They want it so badly to the point where the girls are losing weight to keep jobs. The hardest part, as a costume designer, is watching the parent put so much pressure on their kids, watching the kids carrying the pressure of the job and also the stress of watching the parent fighting with other parents on set. The kids are getting along, but the parents are having issues. One parent may be upset because another parent's kid has more lines or the other kid is spending too much time with the main adult cast. That is the hardest thing to watch because the kids are carrying the weight of that.

*What advice would you give kids who want to try out this career?*

You have to love it. I think when you love it everything falls into place. When the gift is in them and they have what it takes, and they are driven, it all works out. You have to love it because there is no other way to survive it because this industry can be so brutal and hard at times. Some of the dynamics of the business are hard at times but if you love it, the love will carry you through those times.

*What advice would you give parents?*

Back off. Let them be. Let them flap their wings. Parents have to be around to be parents to their children and train them up. I think parents are doing a disservice to their kids when they are spoon-feeding them and making their lives too easy or the parents are overbearing. Kids still have to be kids and graduate to young adulthood. I love it when parents are doing their job as parents by teaching their kids manners, giving them chores, and teaching them right from wrong. I love that, because we don't know if all of these kids who are working now are going to make it past this point. They have to have something else that they can do well. Parents have to make sure of that. The kids can take advantage of these creative environments by going into the writer's room to see what the writers do there. They can sit and talk with the directors to see what they do and how they do it. So, parents should back off and take the pressure off of their kids on set. Let them use that time as a playground of learning wonderful things and flapping their wings and growing. Let them breathe and be who they are, obviously with some boundaries.

# Tyler James Williams
*Actor/Writer/Producer/Director*

*What advice would you give a mother of a four-year-old child attempting to get into the business at the same age you were when you started?*

Wait. Give it time. With us it just seemed to work out for us, but that is not the norm. We had a few things in our favor so to speak. More times than not, it doesn't work out as well or easily for others. As far as the kids falling in love with what they do or doing it for the right reasons, that may not be the case for everyone.

*Suppose a parent says, "If it happened for you it can happen for us. My son is really talented and everyone says so."*

The child's talent is not going anywhere. If the child is really talented, let his or her stage be a bit smaller. Let it be a school play, Community Theater, or something like that. Because the minute you start putting them in front of the camera, the experience becomes a job and a profession. Unless you, the parent, are mentally prepared for guiding your child, you are going to do more damage to the child than any money could ever fix.

*You make it seem like you have regrets about starting as young as you did or that there are more disadvantages than advantages about starting out so young.*

There are more disadvantages than there are advantages. I probably sound that way because I have seen 9 out of 10 of the people that I started off working with in the industry who now live unhealthy lives. You see that they have been doing it for so long, and they continue to pursue it to the point where they want it so much that that is what their lives become. When I bump into some of them, instead of having a natural conversation and asking how the person is doing, the first question is, "What is the last project you worked on, or What are you working on now?" That is not healthy for anyone let alone a child who values his or her worth by the last thing they did or the last project they worked on. There is an unhealthy competition going. It is almost as if the kids don't even have real friends anymore and the parent has to understand that part of it. The minute you get your kid into the industry, for real, they are, most likely, going to have more competitors and leeches than friends. True friendships may become very rare. In my experience, I don't think I developed real friends until I was about 17. I started so young, I was already "in the business" before I knew what a friend actually was.

*If you had to do it all over again, would you have started later?*

Here is where I will, I'm sure, start to sound hypocritical. I will tell a parent of a four year old to wait before getting into the industry but if I had done that I would probably just be a struggling actor right now. One of the things you can't deny and you must consider is timing. If I did not have the experiences in the industry that I had from 4 to 12 years old, living in New York, my career probably would not have taken me to where I am now. Even though my early life experience was what it was, I was fortunately able to adjust and fall in love with what I have chosen as my career path. So I guess the answer to the question is yes and no.

Tyler James Williams

*Go back to that moment when you were four years old realizing that this acting thing was what you wanted to do. What advice would you give your four-year-old self?*

Absolutely none. I wouldn't give a four-year-old child any advice. What was beautiful about that time was that it was all a dream. It was the purest form of a dream. I didn't even fully understand what I said I wanted to do. All I knew was that it actually meant something to me. I just knew that I had fallen in love with the idea of me doing what I saw. I think that that is what many industry people are really trying to get back to. It's a lot like a drug addict who is chasing that initial high. I believe that the average actor is looking for that today. Getting back to the place when that dream was really real and it still seemed real and obtainable. This is before the industry showed you the reality of what really goes on. I wouldn't say anything to any kid who is out there, who is young, except dream. I would tell them to dream and just let that be it. Because they have enough time, when you grow up, for life, in this industry, at times, to tell you just how sucky it really is. In the real world, most kids find out what life is really about after they graduate high school and leave home for college. Kids who start young in this business find out that reality much earlier. That's why many kids in the industry seem to be more mature or older than they actually are. They seem to be old souls because the industry forces them to grow up sooner and much faster.

*So you are saying wait before the child goes on auditions for commercials, or print or anything?*

I would say consider the most important word of your question, the child. The child is only going to be young once. The child is going to grow up and turn 17 so fast. Don't put the possibility of a career for the child before the child. Let him or her be a kid, and do kid things, first. If you are going to pursue it anyway, make it an extracurricular activity. Make it like their soccer team or art class type of activity. Don't put any energy to it as if the stakes are high. I think that is one of the things that you did well with us was, the stakes were never high. Acting was never seen as that big of a deal for us.

I remember when Tylen (my baby brother) as a younger kid would walk into a casting room to audition. It was never a big thing for him. But it was for some of the kids at the audition. Tylen would walk into an audition and because of the amount of work that me and Tyrel had done in the past, some of the kids or the parents would immediately start to get stressed or anxious because he was related to us. Some of them thought that because he was our brother and we worked often that it would lessen the other kid's chances of booking the job.

They would think, "Oh no, there is Tyler and Tyrel's brother. If he is auditioning for the same thing, my son is not going to book the job now." That is not necessarily the case and that kind of stress on a little kid is not healthy. If you are going to let your child work in this business at a young age, make it so that the attitude before, during and after an audition is, "If they book it fine, if they don't book it, it's fine too." Let the focus be on the activity of auditioning for the job and not the job itself.

*Ok, let's play word association. I am going to say a word or phrase. Tell me the first thing that comes to your mind. Ready?*

*A Negative Stage Parent:* The worst…the absolute worst. A bad stage parent does more damage to a child than the industry ever could.

*Child Star:* A burden. The label is a burden that most kids need professional help learning how to carry.

*Hit Show:* What's next? There is a saying in the industry that goes, "You are only as good as your last job." But that is not the way it is out here. You are only actually as good as your *next* job. If you have a hit show, you need another hit show. If you get another hit show you then need a hit movie. It's great! It's the best time you can possibly have - but what's next?

*Hollywood:* Wonderland. It's like Alice in Wonderland. None of it is really real.

*Socialite:* A parasite. The word parasite sounds so bad but we need parasites. They serve a purpose. People use leeches to get their blood clean. You need them essentially but you know that's what they are. No matter how pretty it may be it is still a parasite.

*Entourage:* Expensive. Having an entourage is very expensive. Probably the number one reason many popular celebrities will spend up all of their money.

*Hollywood Parties:* The single most pointless thing on the face of the earth. I reject the idea that many people have that you will get a job from going to a party because you are rarely going to get a job from hanging out at a party. That is never going to happen to most people.

**What is the biggest difference between being rich and famous and being wealthy and successful?**

Longevity. You can get fame and riches tomorrow if you are willing to do what it takes to get them. I can release a sex tape tonight and have fame and riches tomorrow. That doesn't mean that I will be wealthy and have success. With fame and riches you will have to try to maintain that. It's like having a bad car. Wealth and success is a mindset. It is a place that you are in mentally.

**You have been in the industry for 18 years now. You have made the transition from working child actor to working young adult actor. How have you managed to avoid the stereotypical transitional traps of the industry?**

By having people who could tell me the truth without having a vested interest in me. That and patience, I guess you could say. I attribute a lot of my young adult career to my acting coach. Simply because he appreciated the work I had done at that point to see that I could do so much better and he told me when I was BS-ing my way through it. The patience component started in me when I was a child. That is one of the things that inspiring young actors (or their parents) don't understand. As a child, I was taught not to want or need anything. If you want or need anything you are bound to have a dysfunctional lifestyle out here in this industry. I was taught and had to learn the business. I had to learn what the business actually is. For example, a person who is acting in this business, in television, is just selling advertising time. If you look at it from that perspective it will shift your whole perspective of what the job is and what the industry really needs. If you look at it that way, everything stops appearing so personal at that point.

*What is the most exciting thing about being a working actor?*

Hitting the sweet spot. You have done all of the prep work. You have gotten the role. You have done all of the hard work, all of the emotional work. You have done all of it, then you get in front of the camera and it is time to put it all out there and it is effortless. Everything is clicking and everything is working. It goes back to being a drug addict. It's those moments that literally last about 30 seconds that everyone is looking for, chasing for. Everyone is looking for the sweet spot of creativity. That's what we are looking for. At least, I know that is the case for me, and the creative people that I know. Nothing in the creative world is better than that moment. Not the attention or any of the rest of the stuff, although I know that the attention is what some people are looking for, but not for me.

*What do you think happened to those kids who don't make the transition? Why didn't they make it?*

Well, many of them don't know what to do. I am not saying that from a cocky place, as if I knew what to do and they don't - no. I didn't know what to do, either. What happens is as a working child actor, you have worked so long and got used to it. You were cute, you were a natural and everything came easy to you. After a while something changed and that natural thing no longer works for you. All of a sudden people start out-reading you for roles significantly and no one is telling you what to do now. I had the privilege of having a good agent and when I hit that stage in my life and was able to articulate that to her she knew what to do and say. She said, "It's time for you to start going to class." I was like, "Oh, ok" because I didn't know what to do. It's somewhat like being the star football player in your local high school, then going to the NFL. You were the best person at what you did well, in that place. But now you are on a grand scale with people who have been training their entire lives. You will get swallowed up because you are not on that level.

That's why I say let your kids wait because I found myself, at 17-18 years old, reading with adults who went to Julliard who were playing younger roles than they actually were. There were 26 year olds auditioning for high school seniors, or college freshmen roles. Had I not been going to acting class and had the acting coach that I had, I would have never been able to compete for a role that I just recently landed. There is no way in the world I would have been in that film because, if I am doing a scene with someone who is classically trained, there is no way I can measure up to their quality of work. So the scene would be off and it just would not work. That's what happens to kids who get trapped. They were cute and they were funny and they were riding on their natural talent but no one is telling them that they need to get really good at what they do. The teenager who wrapped the last season of "Everybody Hates Chris" would have never booked "Dear White People," absolutely not. The teenager from the last season for "Everybody Hates Chris" was never going to work again if he had not gone to class to get better. Because he was so good at just that specifically, and he did that for so long, he would have approached every other and future role the same way he approached that sitcom. Maybe he would have gotten a role here or there, maybe. Maybe he would have done a movie but that would have been pretty much it.

*What is the most frustrating part about working in the system of entertainment, be it music, sports, etc.?*

It would be two-fold. It is the waiting, and the things you can't control. Many people outside of the system may not realize that the artist, the one with the special skill, as a working artist, sits at the bottom of the barrel where control is concerned. You are always waiting for someone to give you a job, whether it's an actor, singer, dancer, or football player. The artist is always waiting for someone to employ them. Even with singers, they can sing hooks in the studio, record records, and lay down tracks and everything but that singer still has to wait for a label to put the record out. Even if it is done independently, the artist has to wait that much longer to get it out there to the people. Having said that, I know most singers would disagree but singers have it better than actors. Because they can at least generate product. They can sit down with themselves and just sing/write a song. But an actor, the artist can't just sit down and write a television show to star in. The things you can't control piece involves things like, losing roles because I was too old, too young, too tall, too thin or too short. Hearing things like your performance was spot on but you just don't look right next to our lead character. I lost count of how many times that has happened. You are going to be too "something" for a lot of roles. That is something that an actor can't control. That is the most frustrating thing because when you get a note (feedback) like that from casting that is something that you can't do anything about. In those cases, I would have preferred to hear, "You sucked," rather the alternative note.

*In the midst of all of this you still manage to book jobs. How does or where does your faith come into to play?*

Faith is key, because in the moments when I don't have faith, I become physically sick. My stomach is in knots. There was a time, before a project, when I was at my lightest weight. I was throwing up all the time, for no apparent reason. I went to the doctor and ran all of the usual tests, and they had nothing for me to explain why I was throwing up and my stomach felt sick all the time. I realized over time that it was stress. It was stress of not having enough faith in God's plan for my life and my career. I was worried about a project and questioning if it was going to do well and worrying about if I was ever going to work again. You have to have some kind of faith. I believe that's why people in this industry do drugs. That's why there is so much cocaine available in this industry. People wonder, "Why are there people who still do cocaine? It's so bad for you." There is so much cocaine going around Hollywood because it is a power drug. It is one of the few times that an artist feels powerful and in control of the industry. With no faith, life is just terrible in this industry.

Even in the midst of working as much as I have worked, and since 18 I have had at least one job a year to date, your head says the craziest thing. Your head begins to compare and says things like, "Yes, but I am not working as much as this person." So it feels like I am not working. Every year I have had a project come out or I have had a project but still there is a comparison to somebody else. That's when you MUST have faith in knowing that you are going to be taken care of, you are going to be fine. My faith keeps me beyond grounded...it keeps me healthy. It keeps me mentally healthy and physically healthy so I can be clear in knowing that I don't need to worry or stress about anything. I know that there will always be another job. No matter what I might be reading for right now, there will always be another job. I can be reading for an audition for a big role, it can seem like the biggest role ever, and everybody in the industry who fits the profile will be reading for it too. We find out later that the project goes absolutely nowhere. I was looking at my computer the other day and just scanned through all of the appointments I got and all of the auditions I went on. I noticed that most of the projects never came to fruition. The projects didn't even get shot or come out. But I am going in there and fighting for this role. It is never that serious. It just is what it is. If you don't realize that quickly, you will become a disgusting human being and fall apart.

*It sounds like this industry is very stressful whether you work or not. How did you not succumb to the drug or abuse scene?*

This is what I have been trying to say this whole time. If the parent does not value the child more than the parent values them working, the child will most likely become a crack head of some form. It is only because of y'all, that's it. It's because of you and parents like you that I am not crazy, that I (and the rest of the kids who don't have those types of problems) didn't become "that" kid or young adult. I didn't feel the stress of it all until I became an adult like the rest of the world. By then I was prepared to deal with the stress of it all. That's when you are supposed to. It wasn't until then that I ever actually felt it. If you do not value your child's sanity more than them getting the next big thing, you are in trouble.

If you are willing to have Marvel on the phone saying, "We want your child to be the next franchise child superstar hero and make billions of dollars," and you don't consider the consequences, and you sit there and think about it without considering walking away from it all, prepare to fail as a parent because your child is going to be unhealthy. You have to be willing to walk away because your child feels that. Your child feels that pressure of not being able to walk away. That pressure opens the door to ways of handling the pressure or trying to escape from it. Alcohol or drugs always seemed to be the first alternative for many people. At one point, I knew of so many people who were either using drugs, experimenting with drugs or addicted to drugs, I just assumed that everyone around me was doing or addicted to drugs, just in case. When I found someone who wasn't, it was a pleasant surprise. Vices are a terrible thing to have in this industry. They become crutches and most people's downfall. If I can't live without it, I don't need it.

A person is not supposed to feel that his or her entire life. As an adult you are supposed to feel that but not as a child. Just like you are not supposed to drink until 21 or smoke at a certain age. That's because as a child you are not wired to handle it. It is the same as the pressures of the industry, the child is not wired to handle it and shouldn't. But if the parent is not handling all of it the child is handling some of it. That is still wrong. So if the parent is not ready to handle it, then just wait. It's fine. Tap out; the industry is not going anywhere, just wait. I'm not saying don't do it. Some people will just flat out say don't do it, but I'm not saying that. Just wait and send your kid to a performing arts school/college. Let them get trained. Send them to Julliard, send them to Carnegie Mellon, send them wherever, but let them get trained. They will be so much better at it than if you would have put them in it when they were little and they will be able to handle the pressure. If this is what they want to do, there is still so much time for them to do that. There are so many extremely talented adult actors who were nowhere to be found as kids but they stayed away, studied and they are huge now. That happened for a reason. Give your kids time to be kids.

*As I am listening to you, I am thinking about people who are on the outside looking in. They think Hollywood is glamour, red carpets, millions of dollars, and the like. Give them a realistic view of your perception of Hollywood.*

I'll put it to you this way. Imagine your grandfather bought a 1964 Chevy Impala in 1964. That is a great car. Now imagine that he drove it every day, then passed it on to your dad and the car stayed in the family and was eventually passed down to you. This is going to be your first car. You can paint it as nicely as you want to. You can put a new engine in it. You can put new rims on it. But it is still a 1964 Impala. It's been around for a long time and maybe at one point it was the best thing since sliced bread, but it definitely is not anymore. That is what Hollywood is. You are coming into a place that keeps repainting itself. The new paint job looks beautiful, but it has frame damage. Anybody who knows anything about a car knows that if the car has frame damage, that's it. It's done. It's never gonna be good any more. Hollywood will never be good ever again.

*Are you saying that the entertainment industry is a corrupt industry, full of nothing but negative experiences, and that there is nothing good about it?*

I love what I do for a living and I love my job. However, I would say that the only thing worse than the entertainment industry, industry wise, is probably politics, because the system will break you if you let it. It is built to break you. I guarantee that when it is all said and done, 99% of the people in the entertainment industry will be broken on some level. Because that's what it does. It's not like I am just throwing that out there just to say that. I know you are not strong enough. It happens every day. You become one of three people. Person #1: You become a shell of who you used to be, to the point where you are just making decisions and doing things that old you would be completely confused about. Person #2: You become a slimy disgusting human being because you hang around that element of people and they have taught and molded you to do so. Person #3: Or, you sell your soul to buy into the corruption of the entertainment industry.

*Is it possible that you can come into this industry grounded, go through the ups and the downs, and survive it, changed but still remaining true to who you really are and what you stand for?*

It is possible to go to the moon but that doesn't mean that everyone is going to do it.

*Can you say that you know of ten kids who started with you, or that you have met along the way, who are your age now, who are emotionally, mentally, spiritually, financially, and relationally ok?*

Ten people, no - five people, yes.

*You are an adult now. What about the successful, working adult world of the industry? Generally speaking, are they emotionally, mentally, spiritually, financially, and relationally ok?*

Some of them yes, there are a few. However, you read about it in the news just about every day. Nobody has worse marriages and more unadjusted children than Hollywood people. We divorce somebody every other day. Our kids are running all over the place doing every drug they can find. It's really hard to become a well-adjusted human being in this industry because this business is not a very smart emotional choice for a profession. It is a profession that you have to fall in love with to do it well, then get rejected by it 9 times out of 10, but this is something you are madly in love with. It's not like getting rejected by this job that you interview for just because you want to work at any type of job. Where you are just going in and saying, "I need a job."

Its just like that old Chappelle joke, "Why do you want to work at McDonalds?"

"Because I really love McDonalds."

What the person is really saying is, "No, I just want a job." For, actors, there are so many roles that we fall in love with that we don't get. Over time that breaks you. Not just your feelings, but your soul.

So yeah, there are a few entertainers that you don't hear anything about, who are ok. But these folks are more of the exception than the rule. The rule in this industry is typically, you are going to marry three people, and it's not until the third marriage that you are gonna get it right. Some don't get it right after that. If you have kids in those first two marriages, those kids will probably go to rehab before they are 25. Because you, the parent, weren't there. You had to focus on the next job because I could literally have a job today, then, never work again. That's what this career looks like for most people in this business. So in order to provide for your family, you had to be gone all the time. So most likely your kid will suffer from abandonment issues and end up in rehab before 25. But this kind of life comes with the territory.

*If this is the case for so many, why do entertainers stay in the industry?*

Because we love it, we love what we do. At times it can seem like we are a glutton for punishment, but that's why I say that it is such a brave career choice.

*It sounds like the industry is a lot like being in a dysfunctional relationship with someone. When times are good they are really good, when times are bad they are really bad. So you stay in this relationship because the good times are really good and they outweigh the bad. Is that a correct analogy?*

The good moments make all of the bad moments worth it. It really does. That's what keeps you going forward. These are all of my opinions about show business, but when the industry is good to you, and it has been great to me, there is nothing like it. I don't even know what it's like for someone that the industry has not been good for, for someone who hasn't worked for the last five or ten years. I don't know why they stay because his or her bad outweighs their good. So that's a different interview entirely. It is a beautiful thing when it works.

*Do you believe that it is a challenge to be in this business more than ten years and not be bitter, indifferent, frustrated, or empty?*

I'd say, quite honestly, it is almost impossible. To not be bitter in some way, to not be jaded in some way, yeah that is almost impossible. I am not talking about superstars here. I am talking about working actors, which most people, that's if you make it that far, will become. I'm talking about working actors, who make a living just by doing the acting thing without having to get a side job. There are actors who act (and other entertainers in every field) and you will recognize his or her face when you see them, but they don't make enough money to sustain themselves, so they have to get side jobs. I am not talking about the working actor who makes enough money to pay all of their bills, send their kids to good schools/colleges, buy a house, live in a good neighborhood, pay all of their taxes, and go on vacations. That means they book just enough jobs during the year, or have enough residuals coming in from previous jobs that they can do all of the things that everyone else in the real world strives to accomplish. I know working actors who have all of those issues. I know people definitely who don't understand why somebody else is the "it" person right now. Everything they read for that "it" person gets or books. If that happens enough, that will make you jaded. Especially if you don't think that they are very good.

That is another point to make. There are people who are classically trained and they are up against those who are not and for some reason, be it a look, a type or something else, the classically trained person won't book the job. I know people who can act circles around me and I have done scenes with them, but they can't seem to survive as working actors for some reason. That is crazy. Some of them are bitter and some of them see what the other side looks like from a distance and feel somewhat saved from all of the stress of it all. Others are some of the most gracious and patient people that I have ever seen in my life. They are like, "We know it will happen at some point. So until it does, I am just going to enjoy what this is, right here and now." I am not there yet, so I think it is one of the most commendable mentalities to have. They are still passionate about it. These types of people are the "Art Purists." Those are the people who fall in love with auditioning. They are just happy to stand in front of somebody and do it. I believe those are the people who will eventually survive and end up doing very well. For me and other working actors we now see auditioning as that thing you have to do. We see it as being judged by every little thing that we say and do just so we can possibly get this job. The people who are really healthy are those who are just excited to have an audience. They are just excited to be invited to the table to read. They are still passionate. I have been trying to get back to that place for the last year and half. Just being that person at that place. To walking into an audition with the mentality that says, "I appreciate you taking the time for you to see me do what I do."

*Do you think that the goal of the typical working actor is to become a superstar?*

Yes. It is capitalism. Most working actors are trying to get to that 1%. One percent of actors are working actors, .5% of those working actors are super-stars. We are fighting to be at the top of the "A" list. Everyone wants to be in that .5% now. Once you become a working actor, remaining a working actor is no longer ok. Working actors will probably make six figures in a year. That's what's crazy. I was talking with a friend of mine, who is also an actor, who is from the "hood." He said to me, sometimes I wish I could run back to my hood and tell everybody, "They are giving money away, over here! They are giving it away!" Let's say the average person in America wants to make $60,000 a year. Most working actors, if they do a pilot, or a few episodes on a television show (provided they have good quotes), a movie that does fairly ok, have a show that is in syndication, and/or do an independent film or two, will make six figures a year, and that's the very low end. That's what's crazy. It does look like the industry is giving money away. America loves to be entertained. However, the working actor wants to make millions of dollars for one project. That's where the .5% live. It is capitalism in its purest form because we are not ok with just making a good living; we want to make a great living.

*If the working actor is striving to be a superstar, what is the superstar striving for?*

The superstar is striving to stay there! Once you get there, the superstar can take a sigh of relief for a while. But right behind you there is a newer, prettier, stronger, funnier, more dramatic, younger version of you, who is just as talented, making his or her way up the pike. When I get old enough, if my 'thing" is not selling as it use to or "that thing that I do well" is no longer as special or unique, I know they are just going to kick me to the curb, really fast. So I have to make sure that I am great! So no one ever really "makes it." Let me show you what the working actor's road to superstardom kinda looks like for some people.

The Newbie (beginner) just wants to get on television, so they get a regional commercial and lose their minds with excitement! After that excitement wears off, they want a national commercial and, "Oh My Gosh!" They get a national commercial! It is seen all over the nation! They think, "Life doesn't get any better than this. I have made it!" They follow that by getting three more national commercials and they are celebrities to their circle of the world! How outrageous! After a while, that wears off, and they feel like they can be doing more. Now they start to notice the shows that his or her commercials are playing in the midst of. Now they want to guest star in a show. You get a guest-starring role on "Law and Order" and that is it! It's a popular show that everyone watches. Your grandmother loves this show and she tells everybody that her grandbaby is starring on her favorite show! This is fantastic! You have made it! You are a star!

After the celebrity of that wears off, you notice other people who look like you who are starring on television shows. Now you want to be-on-a-show. "I want to be a regular on a show!" Here comes pilot season. You work really hard and study your lines and it happens! I cannot believe it, I am now a regular on a television show! My dreams have all come true. I have made it! I'm living a dream! Red carpets, invitations to award shows, gifting suites, award shows and celebrity events are all a part of my life now! You think, "I have to pinch myself to see if I'm dreaming! This is amazing! I am making so much money per week, and I have all of this exposure! Even other stars are complimenting me now! I am just like them!" After a year or two of that life, you notice that other television stars, just like you, are also doing movies and making a lot more money than you are. Now you want to do movies too.

Oh My Gosh! You get to do a small role in a movie and it does well! Amazing! You love the pace, the schedule, working with the stars and the excitement of the movie lifestyle. It has so many more perks than television! Now you want to "star" in a movie. "Un-Be-Lieve-Able…just saw my face on the poster! People are coming to see me. I have never made so much money in my life! This is a little piece of heaven. Now people want to work with me…wow!" But then an actor friend of yours is starring in a movie franchise and treated like a rock star! Now you want a franchise. You want *Fast and the Furious*. You want eight of these movies with you being the star in all of them! "I can't believe it, I have a successful franchise!" You have made it big for sure! But you notice that although people are going to the movies to see your work, you don't feel like you are respected among your peers so you now want an Oscar.

You have to fight and struggle and study a new craft and land a role that is going to change the way people see movies! In time you get your Oscar but you now have to earn the right to keep the Oscar by continuing to do great work and land great roles. Now you have to maintain the spot that you have at the top. It's harder than you ever expected it to be. It's actually much harder maintaining it than it was booking that first commercial but you can't think about that now. You have to stay relevant because you just read in Entertainment Weekly about a younger, prettier, stronger, handsomer version of you who just debuted in their first movie and it was a runaway hit. The critics are calling the new actor the next YOU! Soon after he signs on to do a franchise and is now, in your eyes, gunning for your spot. Now what?

This scenario is one of the best outcomes for actors. This is not the norm either. There are so many different pit stops, detours and dead ends along the way and tragic stories of people who never even walked a portion of the "Working Actor meets Superstar" road. I believe that the happiest, most successful and least bitter of all of these folks, in many cases, are the novices. They are clueless to the pressures, they work occasionally, they love what they are currently doing and they are still passionate about what they are doing. They still love what they do for all of the right reasons, without the pressures.

### *So why not just get a job working at a bank?*

Exactly. Go for it. That would be my advice. That's why I said at the beginning...wait. Because what you have to understand is if you are going to become an actor you are pretty much saying I want to be a dysfunctional human being. From the inconsistencies in everyday life, work schedules, rejections, successes at the box office, flops at the box office, changes of production plans, lack of quality family time, hiccups in financial income, and everything else, unless you belong to the 1% who survive it all, working at the bank will be a better, more stable, less exciting but more functional and sane way to live your life, and establish a family with a sane group of people around you. If you choose to do this you are also saying, "I don't want to be happy most of the time. I want to deal with deep bouts of depression, and I want to get rejected most of the time, for something I love deeply."

It is kind of like being a child in kindergarten and you are doing a macaroni art project with dried macaroni, construction paper and glue. Your little hands learn how to draw the design you are going to make and then you start to carefully put glue on each piece and lay the macaroni on the paper to dry. You are so proud of it and once it dries you take it home to your parents and as soon as they see it they say, "get this piece of garbage out of my face." They throw it on the floor, then pick it up and throw it in the garbage. You're the kid who cries about it but the next day you go back and make another macaroni project even though the same thing happens over and over again when you get home. You keep making them because you love making them even though no one else seems to. I must admit. I am glad that I am not a girl in this industry. I get notes from casting like, "You are not tall enough or you look too young." You know how many girls get, "You're too fat, you're not as pretty as her, lose 13 lbs then maybe we will see you again"?

Or, "Your teeth are crooked." Your teeth are crooked is a really big note. You can't just get some make-up and cover that up. That's a big note that people get often. That's gonna take some time to fix. But notice how

229

many stars you see now who have perfect teeth but early in their careers the teeth were all over the place. That's why you see them now with those big, white, Chiclets in their mouths. I get a note often that I have a space between two of my teeth on the left side of my mouth. Apparently casting is noticing teeth and they are a big part of your acting career. So, be ready, you can act circles around other people, you can cry, you can drop that tear at the perfect moment like Denzel, but you could still get that note, "Your teeth are crooked," and lose the role. Look at all of these "A" list superstar actors, go back. Their first jobs they had crooked teeth, now, they are perfect. For most people, crooked teeth will prevent you from working. I'm just putting that out there. So, if you want your baby to be an actor, get some braces on their teeth before you get started!

***That's funny! What is your take on parents having a Plan B for their child's acting career?***

The acting should be your plan B. This should not be your child's plan A. If you have already jumped the gun and your child is in the business, let this career path be your plan B and push your kid to go to college or something normal. People ask me all the time, "If you weren't acting what would you be doing?" I always tell them, "It would be some form of entertainment." Then, they typically ask, "Yeah, but what if you couldn't do that either?" I tell them, "Well then, I'd be homeless." Because I am not good at anything else like that. I learned how to write for television. I am becoming a decent television writer. I can't write, like a regular book. That's not what I'm good at. Everything in my world revolves around entertainment. I would find another entertainment door, like writing music for somebody or something like that. These are different skill sets of writing. When you look at journalist, I couldn't be a journalist. I don't know how to write as a journalist or have journalism skills. I could go to school to learn it but I would be 22 going to school. I would be behind the curve and I wouldn't like doing it.

So, I'd say to the parents, make acting the plan B and let your kid do other things. Many actors become waiters because it's acting. You are learning how to act. You are memorizing things quickly, you pretend to be pleasant, and servicing whatever they want. That's all we are really doing. We are servicing our audience and trying to find out what they want. We then give that to the audience so they can remember who we were.

## How important is education in this industry?

Education is two-fold. It is pivotal and it is not. You don't know how many stupid actors I know. They are great actors but stupid people and they work all the time. I don't mean stupid by way of their opinions, I mean by way of the non-smart decisions that they make in life, overall. I am not going to lie to people and say you have to be very smart to do this because you don't. I know people who didn't get out of their freshman year of high school. Education is pivotal if you want your child to be a good human being and have longevity in this industry. If you want them to be smart, make good decisions and good choices, be able to know what's going on in their world around them, and approach that world well and make choices based on that, then yes. But if you want them to be an actor and just roll the dice of chance along the way, they pretty much just need to know how to read. If you want them to excel, do shows and choose to do projects that prove that they are thinking, being proactive and making sound judgment calls, and not just picking roles because they make them look pretty, then yes, school is the way to go. If you think that your child is pretty enough to coast on just their looks then, no, they don't need education. There are many very successful adult actors and entertainers that never graduated from high school or they dropped out of college or never went to college. But they became students of their craft to kind of over compensate and they are some of the hardest working artists out there today.

*What do you say to the parent whose child is now a non-working teenage actor with no work in sight and doesn't have an education to fall back on because of their pursuit for fame?*

For the parents who have already wasted too much time in this industry and your child is now a non-working teenage actor instead of an academic student, your guess is as good as mine. You have set your child up or have given them a skill set that they really can't use anywhere else. That is unless they become a waiter or maybe they can sell real estate, but you need a level of education or knowledge for that too. I don't know. You have to work with what you got at this point and try to make lemonade out of lemons. They can go to college for drama, or something dealing with the arts.

*What if the parent quit their job years before and threw caution to the wind for this pursuit, the marriage has fallen apart, and they have nothing to show for time spent?*

I would tell them the same thing that I am assuming a bouncer says to somebody at a casino in Vegas. "I'm sorry, but it didn't work out. You took a gamble and it didn't work." Like, there is nothing else to say and I know that may sound callous but you put this above everything else and that's not the way to do it. Just like with gambling, if you put your house up as collateral, when they are taking your house, they are not going to say, "Well, uh, I'm sorry what can I do to help you keep your house." They're just going to take your house because you gambled. This industry is a big gamble and when you are rolling the dice with it that is the chance you take. That's why it can't be your plan A. You can play it smart and "figuratively" learn how to count cards and get good at it. You can learn how to hide it, and hope you get 21 before you get caught doing it. Just like gambling, if that is the poor choice of a plan that you want to go with, it's a free country. Either way it is a gamble. If you don't play it smart you could lose everything and literally have to start over, with no skills. So, I tell you the same thing that I'm assuming a bouncer will tell you, "I'm sorry, you have to go home."

### *What is your advice on finances for a child who has had a measure of success?*

Get a good business manager...it is not your thing. Get a good business manager...it is not your thing. Your job is to be the artist. I know very, very few artists who are great at maintaining all of the components of their finances and the business of managing it. It is incredibly hard to do. I am not at all saying that you can't do it. However, if you don't have someone in place to make sure commissions are paid, budgets are balanced, taxes are paid, expenses are paid, on time, while you are being the artist things can get pretty messy, very quickly. Get an accountant that is an expert in all things money because you will be dealing with too much money. So many entertainers are in trouble with the IRS either because they have the wrong people looking after their money or they are trying to address the money matter themselves.

There are some 70s stars who are still making 6 figure income because of residuals from reruns from shows that were very popular back in the day. The same way that even investment people or well known financial business people don't do their own taxes, neither should you. Learn what they are doing and why they are doing it because it is your money and you need to know what is happening with it and why. You might miss a few things that may cost you a lot more down the road. On a personal note, regarding you spending your money and how you handle it, just look at it this way. I recently spoke to an actress who typically books a pilot every year. She has one of the smartest perspectives on how she sees her money. She said that she always makes sure, whatever her yearly budget is, that she has that and another year in her account. That is smart because a working actor can be unemployed for six months to a year in this business. That is understandable because in that time you can be working on your craft, reinventing yourself or diversifying during that down time. But you only need one car, don't go crazy and get two just because you can afford it at the time. You need one place to live, don't get more.

Don't travel, wait until you have a bigger cushion, just in case your dry spell lasts longer than you expected. These are the things you see happening the moment someone gets more money than they ever made before. They buy stuff. They buy expensive stuff that they don't really need, too early in their career. As far as the traveling goes, our job will probably take us there anyway. Just wait a while and you may be able to travel and get paid doing it and get per diem while you're there, just be patient. Always make sure that you have enough money in your account to live on for at least a year and a half, at any given time.

If you have already lost all of your money because you did all of the things that you should not have done, learn from what just happened. I know that guy. I know that guy, but he is like fifteen different people. Learn from your mistakes and don't blow the next million. Don't let your ego get in the way and don't get caught up in the "Hollywood Ego-Image-fest." I know so many people who claim that they are broke but drive an Audi. Sell it. Get what you can really afford. I am not saying it like it's easy to do. It's not, especially if you are poor when you start making money. But if you have lost all of your money, and you are growing as an actor but just waiting for another job, you can eventually make the money back. During this time find out who you are. Find out what you need to work on and the areas you need to work in.

Diversify who you are supposed to be in this industry. You may not be a leading man or a leading woman. You may be a supporting actor or a character. You have to be honest with who you are and what you can/can't do. Whatever it is for you, do that well and don't focus on doing what you are not supposed to be doing. Have a real talk with your reps to find out who you really are and don't waste time going in for roles that aren't you. Most people want to be the leading man. You want to get cut up, rip your shirt off, and be that guy. But that is not who everybody is. You may have to be a character with a smaller role, and the least amount of lines, but still just as significant to the lead and the movie.

*If you were able to start your career all over again, at age four, knowing then what you know now about the industry, what would be different?*

I almost want to say that I wouldn't do anything differently but the only thing I would do differently is I would have learned lessons faster. I would have learned that very rarely do other actors get you jobs. So, I wouldn't have spent so much time hanging around other people thinking that that was going to do something. I didn't do it for very long, but I wasted time that I could have been working on my artistry. I would have started writing earlier. I would have gotten into acting class earlier. I would not have listened to people who didn't know what they were talking about and now I know who those people are.

*Do you have final advice for parents?*

Love your children. Reevaluate what that means…to love your children. Understand that by saying, "My child is going to be rich and famous," as a minor, it's like putting a loaded gun in your house. At some point your kid may stumble upon that gun and accidently kill himself. Understand that by saying, "My child is going to be rich and famous," your child, because of your actions, might grow up to be a dysfunctional human being. So love your kids enough to make that a serious consideration. You should sit down for a while and think about it. If you do ultimately say, "Yes, let's do this," love your kids, be ready to walk away, hold your kid's sanity and mental health above all else. Make them good human beings first, then good actors.

*Do you have final advice for the kids?*

It is never that big of a deal…remember that. I went to a birthday party last night of someone who I had worked with a few years ago. I was about to walk past the red carpet's press line. I looked over and saw all of these kid's faces that are all vaguely familiar from television or from being around the

Hollywood scene. They all wanted so desperately to be noticed, to be seen, to be interviewed, and to be validated. It was very sad to me that they felt worthless or less important if they didn't get their picture taken on the carpet. You are worth more than a picture. You are worth more than a red carpet interview. It is never that big of a deal…if you don't book a role, that's fine.

# Beth Bogush
*Producer/Choreographer/Master Teacher of Dance*

*What would you compare working in the Entertainment Industry to?*

I can't compare it to anything else. It's its own unique entity. It's unpredictable, often based off of popular appeal. You have to be willing to change with the industry's current trends and keep well informed and prepared to adapt to whatever job comes your way.

*What has your experience been like working with children?*

My experience working with children has been a wonderful blessing in my life. It has been full of challenges and experiences that I will forever cherish. It has afforded me the opportunity to teach and direct all types of talented young children in the entertainment business from all aspects. The reward of getting to have a hand in guiding and preparing them to achieve their desired goals is very fulfilling. Knowing you had a vital role in their success is the best feeling in the world.

*What has your experience been like interacting with the parents?*

Most parents have been a delight to work with over the years. Sometimes however it has been difficult to express to parents the truth about their children's talent. Parents often see something different in their child than the teacher, director or producer sees. We all want the best for the child and sometimes it's just not the right time for them. I feel honesty is always the best policy with children, and it's a very competitive field of business.

*What advice would you give to kids about discipline and focus?*

Be realistic about the child's ability to focus on their training and what is expected of them in the business, it's a real deal breaker in the kids business. Get as much disciplined training in whatever type of talent you are pursuing at an early age. If you are pursuing only one lane of training, stay in it, don't jump from one thing to another. If you are a triple threat, give each discipline of training a chance and get the best training.

*As a choreographer what do you feel children need most to be successful in this industry?*

Children need a good personality, the ability to listen, ability to follow directions, and to love what they are doing. Children also need to be exposed to as many teachers, information and formal training as possible. A well-rounded foundation is needed to compete in this day and age. They need to attend as many workshops and meet as many people in the industry as possible.

*What type of formal training do you feel children need in order to stand out?*

I would suggest as much private training with the right coach in the desired area they are hoping to work in can have enormous benefits. Private training with a coach is a great supplement to group classes in acting, dancing and singing.

*How can the parent and child avoid the pitfalls of the industry?*

Don't take everything everyone says for the truth. Ask many questions and stay alert to what people are expecting of you and your child. It's a business that is very competitive and fickle. Stay focused on your true talent and surround yourself with good people.

*Do you have any final words for the child?*

Have fun, stay focused and disciplined in your training and be thankful of every job you get.

*Do you have any final words to the parent?*

Be wise in the decisions you make for your child. Get your child the best education possible in all aspects of their training. Make sure you are letting the child live their dream not yours. Listen to their teachers, most times they know best. Don't be afraid of a plan B.

# Dawnn Lewis

*Actress/Grammy Award Winner/Singer/Songwriter & Producer*

***How would you describe what the culture of the entertainment industry is versus what it is not?***

I have to admit that my perspective of the entertainment industry's culture has changed over the 40+ years I've been blessed to participate in it. I started singing and dancing at the ages of four and seven and haven't stopped yet. My formative years in "the business" taught me that this is a community and culture that few "outsiders" or "normal" people understand, and we have to look out for each other. There has always been an intense sense of competition amongst the "talented tenth," but at the end of the day, we always shared information, and had a sense of responsibility one for the other. These days, it appears to truly be "every man for himself," and "How can I get my 4.5 minutes of 'fame', whether I deserve it or not, trained for it or not?" No one wants to be an "outsider" or "normal" any longer. Everyone wants "in" on the celebrity train, and they are willing to expose or embarrass themselves at any cost, masquerading that as "talent" in order to get it! During my journey, it was also mandatory to have multiple talents, i.e. sing, dance, act, compose, and play an instrument. You were also expected to have depth and variety in your performance "gig bag," i.e. comedic, dramatic, musical comedy, and physical stunts, etc. While special effects existed, the final product still relied heavily on the artists' ability to genuinely deliver.

Today's talent pool appears to be very pointed in its offerings: I'm a comedian/actor; rapper/actor; recording artist/actor; anything/reality star/

actor; film actor; TV actor; strictly comedy...you get the idea. It's hysterical to me, how EVERYONE somehow convinces him or herself that they are actors! "Culturally," instead of "us" and the "normal" people, I believe a class system amongst performers has developed. There are "A" list-bona-fide STARS, then "B" list-very-talented-not necessarily first choice celebrities, "I-Have-A-Huge-Internet-Following-So-I-Get-A-Series & Movie-Offers" celebrities; "In-My-Own-Mind-I'm-A-Star-Cause-I-Have-A-Reality-Show" personalities, and the "I-Used-To-Be-Someone" recognizable & respect-able - very talented - yet unfortunately not now employed - "real actors!" Somehow, all of the above have a legitimate claim, and are all celebrated as long as it translates into ratings and marketing dollars. We don't necessarily look out for each other but now make it a point to socialize and coexist with those we feel are closest to our "class" or "marketing bracket."

### *What are some of the great realities about this industry?*

The amazing opportunities to work side by side with some of the most talented people on the planet, world leaders, history makers & changers. It also allows you to explore the world, and cultures beyond your wildest imaginings, while highlighting realities that effect and change lives around the world. It's incredibly powerful and humbling, all at the same time. Our "privilege" to invent or re-create worlds and realities, people and events absolutely reminds you of how much there is to learn from and pour back into your life and the lives of all those who see or experience your work. On top of all that, it is possible to make more money than most people would ever responsibly spend or less money than most people would consider an option as an adult! Wow, what a rollercoaster!

### *What are some of the disappointing realities about this industry?*

It is possible to make more money than most people would ever responsibly spend or less money than most people would consider an option as an adult!

Growing up, I could be very pro-active in securing work. The individual's willingness to "hustle" and "talk your way into a room," was an admirable trait and an often-necessary tool. Then we went thru a period where you couldn't buy your way into a room without the right agent or manager submission. Now, in a lot of cases, studios and directors are actually casting based on Internet popularity, rather than genuine talent! Or, instead of being in the room to meet you, requiring you to "audition on tape."

- Choice roles for people of color, and women remain at the low end of the spectrum, but there are several directors and production companies doing what they can to make as many opportunities as they can in their projects.
- In too many cases, "new" or "young" still means "better!"
- "Age-ism" in the entertainment industry, I feel, unfortunately, mirrors our current society's mindset that our "seasoned" citizens are unfashionable or somehow inconvenient, and thus less valuable or utilized. They are often used as the "support" or "joke" for the younger performer, instead of as a lead, tapping into the wealth of knowledge and experience in them. It's refreshing to see many of our veteran performers refusing to be put out to pasture, and creating companies that produce films and television product primarily featuring them! I think it is brilliant! Right-On Sylvester Stallone, Morgan Freeman, Cate Blanchett, Bruce Willis, Bill Cosby, etc!

*How would you differentiate between "rich and famous" versus "successful and wealthy?"*

"Rich & Famous" – For whatever reason, you've gained financial abundance and popularity, either because you were in the right place at the right time, or connected to the right person(s) or project(s), not because of any particular talent or impacted skill. You're famous for being famous, and getting

"Paid" for it! Once that status changes, (and it will), you are no longer a topic of conversation.

"Successful & Wealthy" – Because of your effort, talent and/or skill, you have carved out a reputation of excellence that sustains you and those fortunate to be associated with you, in "lean times" and "times of bounty." While in this position, you often experience great financial gain, but you're also aware that you are "blessed" in other areas such as spiritual & physical health, family, security, savings and the opportunity to be your best self-walking in your purpose, and encouraging others to do the same. Your name and contribution usually live long beyond your participation.

*How can a parent keep a child safe in this industry?*

A parent needs to have a realistic understanding of what this business requires, and how it "uses" its performers, writers, producers, etc. It's hard work, for the child, and often even more so for the parent. The parent must make mature decisions for themselves, and primarily on behalf of the child. Learn the union rules for child labor; pay attention to the content of the projects you're allowing them be a part of, particularly the things they are asked to say; pay attention to who they associate with, and do all that you can to preserve their awareness that they are still "children" – not the family meal ticket, nor the shot callers. As in any environment, children need healthy examples from their parents or guardians. Don't be a jerk! Children mimic what they see. They learn to be decent human beings, by watching you be a decent human being. If you can't always be with your child, be sure you assign an adult as a guardian who takes your child's care as seriously as you do.

While they are on this amazing journey of their talents and imagination, invest equal time in their education, both academic and social. I think both are crucial to any young person making a healthy transition from child to adult performer. If you teach them to be healthy, caring, invested human beings, they are more likely to value their opportunity and talents, as well as the talents of others. Make sure they learn the business, and are aware of how to protect themselves when you're not around. Most importantly, LOVE THEM. Be sure they know, that they are loved, regardless of how many movies, TV shows, commercials, billboards, etc. they appear on!

**What does a child actor/performer need to know about the art, work and climate of this business?**

This is a JOB! Take it seriously. Study your craft, practice your craft, study some more, practice some more, and always remember there's more to learn. There are countless other talented singers, dancers, actors, etc. They are being considered just as you are. But YOU are the only YOU there is. Develop what makes you special, and embrace it. You will hear "no" more often than you will hear "yes," and that's ok. Expect it, learn from it then, move on to the next opportunity. It really must be that simple. That's often easier said than done, but nonetheless the healthiest way to maintain an "even" spiritual and emotional balance as you navigate the business. It's very subjective, so all you really can do is your best.

**Is it possible to stay sane, financially stable, emotionally grounded and relationally healthy in this business?**

If you invest in growing you and your child spiritually, emotionally, academically and socially, odds are you'll both learn what it is to be financially responsible with whatever amounts of money you're making, and be decent judges of character to cultivate healthy friendships and relational circles. Once that's done, hopefully you'll recognize the value of protecting what you've invested so much into and worked so hard to create. When times are hard, and friends seem few, chances are better that you won't consider selling your soul to create temporary or damaging "fixes."

*My final words to the child:*

I LOVE YOU! AND IF I FAIL TO MAKE IT CLEAR TO YOU THAT I LOVE YOU, PLEASE, PLEASE, PLEASE LOVE YOURSELF. BELIEVE IN YOURSELF. BE PATIENT WITH YOU, RESPECT YOURSELF! THIS BUSINESS DOESN'T DEFINE YOU . . . YOU, DEFINE YOU! SO, INVEST IN YOU. PROTECT YOU. REQUIRE OTHERS TO RESPECT YOU, AS YOU RESPECT YOURSELF. REMEMBER THAT OTHERS LOVE THEMSELVES AS WELL. SO, HONOR & RESPECT THEIR JOURNEY JUST AS YOU WANT THEM TO HONOR AND RESPECT YOURS.

*My final words to the parents:*

This is your child's journey and life. While you are the guardian and guide, do not mistake this as "your" chance to live out your fantasy, or cash in the golden ticket. This will be very demanding on you and your relationships and sense of self. Get all the help you need so that you don't lose yourself and are able to keep things in proper perspective. If you are able to do that, you and your child will be a force to reckon with, and Heaven's the limit, by the grace of God!

# Tina Pollini
*Craft Service Key*

### Why is Craft Service called Craft Service?

Craft Services is aptly named simply because we serve or support the Crafts. Throughout the years, the job description has been modified, and ask anyone from the "old days" and you will get a completely different version of what the day to day duties did or did not include compared to now. Craft Service is a Local 80 union position, and may include food service, cleaning and/or labor. Duties vary from television, film and commercial projects as well as from stages or location sets. Production Companies and Studio Lots each have regulations, budgets and systems in place that have to be followed. Most of us think of Craft Services as the food that is there for the taking, whether snacks, beverages or hot meals. We do not prepare or cook food, and we provide what we can with the budget we are given. The biggest part of our job is the stuff that is taken for granted, but is absolutely necessary for the production.

### How would you describe the Entertainment Industry?

The entertainment industry is the perfect representation of good and evil. We are drawn to it either as participants or viewers. Those of us who are lucky enough to decide which parts to benefit from will prosper. Our hard work will make it look easy, even though we know it's not.

*Is it generally a safe and healthy environment for kids?*

Yes. It is safe and healthy for everyone, especially kids.

*What are the overall eating habits of most kids in the industry?*

The Craft Service area of any show is usually enticing. The overall eating habits change with time, especially with kids. It starts with sweets, sodas and packaged snacks but after more time is spent on set, even the kids realize that healthier choices are the way to go.

*What is the highlight of your job?*

The highlight of my job…hands down – is the people. And how lucky am I to get to spend time with everyone in a kitchen!

*What has been your experience with parents on the set?*

The experiences have varied from show to show. As a parent, I understand how each parent wants everyone to know how special his or her child is. And they are! But on set, everyone is equal. Once parents know how the production works, it generally goes smoothly.

*What does a new parent/child need to know about the climate of studio sets and production locations?*

Studio and location sets are exciting no matter how many you walk onto. Most productions are run very professionally, and there are production and crewmembers paying attention to every detail. Just enjoy the whole experience and have fun!

*Do you have any advice for the young performer?*

Listen to your parent, teacher and of course the Director! <u>Craft Service</u> <u>Side Note:</u> Let Production and Craft Service know of any food allergies as soon as possible! Bon Appétit!

*Do you have any advice for the parents of the performer?*

Parents, just be the parent. Oversee behavior, manners and meals.

# Tyrel Jackson Williams
*Actor/Producer/Musician*

*Although you are 18-years-old, you have been in the industry for over 16 years. You've been on several televisions shows, done voice over work, commercials, movies, and print work. You've pretty much done all of it. What is your fondest memory to date?*

Hmm…it's difficult to pinpoint one moment that has been the best for me, but I would have to say walking onto the set of "Failure to Launch." That was one of my fondest memories. I felt like I was actually acting. I felt like I was really doing a professional thing that was going to be seen and it was a big deal for me. I was proud of my eight-year-old self that I was able to show up and do good work. I also have very fond memories of the first few episodes of "Lab Rats." It was the idea of being able to do a good job that impressed people on stage and in front of the camera. It was a big deal for me, to show people what I could do and have people like it. It was a positive exchange for me between the audience, the actor and the crew behind the camera, the directors and the writers, the grips and the DPs (directors of photography). Their reactions reassured me that I was doing something good.

*How would you describe the entertainment industry?*

The one word description I would use for it would be crazy. It is pretty much a place to have fun, pretend to be someone else, but give up your job security. There is no guarantee that you will be working consistently. Even if you get a show and things are going well, there is no guarantee that it will be consistent. You can get kicked off of the show. The show could get cancelled. It may not necessarily have any thing to do with you or how well you auditioned because you can get a job just because someone recognized your face from another job you worked on. But that could be the very reason why you don't book a job. You don't look like we want you to look. Casting may say you are too nerdy, too cool, too tall, or too short. There are exceptions to every rule, but regardless of how well you do at the audition, it's a very weird industry in that way because you don't know which way it's going to turn out.

*Is it crazy in a good or crazy in bad way?*

Neither, it's just unpredictable and unusual. Like if you were going into the fast-food industry you know that you could start off by mopping the floors, working the fryers then working your way up to manager. You know that that is something you can aspire to achieve. If you put hard work in, you will eventually get there. You know that you will have a job everyday if you don't do something to get yourself fired. With our industry you can be working on yourself and be totally amazing and still not get a job because you can't get an audition.

*Do you sometimes wish you had a normal life where you would go to a normal school, have the regular school experience, and have normal extra curricular activities?*

I think about it sometimes but I don't wish my life were normal. I don't wish my life was any different than it is because I am doing what I would want to do if I had a normal life.

*About two years ago you discovered that you are a pretty impressive music producer. How did what you were already doing in the industry help you to diversify? What happened?*

I don't believe that it came from a place of wanting to diversify but from a place of wanting to know how the production aspect of music worked. I've always had a love and a knack for it ever since I was really young. Whether it was from playing piano or playing guitar or singing. I always had this kind of natural link to music. So one day I started creating it. When I got my first Mac computer I was super excited because I would finally be able to use a particular music program. Once I started using it, I was on the program all the time. I didn't tell anyone about it because I wanted to get good at it first.

*I'm sure a lot of your musical influences came while you were singing so many genres of music on the "Backyardigans." How can a parent help a child find that space to be creative or the place where the child can express him/herself by doing something they enjoy?*

The one thing that you did that I think helped me out a lot was, whatever I had an interest in, at that time, you helped me pursue it. I remember when I went through my "skating" phase. I was like, "Mom I want to skate! This is my life. I want to skate for the rest of my life." You were like, "Are you sure?" I was like, "Yes. I am completely and totally sure that I want a skateboard. This is going to be my secondary career." You took me out and got me a skateboard and you let me go out in the street with my friends at the time and just skate all day, for an entire summer. After a while, I realized that I was not going to be a hybrid of Will Smith and Tony Hawk so I kinda gave that up slowly. But you let me get into it at that time, and I feel like, at that time, I needed to try and be that skater guy. You got me into Taekwondo when I said that I wanted to do it and you got me into Parkour when I found the studio I wanted to train in. You or dad would drive me out there to learn how to do Parkour, get flexible, do splits and stuff then drive all the way back home even though the ride was crazy far away. You guys did it.

You guys invested a lot of time and money into my interests and you gave me time and space to work on it myself. You were not micro-managing everything that I was interested in. When it came to music you got me started playing the piano and I hated it. I hated it but I had to keep playing until I told you I hated it. So you stopped me from playing the piano. Then later on you got me a ukulele and I got good at playing it. I was a naturally fast learner so you got me a guitar. I fell in love with the guitar, then, I got good at it but then started feeling not so great about it because I wasn't feeling fulfilled anymore. I still play guitar because I love it, but I now feel more fulfilled when I'm producing. So all of those musical steps got me to what I am really interested in and feel fulfilled doing.

*Wow, I never realized that you remembered all of that and connected all of those musical things together until this moment. I talk about your piano experience in this book to help parents better commit to supporting their child but listen to them without putting unnecessary pressure on them.*

Yes, if your child is not passionate about something they will find any and everyway to not do it. That is just what we do. When I was playing piano, and I hated it, I tried to find any and every way to avoid doing it. It became very regimented, very routine, tedious, and boring, serious and painful. I started to feel that way about guitar too. If it got too serious and felt more like I had to do it, I lost the love for it. It started getting super serious and I didn't like that. I was like, if it's gonna get super serious it has to be something I feel fulfilled doing like acting. Acting got super serious when I was much younger because it's a business but I loved it so much. I enjoyed the seriousness of it. That's how I feel about producing now. Things are getting serious but if you love the art side of anything that you do you won't get scared away or bored by the business side of it.

## *What advice would you give to a parent who has an 18 month old, naturally gifted child?*

Allow them to express themselves and show interest in things. When I say express themselves I don't mean sit them in front of a sheet of paper and some paint and tell them to make a masterpiece so that they can become the next Picasso. I mean, let them find things that they like to do and if it is something that they really enjoy, point them in that direction. But if they stop showing interest in it don't force them into the mold. With us we showed signs of being good in academics, acting, and music at an early age. And you got us into all three of those things. So you got us into acting, music and a good school. And you let us do all three of those things. Even when we let something go, we did it long enough that it still became a part of us.

I know a few talented actors who were working often but when the business started to get too serious, they didn't want to do it any more. They had people pushing them so hard to continue and trying to get them to do things that they really didn't want to do. I've seen parents do that. Their kids were not into it, some kids were not good at it, and the parents would say things like, "My kids are amazing, "He's going to be a star!" or something like that. They eventually just stop acting completely. Some of them are still talented. They just realized that after a certain point it wasn't about them anymore. When you are doing anything relating to the arts and it stops being about you, this may sound a bit selfish but it becomes a problem. When you are doing something that has to do with art, it is about you the artist. You have to be able to express yourself in a healthy and natural way. When it is no longer about you, and its about the people around you getting what they need from you, that is not healthy, it's not good. With us, it's always been about us when it comes to our stuff and our art. There are others around us with opinions that would help us, but in the end, it is all about us. We have to be good about our jobs. The people around us didn't have to be good at our jobs. We had to be good at our jobs, because they were our jobs.

*You booked your first feature film and your first television show at eight years old. Did you ever feel pressure from production, the directors, or musicians to deliver or perform?*

No, surprisingly. I think the lack of pressure came from you being so chill about our lives, us being good at what we were doing and you not trying to force us into being good at acting. And also, it didn't really feel like a job. I was really having fun. It felt like a version of school, to be honest. Like you have to be good in school at eight years old, but it's not like you are gonna get a bad grade if you are really focused and interested in what you are doing. I was focused, engaged and paying attention to what I was doing, so I was happy with my life. Whenever I got notes from directors, I just felt like, "Oh I need to do that this way," not, "I need to be better or bigger" or "Oh, here is something I need to do differently."

*How did you feel about working and having to get schoolwork done at the same time? Did you feel pressure or overwhelmed?*

At certain points it was overwhelming just because, I felt like, at certain times, school was getting in the way. Like, I knew that I wanted to act but I needed to do school but I felt like I could be devoting so much more time to this acting thing that I love if I just kinda stopped doing school. I knew I could not do that. I mean there are ways in this industry to get around it, especially in California, where you can take the CHSPE (an early exit exam for high school students) and test out. That test pretty much says that you are a legal adult and you don't need to do school. It's pretty much a GED. But even if I was allowed to, I could not legally do that at eight years old.

*Did you ever wish that I was one of those parents that we have seen in the industry and let you get away with not doing school, did your homework for you, lied about your grades, or turned in a fake report card?*

No. I feel like that is an easy way out. Taking the easy way out is never a good thing to do. It's like cheating yourself out of something better. So taking the easy way out teaches people, and parents teach their children that it is ok to cheat. I learned from everything you did, to be ethical in everything you do. And I learned that you couldn't cheat or skimp on anything. And that's helping me now as an adult actor where I am feeling tempted to cheat or not work or improve on myself and be better at my job. But I have to remember, that if you want to be good at something you can't cheat on anything.

*What advice would you give to eight-year-old kids?*

No matter what you do, do your best, and be happy with the fact that you did your best. Don't worry about whether or not you could have done something better. Just do your best, all the time, and don't worry about it after that. After eight years old, that really affected me. I was growing up and just like anybody else would, just like any eight year old on a softball team, you are growing up and you see these other people who are really good at softball too. You start getting self-conscious because you don't know if you are that good. It's ok, just do your best and know that you could not have done it any better than your best.

*What advice would you give an 18 year old?*

Try your hardest not to stress about life. Work on yourself all the time. Try not to cheat on yourself, because that's…that's the trap. While working on myself, going to acting classes and just getting better generally I really want to cheat. Sometimes, I just want to say, "Forget this, I'll be fine. I can just not feel things when I act. What's the big deal?" But deep down I know that's not true. Over time I will become a bad actor and that's something you can't do if you want to have an "acting career." That's just like saying, "That's all right if I'm bad at building tables," when you're a carpenter. You can't do that! Just do your best and trust the fact that you are in process. I know it's hard because I'm doing it too, but it's ok.

***What advice would you give a parent who is struggling to let her 17-year-old son or daughter go after they have been legally in charge of their contracts, money and personal lives?***

I guess the advice I would give them is stop pushing them and being as active with them on set and start supporting from a distance like you would if they were going off to college.

***What are your thoughts on college knowing that you are still working on a show?***

Well, the situation I'm in is a very complex and unusual one. Growing up, college was always one of those things that was just going to happen. You graduate high school and then you go to college. That was my seven-year-old mind, rationalizing what I needed to do for the rest of my life. Now at 18, life looks different because in the industry that I work in, going to college does not guarantee you a job. Going to high school doesn't guarantee you a job. Some people drop out of high school, test out and work for the rest of their lives. Some people go to high school, then college and never work again. It is very turbulent in the business that I work in and going to college is as dangerous as not going to college.

*It's a tricky situation for you because most people go to college to expand their knowledge, explore new ideas, find avenues of intellectual and creative expression and at the end develop enough knowledge in one area that will allow them to create a professional career. None of us realized it at the time but you started doing that as a toddler and have already invested 16 years in your career. Where do you place that?*

Um…I'm trying to take it one day at a time and not worry too much about the future. This would be a very scary time in my life right now, not only because I am finishing high school but also because my television show is about to run its course and I don't currently have another job to replace the one that I currently have. So, I am going to be just stuck out in the middle of the sea. Meaning, as of the day the show goes down, I will be unemployed. To most people that would be horrifying. So do I go to college because I am unemployed? If I do, what if I get another job while I'm in school? Do I drop out of college or defer so I can work on that job? If I wait too long without going to college and nothing work related comes my way, I may have to dip into my savings and eventually not have enough money to go to college and work on myself. So, there are some very big adult decisions that are waiting for me in my 18th year.

*We've talked about this often and you know the pros and cons of it all. The good thing for you is that you have an emotional support system and all of these years you didn't have to financially support your family. So whatever you decide, you will be ok. You have options and you have some time to breathe and stand back for a minute and weigh those options. What is your resolve?*

Right now? In this moment, my resolve is two-fold. The first part is, to relax and realize that God's got it, just sit back and put all of that in His hands and continue living and keep moving forward. The second part is, whether or not you get work…work. Work on something. Always be working on something. I hate being idle. I hate being still. Which is something that is very apparent even in my physicality. Even when I am sitting in one spot my hands are moving or my feet are bouncing. I have already set up in my mind, whether I work or not I will be working professionally on something, be it a movie, television show, writing, producing and such. I will be doing something that is beneficial for me and that has helped me since my junior year of high school. It was around that time when I started to worry. Like if summer would come around and I didn't hop from one project to another when my show was on hiatus. I began to internalize the situation and question what could have created the disconnect that could be preventing me from booking one job after another. But that's part of the actor's syndrome. The actor's syndrome says, "I'm not acting, I should be acting, why am I not acting?" But when you're working it says, "This is great, I'm working. But I'm working all the time, I'm tired, I need a break." It's funny but for a lot of actors this is true. That's why actors are seen as super whiny, never fulfilled or happy. It's because actors are constantly stressed. It's, uh, its like when we are happy it's like there is always this thing hovering over us like, "Yeah, your happy *right now*...but you wait 15 minutes and you could be depressed." And therein lies a conflict.

By the way, parents, never ask your kid why they didn't book a job, because your child is growing up and developing. They are trying to rationalize what is going on around them anyway. If you put pressure on them for not being perfect at doing something they enjoy, that could break them. I'm so glad you never did that because if you would have come in my room one day and said something like, "TJ clean your room, TJ make sure you get your chores done," and then thrown in, "Also, why didn't you book that job you went up for? You prepared for it all week long. What's your problem?" I would have probably had a breakdown. Because I know that I worked my behind off on that script and the audition. The fact that I didn't book the job is being lumped in with all of the other things I'm supposed to be doing every day. This is not good because booking jobs at that point becomes another one of my daily chores, and a chore that I am not doing well. When parents do that they are putting pressure on a child for something they have no control over. The child has no idea why they didn't book a role and when you are 12-years-old you're not going to realize or understand that the director wasn't really jiving with the choices you made during your audition. The child is either going to rationalize it by saying either I am bad at this or I wasn't good enough. So the way a parent reacts to that can either help or hurt the situation.

It's like that day when Tylen or I fell off of the bed that afternoon when we were babies. We were all laughing and having a good time, then one of us fell off of the bed. If you would have run over to us and panicked like, "O my gosh! What happened, are you ok? Oh I'm so sorry, let me see!" we would have cried. But the fact that you walked over to us and just said, "Did you fall off of the bed? You fell off of the bed, huh?" we laughed about it. Because we weren't really hurt, we had just fallen off of the bed. And your reaction taught us how to react to things like that. Because you built us in that way, it really helps us as people and it gave us a thicker skin. So like if someone makes fun of me I'm not going to cry about it and say, "Oh what is wrong?" Most likely, I will laugh right along with them. Because if I did something stupid there is nothing I can do about that. Responding that way to situations has really helped me as I am developing. The lesson here is, everything isn't that serious. So even with your job everything isn't really that serious. I have been re-realizing that lately and it's been helping me a lot.

*That reminds me of social media and how certain people are treated. What are your thoughts on that?*

Ok...social media and the Internet are great, fun and amazing. At the same time, social media and the Internet are horrible, scary and disgusting. There is no way to get away from either part of that if you are going to go on the Internet. You will see really amazing, cool and perverted things. Social media is a hyper focused version of what the world is right now. You will find people who just love you for no reason even if you're not doing anything. They are going to follow you, be devoted and say nice things about you. Then you will get that one creepy guy, who follows you for the sole purpose of trying to get you to kill yourself. That sounds super harsh and overly dramatic but no, there are people who are on the Internet who actually want you to kill yourself. They want to see it. Why? Because you are there, you are alive. The best way to deal with it is to enjoy yourself on social media, have fun, but try not to take anything seriously. It's going to be hard because so many people are dead serious on the Internet and it is so easy to make fun of someone and degrade them. It is also so easy to be made fun of and be degraded. So it takes a lot of internal strength and discipline to post something and not care about what anyone else says. It's like walking into a room, saying something and sitting down on a stage and letting people yell stuff at you. That's what social media is. It's like walking out on stage, to a packed house in Madison Square Garden, speaking your mind then taking a seat on stage allowing everyone to take their turn and say whatever they want to you.

***How do you keep a balanced social media life and stay integral in the social media world?***

What I try to do is be myself all the time, whether I'm on social media or in person. I am not on social media a lot but when I am I try to be authentically myself at all times. That's helped me because I am just naturally a safe and unproblematic person. But if you are not that type of person you can use something else I try to stay mindful of. Which is, before you post or say something, take a second to think about something you really want the most. Something you are willing to strive and work for, something that you need and ask, "Is this post/comment going to keep me from getting that? Is what I'm about to say or do going to keep me from getting there?" If there is a possibility that it's gonna keep you from getting there, either revise it or just don't post it. If it's going to keep you from fulfilling your dreams, don't do it because it can come back to haunt you. Also, try not to lie on social media because you will get caught in a lie. So find out who you want to be, hopefully its your authentic self, and show those different facets of yourself on some of the different outlets. On one I just post pictures and show my artsy side, on the other I am just weird and funny. You should also have a strategy when using social media because it's your life that you are giving to other people for free. I am also mindful not to say things that may paint my friends in a bad light too. I try to be responsible. Keep a low profile and don't try to be big and brash either because people will want to be combative. If they do it, it's best to just ignore them even though you want to respond sometimes. Oh yeah, can I say something to parents about social media?

*Yes.*

Parents...I know you want to help...and I know you want to be a part... but there are some things that many of you may not ever understand about social media. Because the way technology is moving right now it's moving so much faster than it was when you were growing up. It is advancing faster than ever before and every year it seems to get even faster. If you are not already up on it, please don't act like you are. It's very...ooh...please don't. When it comes to social media, kids pretty much have a strategy. When parents get involved with it to be cool, we tend to gravitate to something else.

*So do some of you think that once parents sign on to certain outlets, you guys leave?*

Yes, they get involved and chime into the conversation on social media. Please don't try to be young on social media. Please be yourself. But if there is a negative issue please deal with the issues off of social media. Don't address or discipline your kids on social media. Please talk about it in person. It's like when you were kids, your parents told you to go outside to play. Imagine when you went outside to play with your friends your parents came outside to play with you and your friends. I know some parents have many different ideas and issues regarding social media. But if you raise your kids correctly *away* from social media hopefully they will act right *on* social media. Talk to your children about how you feel and allow them to talk to you about how they feel. Talk. A lot. Because when it comes right down to it, everybody just wants to be heard.

# Paul Smith
*Celebrity Photographer*

### What advice would you give parents when looking for a photographer?

The biggest piece of advice to give parents is to always do your research. Find a photographer that fits best with your child. Look at the work and the types they shoot and make sure they are reputable.

### What advice would you give parents when prepping the child for their photo shoots?

When people book in with me, I give them a very thorough prep email to help them with that. The main thing is of course, get plenty of rest the night before, drink plenty of fluids, and stay away from sugar drinks and snacks. Most importantly, have fun! It's not about "posing" - it's about moments.

### What advice would you give the child for the day of the photo shoot?

Just be prepared like you are coming to the set. Have your wardrobe ready, your homework (internal) ready, and leave any drama at the door.

### Do you have any more advice for the parent/child?

I believe an acting career for a child can be a great thing as long as it is surrounded by all of the right intentions. The parent has to set boundaries, just like with anything else. You have to know what is most important (family, education, etc.). Just like in academics or sports, parent's involvement and support is crucial. Parents don't let the industry just take your child and trust that they know what is going on. Be there on set and at auditions, always making big decisions in your child's BEST interest. Educate yourself when it comes to the industry, and don't just follow the herd. Most importantly, follow your gut. Children, have fun and do this because you love it!

# Vickie Thomas
*Casting Director*

### What is a casting director?

A casting director auditions, selects and suggests actors to help directors, producers and studios make the best choices for acting roles in a screenplay, movie, television show, commercial, etc. Our job is to bring the best people we can to a project and to use our skills, experience and taste to help a director make the right choices.

### How long have you been a casting director and do you still love your job?

I have been a casting director since 1983. I love some things about it more than others. Some things are more exciting than others, and some things about casting I relate to more than others. Likewise, some projects move me more than others. But I love it and feel fortunate to have the job that I have.

### When I explain what a casting director is I usually say, "First the casting director has a conversation with the director, producer, or studio to see what the casting vision for the project is. Then s/he reaches out to the agents and managers to make appointments for their clients who best fit the description of the character breakdown of what the director, producer and studio hopes to find for a particular role." Is that pretty much it in a nutshell?

Yes. We use our judgment to say, "This or that person should come in," or "Let's take a chance on this person," or "I haven't seen this person in a while" or "What if the character were this as opposed to what we initially thought?" Agents submit actors based on the conversations we have with producers and directors about what we are looking for, so between all of us, we supply choices and options for a project. In terms of what we do on a daily basis, we audition a number of actors in order to narrow them down to the best actors for the director to choose from. We may see a ton of people for one role or sometimes we know exactly whom we might want to offer a role to.

*Have you ever chosen an actor for a role and afterwards questioned your choice?*

Well, I'm a perfectionist, so there have been times when I felt like, "Oh, maybe I could have done better." But there are all kinds of reasons that go into making a decision on a certain actor for a role. My taste may not be the taste of those making the final decision or I might have gone a different way, but I have to let it go because in the end it is the decision of the director or studio. If I can state my case when there is a difference of opinion and they listen but decide to go a different way, I have to be okay with it. At least you were heard. And their concerns may outweigh my concerns. They may be right and I may be wrong.

*Do you realize that casting directors are intimidating to many parents and kids?*

Yes, I think we are intimidating to actors in general. With kids maybe even more so because they haven't had much experience in the world, let alone in a casting office with strangers. But I tell actors all the time, "Listen, when you go into the room, do the best you can." Then leave the room and try to forget it. Go to the next audition, go home or go to lunch or something. I know that it is hard to do because there is constant second-guessing, but they should try their best so they don't drive themselves crazy. I also tell them that casting directors want actors to be good. We're hoping you're the one who will nail this role when you come into the room. It's exciting when you find the right person for the part.

***What should parents know before taking their kids to their first audition or into his/her first casting room?***

Make sure your child is prepared and knows the material. It can be a quick experience but that doesn't mean it was a bad experience. We try to see a lot of kids for roles so don't be put off by the number of kids in the room or the amount of time your child spent in an audition. It's a good thing for your child to get into a room and read with a casting director so they can have the experience of auditioning in front of someone who isn't their mother or father and who may not necessarily be the best coach for their child. I think the more they audition, the more comfortable they will be in that situation in the future.

I see a lot of parents bringing in kids who don't have a clue how to act or be in an audition. They're distracted, they don't focus, they are just looking around the room and this opportunity becomes a waste. I just hope that parents will seek out some kind of basics about acting and auditioning and not just throw their children into the deep end of the pool because they're cute. If auditioning or pursuing acting doesn't seem to be working out, it doesn't mean that there is something wrong with your child. They may or may not be that interested in acting. If they are, try to get honest feedback from the casting director and agents to see what can be improved.

***What advice do you have for a "nervous" child when s/he walks into your casting room?***

"Take a deep breath. Let's talk for a minute. How was school today?" Something to make them a little more relaxed. I might ask them, "Do you want to go back out and look over your lines for a minute? If I have the time, I will ask, "Do you want to read it through once?" If I feel the child has potential and they are just not ready, I will usually tell them, "Come back another day but make sure you know the material." It's all about the child doing the best job that s/he can.

*What advice would you give to a parent whose child is as talented as they think but you can tell that the parent is going to be a future nightmare?*

I don't know if you can do anything about that. I guess I would say don't live your life through your child. There is a life beyond acting and show business. You need to prepare your kid for a real life as much as you prepare them to be an actor.

*What do you do with a child who is not interested in the business but the parent is?*

When I see that, I don't push them. I would make a decision probably not to bring them in again. If I were asked I would probably say to the parent something like, "I don't think your child is that enthusiastic about acting."

*Can a child star survive the pitfalls of this industry?*

Yes, I think it's possible, if the parents are solid and have strong family values. If the parents are able to separate real life from this industry, it can be done.

*Do you have any final comments for parents?*

Parents, make sure your kid enjoys acting and wants to do this. Make sure you are not pushing them into something that you want but they don't want. Know that there is life on a set and there is life off of a set -- and you have to be able to navigate both. Make sure that they are growing in other areas as well. The parents are going to have to be the ones who guide that child. That child has to be able to go home and play with the kids down the street as much as they need to know how to come on a set and do the work that they need to do there.

# Nancy Flint
*Studio Teacher/Welfare Worker*

### What is a Studio Teacher/Welfare Worker?

Studio Teacher/Welfare Worker is a classification established in the California Child Labor Law for the education, supervision, and protection of minors working in all aspects of the entertainment industry in California or on projects in which a California resident minor travels out of the state or country to work in the entertainment industry. Studio Teachers are certificated teachers holding Elementary and Secondary credentials and are hired by production companies to (1) provide 3 hours of educational instruction within the hours allowed on set for the varied age groups (6 years of age to 18) and (2) to provide health and safety supervision and enforcement of the California Labor Laws for 15 day old babies through 16 year olds. They are required to be on site of all entertainment productions, which include minors even when school is not in session.

### What is the best thing about teaching children while on commercial, television and movie sets?

What I like best about Studio Teaching is challenge and variety: the challenge of creating a learning environment within whatever physical location is presented, the challenge of meeting the needs of potentially 10 different grade levels at the same time, and the variety of locations, venues, and personalities I encounter.

I love the opportunity to help provide those "light bulb" or "ah-ha" moments when a child is struggling with a concept or task no matter the age or topic. You get to see and feel the frustration ease and the confidence grow.

*What is the most frustrating thing about it?*

I am most frustrated by time, space, appropriate assignments and resistant individuals: *Time* because we must provide 3 hours of instruction sometimes in small increments of 20 minutes. *Space* because we are often provided inadequate "classroom facilities" such as tents or crowded rooms that are not conducive to the students access to teacher attention or their ability to concentrate. *Appropriate assignments* because students often bring busy work or nothing at all which requires us to create curriculum for a wide range of needs and ages. On long-term jobs, the frustration that the teacher, student, and parent struggle with is that there will be homework. *Resistant individuals*, be they production, parent, or student, who neither acknowledge the importance of the educational aspect of our job nor the significance of the welfare aspect.

*What is the greatest educational need for child actors?*

The child actor and his/her parents need to recognize that their education should be a top priority. Be they home schooled or enrolled in a brick and mortar school, their time spent on their education should be paramount and protected. Many times I find that the desire to meet the needs of a production for wardrobe, auditions, meetings, etc. are "scheduled" during the time that the student should be attending to his/her education. Parents can help prevent this by asking that these things be scheduled after school hours. California Child Labor laws stipulate this.

*What concerns you most about children working in the entertainment Industry?"*

I am most likely concerned with the fact that this is really an adult industry and that minors are often placed in surroundings that are not meant for their age group. This calls upon the parent to help make appropriate choices for their child and to be there and aware at all times.

*What are your definitions of a "good" stage parent and a "bad" stage parent?*

"Stage parents" often get a bad rap and it may be dependent upon which you are speaking about. Is it a matter of style, a need for attention, or who wants something done their way? Good parenting is not unique to "the stage." A good parent is aware of their child's goals and sensitivities. A good parent supports their child's goals and interests without neglecting their child's need for an identity based on who they are as an individual person, a student, and a member of a family. I have been blessed to work with young actors most of whom have had parents that *were present* in their support of their child as a child actor and as a maturing young adult. This presence was most often demonstrated by their attention to what was best for their child with a demeanor of calm strength. This calmness and strength not only protected their child, but also served as a model for their child's personal sense of self. A "bad" stage parent would be one whose style and motivations may have been more about themselves and their goals and needs and not those of their child.

*What does a new parent/child need to know before pursuing a career in entertainment?*

A parent/child needs to know that this industry is based on competition, but is not a team sport. In team sports there are usually definable skills that will make you a successful player. In this industry decisions are more often based on undefined criteria. Your child will be invited to "try out for the team" without knowing what the industry is looking for. Disappointments are to be expected. The parent needs to know how to support their child in a way that treats each experience as an opportunity to learn. If the child loves what he/she is doing or wants to do it, support that love of acting through all avenues available without setting goals only tied to fame or fortune. Support them through the disappointments and provide other outlets that will balance their lives as actors and future adults.

### What should parents know about the demands of the industry?

The entertainment industry is a business and as a business it is most interested in their needs: their schedule, their budget, your performance in their project, and your punctuality and focus on it.

### What are the benefits for a child who is able to balance school and work in this business?

The benefits for a child who is able to balance school and work are most notably the skills that they will carry with them into adulthood. If you are successful in this environment, you will be able to transfer these skills into whatever profession you pursue.

### How challenging is it for a child to balance school and work in this industry?

It can be very difficult for a child to balance school and work especially since they happen in the same physical location. Most parents and students don't realize that 3 hours is not always enough time to complete the work that they would have encountered had they attended a full 5 to 6 hour day at their school plus homework. These students have two jobs: their school and their part in the production of whatever aspect of the industry they have chosen. Their frustration and stress increases with each grade level and must be acknowledged by all those involved: their school, the student, and the parent and, of course the studio teacher.

### *Is it possible for a child performer to survive this industry without having a tragic story to tell?*

Of course it is possible to avoid tragic outcomes; however that depends on the individual. The few individuals that I have known who made bad choices were not people who would have avoided those choices had they not been in the industry. The industry does/did not make them do what they did. They chose their own path. The caution I would note is that, again, this is an adult industry and not all of the adults who will surround your child have their best interests in mind. Strong parenting including presence and awareness will help just as it would have had the child not ventured into the entertainment industry.

### *Do you have any final words to the child?*

The skills that you bring to and will develop in your experiences in the industry will affect you beyond your imagination. Use every opportunity to learn and grow from these experiences while realizing that there are no guarantees of a life-long career in the business. The skills that you gain from these experiences will shape you in a variety of ways and will affect how you grow and mature in the future.

If you love acting, singing, dancing and creative activities and want to pursue a career in the entertainment industry, I wish you well. Be prepared to work hard at whatever aspect of this industry holds your interest. Don't forget that once you get a job, you will actually have two jobs: the part you will play and your most important role as a student. Don't set aside your education and other interests. You will grow as an individual and future adult by being smart in all aspects of your life.

***Do you have any final words to the parent?***

I applaud your support of your child's interests. Be conscious of the time involved, the emotional ups and downs, and the stress that this will have on your child as well as you. Be there with support and comfort, as well as high expectations for his/her growth through the experience and his/her continued attention to their formal education. Being present in all aspects of this endeavor will make the difference.

I am most appreciative of the parents that bring their personal and family values to this experience. This will be an important aspect of your child's development as a student, a performer, and a developing adult. Realize that the demands on you, the parent, will be great. Your time will no longer be yours to schedule. This can be an all-consuming endeavor and will impact your whole family.

## *Life Skills*

While the entertainment industry is usually viewed with an emphasis on the performing arts, there is perhaps no other time or situation that will offer your child the opportunity to observe and participate with so many members of this creative industry. Be sure to encourage your child to recognize the myriad of skilled people and potential career choices that offer opportunities to be creative as a part of this creative industry. Lawyers, accountants, production staff, wardrobe, props, camera, greens men, set designers, painters, writers, publicity...all of the departments that work together to make the magic happen. You may be surprised by what potential career opportunities might interest your child. I wish you well.

# Victor Gonzalez
*Director for Disney & Nickelodeon Television*

**What is the most fulfilling thing about directing kids?**

The most fulfilling part of directing kids is that they are, for the most part, unspoiled by the business. They really don't have any preconceived notions about our process, therefore they aren't jaded or cynical and don't have the large egos that adult actors can have. Kids are also fearless. They will try things as actors without giving it a second thought. For me as a director, this is invaluable because the "kid shows" are usually big in scale and require a certain amount of letting go as an actor. They might have to be covered with goo in a scene, or hit in the face with a pie or any number of other things that adults might have a problem with. Children tend to just go with it and usually end up enjoying themselves in the process.

**What is the most challenging thing about directing kids?**

The most challenging thing about working with children is their short attention span. Kids shows have elements that adult shows do not. They usually have stunts, special effects, and visual effects, which take time and patience and require kids to be extra-focused. This can be exhausting for them and sometimes they lose their focus. I, as the director, must always remember that while most kids are in regular schools, playing in playgrounds, and doing regular things, young actors must be on a soundstage most of the day with cameras and lights in their faces. So the challenge for me is to be patient with them and keep a balance between allowing them to have fun and getting the job done.

*What do you think the key is to keeping a child grounded, sane, and normal in this business?*

Without a doubt, parents are the most important factor in keeping their kids grounded, sane, and humble in an industry that is known for the opposite. In show business, when an actor attains some level of success, they enter the world of "YES." They will be given things, allowed to do things, and told that they are great or special in order to keep them happy and working. I think we all know examples of kids who have gotten into trouble because they fell into this trap and thought they were better than most and above the law. The key to keeping them grounded is to make them understand that they are no more special or important than anyone else. The parents must shoulder this responsibility, for the most part.

*What does a new parent/child need to know about the climate of studio sets and production locations?*

Be professional at all times. This doesn't mean that young actors can't have fun on a set but remember that, in this business, time is money. Also, it's a very specialized freelance business where everyone you work with is probably at the top of their game and has built a reputation by being great at what they do and professional at all times. Be just as or more professional than they are and you will be rewarded with great work, which only makes you and the production better.

*Do you have any advice for the child performer?*

The best advice I can give a young actor is to not believe the hype and remain humble. You are just one piece of the puzzle that is a TV show or film. Don't believe that you are more important than anyone else. Be grateful always and don't take anything or anyone for granted. After all, we are all very lucky to be in such a creative and personally fulfilling industry!

*Do you have any advice for the parent of the performer?*

Parents can make or break a child's career. The best advice I can give a parent is to be a parent. Let agents, managers, lawyers, producers, etc., do what they do. Parents just need to love, guide, nurture and set boundaries for their kids. Young actors can face immense pressures. Parents can alleviate these pressures by making them feel like any other kid.

# Octavius (Ted) Reid III
*Sports & Entertainment Director/Wealth Advisor*

### What is a Financial/Wealth Advisor?

A financial advisor is a very broad term, but generally speaking, it is a person whose job is to help you plan out your financial future. They should help you financially map out your short, medium and long-term goals. A financial advisor helps you plan to pay for your kids to go to college; to buy the dream home you always wanted and worked hard for; and helps you plan to retire comfortably. All of these are long-term goals, but our goal is to point you in the right direction with the proper financial instruments. A good financial advisor should also be asking and listening to you about your comfort level of risk because with any investment there is a tradeoff between risk and reward. Once a person understands what their comfort level is, we then aim to achieve the most effective way to maximize the level of reward.

### How does a person/institution qualify to become a financial advisor?

Anybody can pretty much throw out a shingle and say that they are a financial advisor. A financial advisor can be anyone from an insurance agent, to someone that can only solicit mutual funds, to a full service financial advisor who can show you many more types of financial assets. The first thing you want to look for is what type of license does that person hold? Can they only offer you insurance products? Are they series 6 licensed? This means that they have the capability of offering mutual funds. Or are they series 7 licensed? This means that they have a general securities license. They can offer stocks, bonds, mutual funds, and other types of investment vehicles. If a person is looking for a financial advisor, he or she would typically want to look for someone who at least has a series 7 license. There is also a registered investment advisory representative, which holds a series 66 or a series 65. Passing exams for these licenses will allow someone to offer the services of money managers, on a fee basis.

**How can a person choose which licensed advisor to go with?**

When looking for financial advisors, the first and professional way is to log onto a major resource website at www.FINRA.org where you can go on and put in the name of any financial advisor. The Financial Industry Regulatory Authority (FINRA) regulates both the firms and professionals selling securities in the United States.* It will tell you what firm they work for, every firm that they've ever worked for throughout their career, if there have ever been any complaints, and what the end results were. Needless to say, anybody who's been in the business for a long time can have a complaint or two, but if you start to see a pattern, there might be an issue there. So, don't just trust a referral, do your own homework.

The second and practical way is to determine what you are looking for. Some advisors focus on one area while another may have more options. I liken it to a person who walks into a place preparing to buy a balanced meal to cook for dinner. Let's say the store only sells oranges, but then the person walks into a supermarket. Which one would you prefer to shop at?

**The supermarket.**

Exactly. So when you go with someone who has a series 7 there is a lot more that they can typically offer you.

*Would it be better for a parent who was intimidated by the whole idea to start with the oranges?*

No. In my opinion, it would be better to start where you had more options. But, again, it's all determined by what the person is looking for.

*So as I'm listening to you, I am thinking about the medical field, particularly general practitioners. Is it safe to say that many financial advisors are general financial practitioners?*

Yes.

*What field of entertainment do your clients come from?*

They come from music, television, film, football, baseball, basketball, track and field, fashion and broadcasting. They could be artists, athletes, lawyers, business managers, producers, writers, and even some of the institutions that back these industries.

*How would you describe the entertainment industry?*

Wow, this is an interesting question. The entertainment industry is really an industry that drives the economy. It drives fashion. It drives what we talk about around the water cooler; it creates what we listen to in our cars or what we listen to when we're working out or what we do to relax. Much of what we do is run by the entertainment industry. When I look at the amount of revenue that comes into cities from the entertainment industry, it is amazing.

But most people only see the sausage; they don't see how it gets made. They don't see all of the rough patches that you go through to get to a certain place or what you have to do to become an entertainer or become an artist. They just hear the song that comes out, or watch the television show.

They also don't realize how short an entertainer's career tends to be in this business. That's where the financial advisor steps in. For many of the people, especially on the talent side, they are going to make a lot of money, for a very, very short period of time. Then they are going to live off of that same money for a very long period of time. So, they can't afford to take the risk that the average person, or working class person, will be able to take. They are not going to have to get a cost of living adjustment every year for the next 40 years. So we have to treat their investments much differently. It's really more about preserving the capital that they already have as opposed to going out and taking risks to get these high growth investments.

Let's say that a child gets a show at 12 years old. The show stays on the air for five years, which typically equates to 100 episodes and takes the show into syndication. The show is off the air when he or she is 17 years old. If he or she doesn't get another show, he or she has made the bulk of the money at 17 years old. The residual checks usually aren't enough. The money that is made in that short period of time has to last for the rest of his or her life. What are you going to do when you are 30? That is the message that I try to emphasize to parents. Athletes are the ones we hear about most often, but it is happening everywhere in entertainment too. The average NFL player's career span is 3.2 years.** The average NBA player's career is 4.8 years.** So when a player comes in at 19-years-old, he could be retired by the time he is 25 years old. There are many guys who go way past that but there are many who don't. One of the problems I find is that many actors and artists make financial decisions based on emotion, or trusting that someone is a good person or they are going to look out for them - as opposed to checking people out. Many times they hear about this "great" idea that is going to make a lot of money over a short period of time. You should be focusing on preserving capital. Yes you want to get some growth out of it, but there is no reason to take excessive risks.

Unfortunately, many of the risks are not investment related. In my experience with athletes and entertainers, the first thing many of them want to do is spend money, and because of that, the money quickly vanishes. It typically starts with wanting to buy an expensive car and house. So they purchase a $100k car, they purchase a huge house that they don't need. Then they want to buy their parents a house. I have never in my life seen an athlete cut their own lawn so they pay someone to do that. They buy the top of the line entertainment system, and brand new furniture for the huge house. You know you can't have your parents taking the bus so they need a new car(s) to go with the house. But you didn't realize that you have to pay to maintain their stuff and your stuff. By the time all is said and done, the player has pretty much spent every dime of the contract.

One big difference with athletes vs. entertainers is that athletes know how much money they are going to earn at the beginning of the season (not including endorsements & bonuses) because they have a salary.

In most cases, the first couple of years when a player goes broke, it's the parents who share part of the blame. Some parents sacrifice their lives, jobs, and free time for years to help the child become this top athlete, until draft-day. So when draft-day comes, the statement that comes out of the parent's mouths is, "We've made it!" The next comments from the parents tend to go something like this, "You need to focus on the game, so let me handle your finances. I knew how to raise you so I know how to handle your money. I will take care of everything for you. You don't need to hire all those professional people to handle your money. I'll do it and you know you can trust me. You've been working so hard. I'm gonna get you everything you need to make your life comfortable. You deserve it."

Let me paint a picture that I see all too often. Mom picks out the house for him and she furnishes the house, she opens a bank account and begins to manage the money by getting advice from other parents in the space. It's never with bad intentions, because she actually thinks she's doing the right thing. In most cases, she knows nothing about the real estate market, investments, or business contracts. They will typically hire someone from their old neighborhood, a family member that knows nothing about the business or how to deal with this size or amount of money and they put the money in the riskiest investment as they can because someone has offered unrealistic guarantees. Next thing you know half of the money is spent and the other half has gone into horrible investments before the athlete ever shoots or catches his first ball in his first professional game.

*What percent of the industry is business and what percentage of it is entertainment?*

I'd say it's all business.

*How would you describe money management to a child?*

Children are smart. They catch on easily. I would say establish a budget. Look at all of the money that you have coming in, no matter how many streams it's coming from, and match that up with how much money is going out. The difference is what you have left for savings or to invest. The average person should be saving at least 10% of their income. For the average athlete or entertainer, my suggestion is that percentage needs to be closer to 50% because the success may not last. So you really have to concentrate on those numbers.

*What do parents and children need to know before they begin managing their money?*

Parents need to educate themselves about how to hire a financial advisor, how different investment vehicles work, and how to budget money. The three important things that I learned as a young investor in my early teens, after I made, then lost a ton of money, were: (1) what diversification was really about (2) what risk really meant and (3) why you should hire a professional to do things for you. Diversification is extremely important. Diversifying amongst, assets classes, like cash, bonds, stocks and real estate is the key. The parent and the child can learn these things together.

It's about having a balanced portfolio. As the parent learns it, they can teach it to their child.

Giving has become a big deal in our business as of late. Many athletes get caught up in creating these big foundations but for some, it's really just an excuse to throw a big party or give family members a job and very little of the foundation's money goes back to the organization. An alternative for entertainers is to find an organization that is already established and loan their name and their time to that organization instead of starting their own. Besides, what do you really know about running a foundation?

*Can the average parent realistically manage their child's money without outside or professional help?*

Yes, they could, if this was their expertise before. When the financial climate changes, so should your plans of handling it. I could stay healthy without going to the doctor, but at some point I'm going to want to seek out the services of a professional. For example, if a person gets a sore throat they may try a friend's remedy, but if that person has a brain tumor, he's going to want to seek out a specialist. Can the average person stay in great shape without the help of a trainer or going to the gym regularly?

*It's possible but not probable.*

Exactly.

*What advice would you give the parent of a child who just booked their first television show and showed up to set for the first day of shooting?*

Sit back and observe. Sit back and learn first. Don't come on set acting like you know everything because you don't.

*Final thoughts?*

I will leave you with two quotes I say all the time:

- Rich people can buy things they want but wealthy people can afford to keep them.
- Many rich people I know finance a Bentley. Many wealthy people I know own a Prius.

\* FINRA website

\*\* http://www.businessinsider.com/chart-the-average-nba-player -will-make-lot-more-in-his-career-than-the-other-major-sports-2013-10

*Octavius "Ted" Reid III is a Financial Advisor with Morgan Stanley Global Wealth Management in Marlton, New Jersey. The information contained in this article is not a solicitation to purchase or sell investments. Any information presented is general in nature and not intended to provide individually tailored investment advice. The strategies and/or investments referenced may not be suitable for all investors as the appropriateness of a particular investment or strategy will depend on an investor's individual circumstances and objectives.*

# Tia Mowry-Hardrict

*Actress/Producer/Author/Entrepreneur*

### How would you describe the entertainment industry?

Fickle. You're in one minute and out the next. While the business is a place of freedom where you can do what you enjoy, it's important that you don't let it define you.

### What are some of the great realities of working in this business?

For every hundred "No," there's one "Yes." You become very grateful and thankful for the yesses because they're so few and far between.

### What are some of the pressures of children working in this adult industry?

The biggest pressure is that people in the industry treat you like an adult. Often people forget that you are a child. At the end of the day, it is a business. That is how people approach it, no matter what the age of the child is.

### How important are education and family to a child performer?

They are very important. These are two things that can't be ignored. Money is not everything. It's great, but it doesn't keep you grounded. Money doesn't give you integrity and character and family and education do that.

*How important is it to have a life that is separate from this industry?*

It is very important. It's easy for this business to suck you in and define your happiness. Having separate desires and participating in separate activities can help keep you in touch with real life.

*How did you escape the traps and distractions of the business?*

God and my family helped me escape both. My family allowed me to be a child. A lot of what you see in this business is children growing up too fast and being robbed of their childhoods and that's not healthy.

*What was the key to your transition from child star to adult star?*

The key to my transition from child star to adult star was going to college. It was really important for me to experience that and to get out into the real world. After being a part of the Hollywood "scene" for such a long time, college really humbled me and allowed me to grow up.

*Do you have any final advice for the children?*

Stay true to whom you are. Don't allow money and fame to change you.

*Do you have any advice for the parents?*

Don't treat your child differently because they are bringing in money. Remember, he or she is your child.

# Jerry Levine
*Director/Producer/Actor*

### How long have you been in the entertainment industry as an actor?

I've been doing theater since I was eight years old and I've never stopped. I can remember always wanting to do it. I remember singing and dancing to "On The Good Ship Lollipop" and wearing tap shoes in kindergarten. I was always musically inclined. I've been playing the drums since I was in the second grade. I like music, art, and all that stuff. So music brought me toward the industry. I was acting in school, during the summer, in plays, theater and musicals in college as well. All of my training was from theater and I did many many plays as an actor and director. I have had experience in just about every area of theater. I've worked in casting, production, directing, lighting, and they are all connected. They all inform the other. It is important to learn as much as you can and diversify within your field of experience. For me, one thing sort of led to another. One day I was in the pit playing drums for a musical and I looked up and said, "That's looks like fun, I think I can do that, too." I auditioned for a role and I got the part and began to enjoy it because it was a way for me to express myself. It was a form of expression and something that I enjoyed doing. I was good at it and was getting positive feedback. There was escapism and a certain kind of freedom that I got from it. There is a certain connection that I get while I'm acting. It's as if I leave the planet that I'm on when I'm focused on what we create. It is the safest place in the world for people who are meant to act. You are in the zone. I eventually got a recurring role on a sitcom in LA when I was 27 playing a teenager. I was cast in my first movie called "Teen Wolf" playing the role of Stiles.

*Tell me about Jerry the director?*

As a director, one of the things that I do for my actors is recognize their insecurities and use them to our benefit. My favorite direction is, "You are all I need." This comment relaxes the actor and allows them to feel comfortable in their own skin. Sometimes actors will ask, "How was that last take?" I'll just say, "You're in the zone" - which means if you're in the zone, you can't make a mistake. You may make a different choice, you may attack your scene differently, but it can't be wrong because you're in the zone. You're where you need to be, so stop thinking. You see, acting is about not thinking. With acting, you don't want to use your brain. You want to be a leaf in the wind. Acting is reacting...acting is a verb. You are doing something. Like right now, I'm teaching. That's why it is important to go to acting class. While you're in acting class, you are downloading new information into your mind. Don't ever "try" to use the techniques you learned in class while performing. Those are exercises and techniques designed to awaken certain aspects of you or the character you are playing. At some point, during the performance, it will happen naturally. Let it happen naturally.

When I direct, I don't say things like, "Act like this." I will ask a question. Like if someone has to react to what someone is doing, I will ask, "Do you see what this guy is doing?" Automatically the actor will start thinking about what I said. Then I just say, "Ok...let's roll." Now he is aware and will react to that. Babies and dogs are the best actors on the planet because they are not thinking; they are just listening and reacting. They give back what they get. I never tell my actors what to do, but I always ask them questions. I know the actor's instrument and how it works and I know what an actor needs and it is my goal for it to be organic to them. What's cool is when I am editing its rhythm, I can cut a show by closing my eyes and listening to the dialog, I can hear the way a scene plays. There is musicality to it. I still use all of it.

Jerry Levine

*How would you describe the entertainment industry?*

It can be a treacherous and dangerous environment that can confuse and misguide your children into believing in things that are not real; and in things that will eventually go away. When these things do go away, without giving your kid the right background and the right information, it will leave a hole in them that they may not be able to fill. I have read that "fame" is clinically classified as a drug. Some people, when they achieve fame, can lose their perspective, the love of the art and why they got into the business in the first place. That's when fame becomes the goal and the love of your art becomes secondary.

Hollywood is also image and youth driven. Most entertainers experience the pressures of the natural aging process and how it might affect their career. Parents of children in the industry need to protect their children from these pressures, so that when they are older they can evolve as actors as they age. Getting older doesn't necessarily mean that one's career is over. Parents must give their children support and permission to grow and evolve emotionally and creatively. If the parents don't teach this to their child, the child won't learn it from the industry. What concerns me about this business is, as an adult, the rejection can break your heart. So imagine how it can affect a kid's heart. The rejection can be very hurtful and damaging.

*Explain the set atmosphere as it relates to children.*

Production doesn't see the kids who are working on the set as kids really, because they are working. When the parents become enamored by the Hollywood of it all, that's when it goes wrong. When parents stop doing what they are supposed to do, it goes bad quickly. When kids are not ok at home, they are not ok on set.

If a parent creates a confident kid at home who knows who he is, he will bring that with him on set and his skills, as an actor will show that. It will be instinctual and impulsive. Kids need to feel their parents near them all the time. When they are, the kids don't ever have to be afraid. They will be confident. Listen, kids cook early. Either they get it or they don't. This life is not real. You can't lose the balance between what life is and what balance is. If this becomes your real life and real life becomes this fake thing, you have a problem.

*What do you have to say to parents in general about parenting?*

Raising kids is like dropping things in wet cement, metaphorically. You drop things in wet cement; the cement dries and it hardens. Now if you want to change the positioning of that object, if you want to change it; you gotta break it. If you want to drop an object in the cement and make sure it dries the right way, make sure you put it in right. If so, it's gonna harden and sit the right way. It hardens for life and you have to break it to reset correctly.

*Can you share some sobering truths about the entertainment industry?*

The success and the failures in this business are both imposters. Should you succeed? All right, you did ok. But you have more roads left to travel. So don't buy into your success and don't buy in to the experiences that don't go so well either because they are all going to happen.

The other thing is, I hear people say all the time when they get on a new project, "Oh, we are like a family." Well, the only difference is, my family can't fire me. This is a job. I am having a good time on set, but these folks are my colleagues. Nothing is permanent, so just live for this moment.

*What advice do you have for kids?*

I try to tell kids do something that is meaningful to you and the rest will come. Find something that has nothing to do with money, nothing to do with fame, and nothing to do with movie stardom. I had been doing theater all this time when I got a check from booking a recurring role on a sitcom that lasted for a year. I loved the theater whether I made money or not. The love of the art was driving me. The drive is coming from God. It's coming from some other spiritual thing that is as meaningful in my life as anything else. It was a necessity for me. But the drive had nothing to do with Hollywood because I didn't know what that was. Hollywood was a surprise to me. I booked a job in New York and here I come to Hollywood in the middle of this thing. The goal was always to pursue the art that I loved.

*Which do you love most, acting or directing?*

I love my family, my children and my life with them. I love dinner around the table, Christmas, Chanukah, and the beach. It's about real relationships and friendships for me. What I love most about my work is, at this point in my life, being finished. I have done this for so long, traveled so much and directed so much that I look forward to hearing, "Please return your tables and chairs to the upright position."

There is a feeling, as a director, of extraordinary relief when I have completed the work. Because the pressure of what the director is going through is so intense that I am relieved when it's over. I do have favorite creative moments. When I see two actors surprise me with the magic. That is good! My favorite moment is when an actor or actors do something special with their art and surprise me. My advice to actors is often, "Don't stop living to act." As a director, my task is to answer three questions, "Why here? Why now? Why this story?"

*Do you see yourself as a teacher because you are?*

Yes I do.

*What advice would you give a teenage or young adult actor who is trying to make a creative transition?*

When you come to a cross in the road, take it. If that window of opportunity opens, no matter what it is, casting, directing, acting, producing, or executive producing. You don't know where it's going to take you. Even though you have no idea where you're going to go. If you are outside an arena at a ballgame, you don't know the score inside. But if you're the guy throwing peanuts and someone does something, you get to see the game. You are in the arena, you see the game, you see the players, and you now know what's happening. If you're in the theater, you're gonna watch the performance. Go to the game, go to the performance, an opportunity may be waiting for you.

*How would you advise a parent to pursue a career for their child?*

Watch your children fall in love with the art. They don't have to run out and start auditioning for commercials. Do the school plays and let them fall in love with the acting piece because the professional side of it can become difficult and cruel. They can be rejected all of the time. When that happens, is it going to break their heart or kill their spirit? Not if they love doing it first. Start in your church. You should get as much satisfaction doing it at your church as you do in the theaters and professionally. If you can see it you can get it.

The experiences in the industry can be challenging; encourage the love of it and what it gives you in the community theater. Wanting to be famous, walking the red carpet, wanting to be on television, signing autographs, your own narcissism, or the glamour of the awards shows is not what the focus should be. If you don't love it, it's like a marriage, when times get tough, you can break up. But if you love it, that thread of love holds you and somehow, binds you some how to that relationship. Just when you're out the door, you hear, "Where do you think you're going?" That's the very thing that kept me married for so many years. With a strong foundation, a strong faith, a strong belief, and a strong moral compass, it can be done. Use that as your standard as to what you are not going to do. Stick to that and say, "I'm not going to do that." You have to find a way to set the foundation so that it is stable. So make sure that your kid is in love with the right man or woman (metaphorically). Not the stardom, not the fame, not the money.

What you bring to your art, your skill or your talent is what makes it valuable. Convey to your children that you must love what you're doing and find it meaningful and if it is meaningful to you, you will succeed and the rest will come. Don't get it backwards or you will lose your mind.

# Kokeeta Douglas
*Make-up Artist for Television & Film*

### How long have you been a make-up artist?

I have been a make-up artist for 30 years. I began my career as a make-up artist in 1985 while practicing as a hairstylist in the industry.

### How would you describe the entertainment industry?

The entertainment industry is a huge, energetic, influential, static, creative, experimental medium whose overall success is based on the viewer's ever-changing interests. I feel that the industry is a pretty accurate indicator of what the general population is thinking. It is filled with people (in all departments) who are looking for fame and fortune. It is not an industry for those looking for a secure environment and a stable existence - whatever that is!

### What is a day in the life of a make-up artist like?

A day in the life of a make-up artist comes with so many variables, depending on the job. Make-up artists are usually the first team to arrive at a specified location in order to have the actors ready for the set at a scheduled time. The make-up has to be maintained for the duration of the scene, and/or changed for another scene. A continuity log is kept for all make-up rendered to each actor in case the same scene is revisited at a later time. A supply inventory is taken so that everything that is needed is on hand for the day or at a later time. If we have to move to another location, the trailer has to be wrapped down and secured so that all equipment and other products remain unharmed from the move. It is our duty, at all times, to keep our actors comfortable. Make-up artists are usually on set from 10 - 16 hrs a day, depending on the type of production. When the day is over, sometimes the actor may need their make-up or special effects removed before leaving. That is also the make-up artist's job.

*What has been your experience working with children in the industry?*

I have had many experiences with children in the industry in all mediums. My first experience was on a sitcom that took place in an elementary school. Since then, I have done loads of commercials, promos, comedies, and dramas that feature children. Overall, I've had fun experiences dealing with them.

*What has been your experience interacting with parents in the industry?*

I haven't interacted with parents that much, but have observed many interesting techniques used by the parents on their children, such as making their child drink large amounts of soda (soft drinks), eat handfuls of candy to "keep their energy up," even when the child expresses that they've had enough of the junk food. When I am talking to the child, the child can't even speak for himself or herself without the parent interrupting and taking over the conversation. And there is the parent who is clearly pushing the child into acting against their will, which I assume is to fulfill one of their own latent dreams. Then there are the parents who will allow production to do certain things like using paint on their small babies without asking one question as to the contents or possible negative effect of the product being used.

*What would you say were the benefits for children who work in the entertainment industry?*

Some of the benefits for child actors would be: Having exposure into a world of luxury that he or she may never come into contact with at such an early age; the opportunity to explore the possibilities of their own creativity by playing different roles; developing a certain amount of maturity and comfort around all kinds of people; and the ability to grow into each upcoming role in their age range, if they're in the game of show business long enough to reach adult status. They also have the opportunity to become a seasoned acting professional.

*What would you say were the disadvantages for child actors?*

Disadvantages for a child actor would be having a parent who cares only about getting their child "to the top" at any cost and not thinking of their child's welfare. It is hard for me to think of the disadvantages without putting full responsibility on the parent to be aware of every situation that the child encountered.

*What advice would you give to a child who is just getting started?*

I think that any child getting started should keep an open dialog with his or her parent about everything. Trust your instinct. Listen well. It's ok to ask questions. Be assertive so that you are heard. The phrases "Please" and "Thank you" go a long way. Set goals. Equip yourself with knowledge of the business.

*What advice would you give to a parent who is just starting out?*

Make sure that you are working in your child's best interest, and NOT living vicariously through your child. Set short-term and long-term plans.

Discuss the business so that they are aware that it is a business. Keep an open dialog with your child. Trust your instincts. Basically, this is the same advice I would give to the child. Keep an open mind that the entertainment industry may not be for your child.

# Derek Stewart
*Industry Dad/Filmmaker*

*How did you end up in the entertainment industry?*

In 2008, our then 10-year-old son started taking acting lessons in our hometown of Columbia, SC just as a summer activity. After spending a day on set as an extra in a feature film being filmed in Columbia, he told us that he wanted to be an actor. Our support of his dream led us to the entertainment industry.

*What was your original goal?*

Our goal was simply to support our child and help him pursue his dream.

*How would you describe the entertainment industry?*

It's a place where dreams come true…but with a price.

*What were you most surprised to discover on your journey?*

How many people it takes to film a television show or film. I had no idea.

*What has been one of the highlights?*

Just watching my son grow and start to see his dreams coming true.

*What has been most disappointing?*

Since I had no expectations when entering this business, I have nothing to be disappointed about.

*Let's play word association. I will say a word or phrase and you say the word/phrase that best describe it.*

*Hollywood* - Fake
*Fame* - Fleeting
*Stage Parents* - Sad
*Television Show* - Chaos
*Child Stars* - Wonderful
*Family* - Everything
*Production Schedules* - Crazy
*Identity* - Crucial

*What advice would you give to kids?*

You must have a strong sense of who you are and never let ANYONE else define that for you. Be willing to take the road less traveled and stay true to yourself. Keep God first in all you do.

*What advice would you give to parents?*

Remember that this is your child's career, not yours. Your job as a parent has not changed-to raise a decent, respectful person. That should ALWAYS supersede anything else.

# Jurnee Smollett - Bell
*Actress/Activist*

**How old were you when you started in the entertainment industry and how did you get started?**

I was 10 months old when I started. My three older siblings were already modeling and doing commercials in New York. My mom would bring me along with them. I believe there was a photographer who put me in a shot at a photo shoot and I just started modeling and doing print work. When I was three-years-old, I booked two national commercials. The first one was a Pepsi commercial and I got to work with Joe Montana. The other one was a Cheerios commercial that I got to shoot right outside of Orlando, Florida. It was so cool because my mom and I got to take a plane trip and stay in a hotel.

I have four brothers and one sister and we have all worked in the industry to some degree. We all had a show together on ABC called "On Our Own" when we were kids. It was originally supposed to be a spin off for me when I was on "Full House" on ABC. The producers of "Full House" approached my mom and said, "We want to give her character a spin off." My mom had been stretched and pulled in so many directions with all of her kids working on many different projects at the same time. She said to our agent at the time, "I am not doing another television show unless they are all in it so they can all be in one place at the same time." She was just throwing the idea out there. She wasn't really serious; she was just sharing her frustrations out loud.

Our agent took the idea to the producers and they said, "Oh, there are more of them? Bring them all in." So my mom had us all rap and sing for them. I can remember; us performing songs from the rap group Public Enemy and a Heavy D song. We were signed to a development deal with Warner Brothers and shot the show "On Our Own" for a season.

*As a child, what did you like most about the industry?*

At different parts of my life, I guess I liked different things. As I became more aware of the craft behind acting, there was a scene, in an episode of "On Our Own" where I had to cry. It was my first time being emotional and having to tap into a place that helped me cry. There was also a scene in the movie "Eve's Bayou." It was my first real moment where I could appreciate the actual craft. My mom, who was my acting coach, Kasi Lemmons, the Director, and Sam Jackson were the ones who really pushed me beyond what one would normally get out of a 10 year old. There were things that I could relate to in the script. Then there were things that I couldn't relate to at all. Over time, I started to appreciate the pretend aspect of stepping into another character. It can also be very therapeutic, you know. I didn't realize I was doing this of course, but I was also able to work some things through in my own life. As actors, we work stuff out through our characters. That started to become somewhat of a high for me thinking, "Oh, I can get lost in this character."

*Did you feel a certain emotional gravity because "Eve's Bayou" was a weighty story?*

Oh I totally did. People used to always joke with me and say, "You're really a 40 year old in a 10-year-old body." I was definitely not a typical child, in my mind. I was very well read and I was always around adults. The way I was raised, my family and I were always debating topics around the dinner table. I was exposed to a lot of stimulating conversation at a young age. So I was wise beyond my years in some ways. I was aware and was just able to dissect the character of Eve. My mom really talked to me about it. She would say things like, "this is what your character Eve is experiencing."

Between my mother, the director, and being blessed to work with other talented actors, I was able to really internalize the gravity of Eve, the character. Every time I had to do a crying scene, my mom would hug me when the director yelled, "Cut." Getting emotional takes a lot out of you; even to this day, to go to that sad place is tough. My mom would be there every day and hug me after a tough scene.

*How did she know to do that?*

I don't know. She was just being a mom. She took drama classes in high school but that was about it. She was always obsessed with old actors like Joan Crawford and Katherine Hepburn (who is my favorite actress) and we would always watch the *Sound of Music* and all of these old films. We would study Sidney Poitier.

She would work on character development with me. When I was young, she was the only acting coach I worked with. She had an interesting way to coach us, too. She would make it a game and to us it was fun. My brothers and sister and I would all be in the back seat of our car driving home and my mom would call out, "Ok, I will give 50 cents to whoever can cry on cue," and we did it. And it was fun. She made it a game.

It's funny the sort of methods she used in training us. I don't know if she knew it at the time, but many of the pros do the same type of thing. She would get us to internalize and personalize the scenes just like they do it. I didn't realize it until I got older and was introduced to some of the masters. I was like, "Wow, Mommy used to do that with us when we were kids." I believe she just instinctively knew what to do.

I was blessed to have her there and be able to download that. I understand the process better now but when you are in it as a child you don't realize what you are doing. I felt that way when I saw Quvenzhané Wallis in "Beasts of the Southern Wild," I thought, "Wow! That is just extraordinary to me. To be able to get a little baby to tap into those emotions is really extraordinary."

*I believe that having a measure of maturity and focus is the component that separates the average kid from the child who is destined for the industry. Not all kids can do that, especially not in front of a camera, in front of a director, or an entire cast and crew. What are your thoughts on that?*

I agree. For some reason, I never was intimidated to perform in front of a camera. I was always comfortable and ready to perform. I would sing and dance for people in meetings, I had my own little shtick and routine. I'd watch Janet Jackson and Madonna on television and try to copy them. I got in trouble a few times for copying them too well. Yes, so there is an element that separates some kids. Some kids are just gifted in that way.

*As a kid, were you excited about working with your talented casts?*

I honestly had no idea who they were. I was a little kid so I didn't watch any of their adult movies. I was too young to watch a Quentin Tarantino film. I didn't know how famous Samuel L. Jackson or the others were. In my house, all my mom (or we) would watch were old films or cartoons. There was no in between. So to me, these actors were just really nice people who were auditioning, rehearsing, teaching me things and acting in this movie with me. I was confident that I could do whatever they threw at me and I could tell they liked that. I was later told that that was one of the reasons why I got the job. I wasn't enamored like that because I was so little and it was only my second film.

My first one was "Jack," a Francis Ford Coppola film with the late Robin Williams. It was so much fun working with him. I learned how to improvise from Robin. *He* taught me that. Francis was all about improvising, and Robin, forget it, he was amazing! That's how I booked the audition.

Francis flew us all, including the other kids who were auditioning, out to his ranch to rehearse. Me, Robin Williams and Bill Cosby were in the room, and I was reading with Robin. All the kids took turns auditioning and we all had to read with Robin or Bill. Robin taught me how to improvise on the fly while auditioning with him. I had fun shooting that and I remember going to the premiere and seeing myself on screen thinking, "This is so cool, I am up there on the screen." But I wasn't really caught in the moment of how it affected my acting career.

Even when I worked on "Full House," I didn't really watch the show. I saw it, but it wasn't like we all sat down to watch me on this show. It was just something else I was doing in my life. In my family, you were not going to act like you thought you were famous. Not in my house. Between my mom, my dad and my brothers - no, that was not going to happen. In my house you had to do the dishes and all of the chores like everybody else! It was almost like when you were working on a project, you were the one who had to do even more chores!

*As a kid, what was your least favorite reality about the entertainment industry?*

Auditioning. I did not like auditioning. I still don't like auditioning. It is very cold, intimidating and it is really not even about the craft. I have memories as a kid of walking into a casting room and the kids and their moms staring at me as if I was some type of threat just because I was auditioning. And that bothered me. I remember one time, after our family-show, "On Our Own" was cancelled, I was at an audition and my brother Jussie was with me while our mom was waiting in the car. One of the moms of a girl who was auditioning looked at me with this smirk and said, "Oh, I heard about *On Our Own*. Too bad you guys couldn't get a second season...best of luck next time."

The tone and the way she said it was so condescending, almost like it brought her satisfaction. It was very inappropriate to have that kind of competition with two kids. So the politics of that is what you sometimes feel at auditions and I never liked that. I don't believe in competition.

That was so weird to me because our family was so not Hollywood at all. We are New Yorkers, black and Jewish, big suburban, basketball playing, bagel eating folks. We were not Hollywood. So moments like that were probably the realities that were my least favorite. I didn't have a lot of friends who were actors growing up. We were friends with everyday kids. Because they treated us like we were normal, everyday kids.

### What don't parents realize about the auditioning process that they should know?

I don't know if it's really possible to verbalize the level of criticism the child is exposed to in those audition rooms…they internalize that. And at such a young age, how do you protect them from that? When your child goes into the casting room, they are critiqued. Whether or not the casting director is doing it on purpose, it's a part of the process of auditioning. You have to build your child up to be so strong and have such tough skin in spite of that criticism and critique. The kid tends to pick up on every single thing. In the audition, they usually want you to be something that you are not. It's important to build the child back up when they walk out of that room, so that they don't think that those casting people's opinions define them.

Some of the best advice I'd ever been given came from Quincy Jones. He told me, "You can't believe them when they tell you you're great, because you'll believe them when they tell you that you're not." Now with the criticism that you receive in that casting room…you have to know who you are before you walk in there. When the parent asks questions like, "So, what did they say, how did it go?" it tends to make it worse sometimes. My mom would do something that was cool. She would ask us how did it go of course, but then she'd say, "All right, we're going to McDonalds." She'd get the info and then change the subject and we'd move on to the rest of our day. When she would get calls from the agent with feedback from our audition, especially if it was negative, she would say, "Yeah, well…my kid is the best so whatever…it's their loss!" Because of her comments, I never had to feel like I failed at the audition because my mom thought I was the best whether I booked the role or not. I never really struggled with thinking I wasn't good enough because of that.

Because parents don't go in the casting room with the kid, they don't know what it feels like to go in or come out. Don't make a big deal about it. Parents, you really don't want the child to sense the importance of booking a job. That's too much pressure. Many times, if the child is devastated when they don't book a job, it's because the pressure is coming from the parents. That kind of pressure should not exist for a kid. It should be fun. It should be about creating the character, displaying it then walking away. Also, if they don't book a job, the parent shouldn't focus on what the casting people said. It's irrelevant at that point. It's not going to change anything, so why tell them? I think one of the reasons why I still love acting and I'm still in the business is because my mom never made a big deal about auditioning, or getting approval from others. Sure, there were pressures and you can't shield your kid from everything but you can do the best you can. The good thing was my mom was able to preserve a part of me, or my innocence that allowed me to stay in love with my craft.

***What advice would you give a child, maybe 10 years old, who watched something on television and wanted to be an actor?***

Hmm…that's hard. I mean…I sometimes question if kids should even be doing it that young. I don't know if I can really answer that, to be quite honest. I'm just not sure, because so many kids who start that early, they are not fine now. But if I actually said that to a kid, I'd be a hypocrite because I did start off in the business very early and that young, and I am fine now. So, I'm a bit conflicted on this. So many things can fall apart. The child's education and schooling experience can fall apart. Their self-esteem can be broken, wounded or injured. It's hard because so many things can happen.

If they don't have the foundation of the parent being there and supporting them and not pressuring them to be little moneymakers, it's almost impossible. If they have the parent that only sees green, it will be very difficult. When your child is bringing in eight grand just from shooting one national commercial, the parents tend or begin to look at the check, the child, and the opportunity a little differently. I have seen good parents turn into something completely different, and stop parenting all together and it is very disturbing to watch.

But if I had to answer this question, I'd say, study your craft. So that as the child gets older the focus will be more on the craft as oppose to the dollar signs. If it is about the craft and if you are studying, there is real satisfaction and gratification in stepping into a character. As artists, we are able to help society see another aspect of the human experience that they might not have known. We are able to help society live in and walk in other people's shoes that they might have never stepped into. It's no different than reading a great book. You get to live in this world and learn to understand the wonderful experiences. Like the story of Helen Keller, for example; you can better understand her unique experience just by reading about it, and you're not blind. You are able to, for just a moment, feel or imagine what she experienced when you read her story. There is no difference between that and a great film, a great television show, or a great play. That, as actors, is what our job is - to tell a story.

So I would say, study your craft and stay in school, because the academic side of me has helped me with research. It has helped in developing characters, building personalities, to be really authentic. I spend a lot of time in the library when I'm taking on a new character. When I don't, I get really nervous. I am constantly reading everything about the world and researching it. Reading or wanting to delve into history doesn't intimidate me when researching new characters because of my academic background. You won't hear about Jurnee not paying her taxes and not being up on her business side because I was good in math. My dad taught me how to budget accounts and pay bills. My agents weren't all in my money because I knew how to handle my own money. So please stay in school.

There are real sharks out there that will try to take more commission and try to get you to sign contracts without reading them. I read every single contract…every single one. Then I get on the phone with my attorney and talk to him about what I read and what I don't understand. Also, have your own opinion because every single person is going to have an opinion for you. When you don't have an opinion, someone will fill one in and that will become your opinion.

### What is your definition of a child star?

My definition of a child star is a kid who started out in the business very young; works/worked all the time in lots of commercials, on a successful long-running television show or a blockbuster movie (or a string of movies) and made a lot of money. Whenever people ask me what's it like to be a child star, I tell them that I don't know because I don't consider myself to be a child star. I only worked a few times on a few projects that did well. I wasn't necessarily the "star" on all of the projects that I worked on nor did I work on project, after project, after project. I was more of a ubiquitous child actor. You know, the kid who looks familiar but you're not quite sure what you saw her in.

### What advice would you give the parent of a 10 year old?

Everyone's situation is different but I would say a few things. Have a job outside of what your child is doing. I have seen parents resent that the child is consuming their life. They didn't get the chance to pursue their own dreams and desires and the child is now the moneymaker. They began to live through their child and that's not healthy. The parent should know that the pressure should never be on the child. So even if it's a part-time job, do whatever you have to do to make that happen for yourself. Whatever you do, do not look at your child as if he or she is a dollar sign. There is no way to maintain a healthy parental balance when your child is an employer or employee in his own house.

The money that the child makes should benefit, bless, help and improve things within the family but the second the parent starts to look at their child and see money first, that relationship becomes dysfunctional. Fortunately for my mother, it wasn't necessarily about the money and that's why I don't consider myself a child star. I didn't work all the time. There was a time when I was offered roles on certain child centered programs and networks and my mom was like, "Gosh, they want to pay her a lot of money but – no. We will wait for a better project." I am able to have a career now because I didn't take those jobs. At the end of the day, it was about the craft for her and she wanted to be proud of the body of work that I did.

Not everyone liked her and she didn't care because that's not why she was there. She wasn't trying to make friends. She was there to protect her children. My agent, reps and executives on set didn't always like the extent of how she handled situations, but she didn't care. She was a strong parent and the industry doesn't really like strong parents. They want to be able to go around the parent to get to the child. They want to exclude the parent and talk to the child directly so they can get what they want. People still come up to me saying, "Yo, your mom was gangster!" She would straight up be in a meeting and start nursing my baby-brother.

### *How did you make the transition from working child actor to working adult actor?*

It was not easy. There were some lulls. Sometimes it was hard for casting to see me as anything other than that little girl actor. I went through an awkward phase and I also had severe acne. I had to cancel auditions as a teenager because it was so bad. I got a lot of no's for a while. Not because of my acne. I fortunately never lost or didn't get booked for a job because of that. But I didn't work all the time. This is one of the reasons why I'm glad

314

I wasn't over exposed as a child and intentionally said no to certain projects I turned down, because when people see you as only one thing its hard for them to see you as anything else. When you are overexposed, that's what happens. It seems like a great thing for a child to be on a long-running hit show, but that is not always so. Overexposure is not always a good thing. It can kill a potential career. I was blessed because I worked with so many very talented actors. Just working with them helped me to get better as an actor. I have to earn the roles that I book. I am still earning it. I still don't feel that I have arrived.

One of the things that helped me transition, especially as I waited for the right role, was the fact that my mom did something that was so cool and most parents didn't do. From the time I turned 12-years-old, she stopped reading the scripts that came in for me and let me read them and decide for myself if I wanted to audition for them or not. After I did "The Cosby Show," I did a film with Angela Bassett called "Ruby's Bucket of Blood." That was the first script/movie that I read and decided to do on my own. From that moment on, it was up to me what roles I decided to take. It was 100% my choice. I was having meetings and talking with my agents, though my mom was in the room and was supportive, of course. She put the creative stuff in my hands. That is one of the reasons why my resume is not 50 pages long. I was very selective in what I chose to do. And learned how to mature in it and look at my long-term plans instead of what the role could do for me at the moment. I live a comfortable life and I am a working actor but I am also very proud of the work I have done. I am patient and selective.

***Did you ever get to a point where you didn't want to act anymore?***

I went through a period as a teenager when I was so awkward and so unsure of myself. I wore my hair in my face because I was trying to hide my acne. My acne was out of this world. It got so bad that I was working on a project at 15 years old and one of the producers came up to my mom and said, "We have to do something about this, its showing up on camera." Most of the time, the makeup made my acne even worse. So my self-esteem was destroyed. I struggled with it for years, trying every product on the market!

Even in the midst of all that, I didn't necessarily want to take a break from acting, I wanted to take a break from *everything* and just curl into a little ball. I didn't even want to go to the grocery store. I would cancel auditions when I felt that way. It was usually on days like this when people recognized me on the street. One day, it was very bad. I was recognized on the street and a woman walked up to me and said, "Oh my gosh, you are so and so," then paused and said, "I'm a dermatologist, I can fix that." Of course, I was totally embarrassed but I had to get over it. I rode all of those stages out and some days were better than others.

But eventually, I had to get to a point where I had to learn to stop caring about it so much. I had and still have to sometimes try not to be so self-aware and just go with it and just resolve that it is what it is. So, I had to learn to get over myself, and what I was feeling. Once I got over those phases, I was ok.

*Any regrets?*

None. Even when I think about the roles I turned down or the ones I didn't get. That's why I'm still in the business. I don't have any regrets and I love what I do. I also believe what is meant to be mine would have been mine or it will be mine. There is room for everyone. So, no, I don't have any regrets.

*Do you have any final words for kids?*

Find a passion that is outside of the industry. My passion is non-profit work. Volunteering, speaking to my peers about HIV/AIDS, traveling to South Africa, sending books to Africa, and traveling to Europe with the organization are big passions of mine. I enjoy speaking to kids in L.A. I have worked with an organization called Artists for a New South Africa that is dedicated to dealing with HIV/AIDS since I was 12 years old. So, a lot of my time growing up was spent focusing on charity work. The industry will make you think that it is the most important thing in the world and it is absolutely not. I had so many passions outside of the industry, like spending time with my family and friends. Don't allow the industry to consume you. I didn't care about the parties; I didn't care about the red carpets and the rest of that stuff. Life, for me, was bigger than that stuff.

### Do you have any final words for the parents?

For the parents, I would say the same thing. Make sure your child has a passion outside of the industry. Even if it's knitting, volunteering at an animal shelter, baseball, or ballerina class. This kind of stuff builds their confidence and their character.

While you can't let this industry consume your life, it does take a lot of hard work, and endless hours doing work that no one sees. If people really saw the hours invested in being good and working at your craft in this industry, it would surprise them. It's an endurance test.

That's why studying is the most important element. If I think, "Oh I'm a good actress now, I don't need to study any more, I am eventually going to suck, and then...I am done. I am not going to be ready for the next challenge. Every new project you start, you are starting from zero. You can't bring your old audition from that old role to your new audition. That is crazy. But that's the exciting part about it. You are never bored, you are always challenged and you always feel like you can get better. Do you think Kobe Bryant stops practicing because he's a professional basketball player? No, he still practices, whether he is sick or not.

### Do you have final overall thoughts?

I am glad that you're doing this. This is a taboo topic. The way in which society defines children and parents in the industry is not good. People kind of expect child actors to grow up and become drug addicts and for the parents to be stage parents. It's a really negative stereotype and it's sad because it doesn't need to be that way. At the end of the day, what we are doing is an art. Art is very noble and important. But our industry has been really tarnished. So the fewer stories about a child going off the deep end because they didn't feel loved, or get the attention that they needed, or didn't have a childhood, the better. Hopefully this can be a tool to help parents prevent that. So I applaud you, Angela.

# Sarah Jackson

*Seven Summits Pictures & Management - Owner*

**What is a talent manager and what are you responsible for?**

An agent covers a "project" comprehensively, but a manager covers an "actor" comprehensively. Many actors are interested in working in a multitude of different areas of the business, and supporting them not only requires looking out for great material, but also keeping all their projects and goals focused and moving forward. Promoting a TV and film career, an online presence, a music career, an endorsement career etc. requires a motivated and dedicated manager. A manager must have the skill set and vision to really become an architect of a client's brand, not just an acting career.

**Does everyone need a talent manager?**

I believe so. The job of a manager is ever evolving - as an actor gets more and more successful there are always new hurdles to overcome. Going from working actor to a respected actor to an award-winning actor all require support and specific skill sets. Success and new opportunities come with one drawback, competition. With each echelon of achievement in one's career, the circle of consideration narrows, and the competition gets tougher. An actor that wants to find great roles and work with great directors needs a strong team of representatives and that includes a manager. Successful actors employ every means available to get great work.

*How would you describe the entertainment industry?*

"Show business" is made up of businesses that produce and exhibit film, television, commercials, music, radio, podcasts, and videogames.

*What is your definition of a Stage Parent?*

A "stage" parent cares more about the money and perks of a job than the child's happiness or creative ambitions. A stage parent lives vicariously through the success of their child.

*What is your definition of a Child Star?*

A child star is a performer who has gained a relatively large amount of celebrity or recognition at a young age.

*What are managers looking for in a child actor?*

Not so different from what we look for in an adult actor. A child who has the ability to overcome challenges, who will perform at their very best under intense pressure, who will surprise us all by delivering beyond all expectations…and of course, who possesses talent and charisma.

*What are managers expecting from parents of child actors?*

Parents who are courteous and care more about their child's happiness than anything else. Managers expect that a parent understands that the child will hit a lot of walls; and will help them to see it as an opportunity to learn and grow. If you aren't a learner, you won't get very far. I would hope that the parent would enjoy the process along with their child and yet be willing to give it all up, if the child grows to realize that they have other ambitions. A parent should be in it for the long haul and remain loyal to the team of representatives over an extensive period.

***What advice would you give to a parent of a child just starting out?***

Place the child's needs and desires above the demands of Hollywood. Do not force them to skip school for an audition, miss homework or stop hanging out with friends in order to rehearse lines. A child should not be forced to work, but should feel encouraged and supported if it's something he or she would like to pursue. And please be patient…there is no overnight success.

# Tylen Jacob Williams
*Actor/Musician*

*Describe the entertainment industry?*

Hmm…

*What do you like most about being an actor?*

I just like it. It feels natural to me. It's not really about what I like most about it. There isn't one thing. I feel like it's what I'm supposed to be doing and I feel like it's a part of me.

*Are you ever afraid when you are in front of the camera?*

No.

*Do you feel just as at home in front of the camera as you do when you are watching television?*

There's really no difference for me. I'm comfortable doing both.

*What don't you like about acting or the industry?*

Hmm…there isn't one thing that I don't like about the industry. If I'm not a fan of something or a certain part of it I know I have to deal with it and do it anyway. Like working and going to school.

*What do you see yourself doing in 10 years? Do you think you will still be an actor?*

Yes. Probably doing movies…I'm not sure.

*What would be your ideal role?*

I'd say being a super hero of some kind.

*What kind of Super Hero?*

Like a Marvel or a DC super hero, or someone in the Avengers.

*What has your experience been like working with other kids in the Industry?*

It's either been good or bad, there's never really been an in between.

*Give me an example of a good experience?*

Hanging out on set then having lunch with my cast mates, like Damarr Calhoun. We have fun on set.

*You are now 13 years old and you have been working in the industry since you were three months old. To date, what has been the highlight of your career?*

Being a cast member and working on "Instant Mom."

*What can you say that you learned from your brothers that relates to the industry?*

To always be professional.

Tylen Jacob Williams

*Have you ever been jealous of your brothers when they were working on a project? Or is there competition between you and your brothers?*

It was more like I wish I could do that. Competition, I don't think so, no. We cheer each other on. I feel like they are happy for me and I am happy for them.

*How do you balance going to school, practicing your bass, and learning your lines?*

Well, they all happen at specific times of the day. Let's say that my call time is 8 a.m. and I wrap at 3 p.m., I can just come home and do school and then practice my bass. I still have a large amount of time of the day left. But even if there isn't much time, I can't exactly do everything. Some days you can and some days you can't. But I do have to make sure that school and work are the priority.

*How do you feel about the other parts of acting, like award shows and premieres?*

They are fun. It's just that they're not needed. They are fun to go to. You get to hang out and see other people that you know and walk the red carpet but it's not exactly like the best time on every occasion. I don't really like it, but it's fun to go to sometimes. I like doing them but it's not like it's my 100% favorite thing to do. If I had to pick between working and the other things I would choose working.

*What advice would you give to kids about how to prepare for their lines?*

Hmm…well you have to go over them, of course. It doesn't matter if you go over them at your house or on set but you have to make sure that you know them. It doesn't matter if you mess up once or twice. You will mess up; it's just that you have to make sure that you know them well. Even if you don't know them exactly, you can sometimes throw in a word that's similar because the director or script supervisor want to make sure that the lines match perfectly. They want to make sure that you say exactly what's on the page. Even if you don't get it on the first take, they will correct you and tell you what the lines are supposed to be. You will have a chance to go over them with a coach or someone from the cast. If you are doing a commercial job, you can always look at the script or have someone run them with you.

*How would you help a child get ready for her first audition, especially if she's nervous?*

I'd say you have to walk into the audition like you want it. You have to prove that you want it. Even if there is a line that may not be your favorite, you still have to deliver it the way the casting director would want you to.

*Suppose she studied her lines and she's ready but she walks in the room and goes blank! She forgets everything. She doesn't remember any of her lines?*

You say, "I'm sorry, can I take a look at the script?" It's not a big deal if you mess up in the casting room. Just say, "Line please," or "Can I take a look at the script?"

*You make it seem so easy. Why do you seem so confident and nonchalant about it? Have you always been as confident as you sound?*

No. It was about three years ago that I finally understood what I was doing, technically. Right before I booked "Instant Mom," right before I started auditioning for it. I was about 10. Something just clicked and what I was doing made sense and I knew what to do as an actor.

*What advice would you give to an excited parent who really wants their child to do this? They want them to be famous and book a movie. So they want the audition to go really well.*

Well, it doesn't matter what the parent thinks about the audition unless it is parent-driven. Unless it is parent or family-driven, their opinion doesn't really matter. It matters what the kid is thinking about because the parent is not physically doing the acting or booking the role. So it's not their decision as to how the child should audition. If they are working on something specific, have the parent bring in an acting coach to help them run lines or help them understand the role or the character.

*Great point. What advice would you give a kid who has been auditioning for years but has never booked anything?*

If you have been giving 100% during your auditions, that one role will come. The other ones probably just weren't for you. But if you aren't really giving 100% and you're just going in and you're just reading the lines and there is no emotion behind it, in your face or your body, you probably won't get it. You have to go in there and fight for it. It doesn't matter how many times you didn't book anything, you still have to go in there and fight for it.

*What if he finally books a role and is on set, and at the last minute the director changes a line and the kid feels uncomfortable saying the new line. What should he do?*

He should walk over to the director and tell him that he is uncomfortable saying the lines. The director is an adult but in that situation you are both professionals and this is business. If you are uncomfortable, you have a right to tell him that and they can adjust the lines. It happens the other way too. If they give you a line and it is not funny or the line is not working, they will change it and you will have to conform to that change. But you don't ever have to say anything that you are uncomfortable saying. No matter how young you are.

*At this very moment, we are in the car driving to set, early in the morning. If you could be doing anything else right now what would it be?*

Sleeping.

*Would you prefer to be headed to a traditional school setting to hang out and play with other 8th grade kids?*

Hmmm…No.

*Do you miss going to a traditional school?*

I've never been to a traditional school so I don't know what it's like to have gone to one.

*What do you like about being schooled on set with your studio teacher?*

I like that it's just a one on one experience. There aren't any other kids in there. It's just the two of us.

*How do you feel about being home-schooled after you leave set?*

I feel like it's just something that I have to do. I don't think about what life would be like if I didn't do it. I just do it because I know I have to.

*How do you find time to hang out with your friends?*

I have to fit it into my schedule. I have to find time to do it. It's usually on the weekends. It's always on the weekends actually unless I'm on vacation.

*Do you have friends who aren't in the industry and do they treat you differently?*

I do have friends who aren't in the industry, and no they don't treat me differently.

*Do you have friends in the industry who struggle with all of their responsibilities or don't want to do school but really want to go to all of the parties and events?*

Yes, that is the case for a few people I know.

*Do you have any final words for kids?*

It's a lot of work and it's not all-just fun. You can't do everything that you want all the time but just make sure you get what you have to get done.

*Do you have any final words for parents?*

Your job is to be the parent. You don't have to be the manager or everything else. You are just the parent. If you want to be like their personal manager you can do that, but just be you. You can get a whole group of people together to do the other stuff. You are also not the children who are acting, so don't tell them what to do with their acting career. Instead, ask them what they want to do.

# Karin Farrell
*Vice President - On Location Education*

### How would you describe the entertainment industry?

I suspect that the perspective from my desk is somewhat similar to that of young performers and their parents. As my late mother-in-law said, after spending a weekend in surgery, when asked how everything went: "All I know is that a lot of people have a lot of demands on my time." Such is the world of entertainment. It is a 24/7 industry that includes film and television, theater, music recording, circuses and other "extravaganzas," press events, ADR, commercials and print, with call times arriving late and days starting early. It's the epitome of "hurry up and wait," as there are changes to schedules, delays in filming on the set, location changes, and script adjustments. Being flexible isn't a suggestion—it's a must if one is to survive the chaos. And, with all that, it's an exciting, vibrant industry that any young performer with the talent, dedication, and true love for performing should be thrilled and honored to be a part of! I know I am.

### What is the one thing you want all parents to know about their child being educated in an industry setting?

Choosing to allow your child to perform professionally is just that: a choice. With that choice may come some sacrifices to your child's educational path. This should NOT mean sacrificing the education itself, and no one should ever convince you otherwise. However, it may mean switching to a more flexible school program or choosing not to take as many AP courses. Being flexible and open to change is important, and keeping a positive attitude about the change will help your child to feel comfortable and free of anxiety. Remember, your child is wearing two important hats: that of a professional actor with expectations that are the same as the adult actors on set, and that of a student, with teachers, parents, and even the production company expecting him or her to keep up the grades. That's a lot of pressure to handle, so helping your child to make wise academic choices can alleviate a lot of stress.

### What are some of the benefits?

One benefit to on-set tutoring can be more individualized academic attention. Depending on the number of students in the show and the student to teacher ratio in the classroom, on-set tutoring can allow for more 1:1 attention from the teacher than a student would receive in a traditional classroom. This can mean spending more time, or less time, on specific topics or assignments, allowing the pacing of the material to be dependent upon the level of understanding of the student.

For those students who perform and travel, such as in a touring Broadway show or other live performance production, on-set education can allow for wonderful experiential opportunities through field trips. I firmly believe that travel is one of the best forms of education and, when on tour, students are able to fully experience the culture and geography of each city that they visit.

### What are some of the disadvantages?

As a contrast to the advantage of having a small student to teacher ratio, some shows may have as many as ten students per teacher in the classroom. While that may seem small for a traditional classroom setting, it can be a lot to handle on set. Generally, each student comes from a different school program and is studying different courses, and, often, there can be a wide age span among the students. This can make it difficult for the on-set teacher to assist each student as much as they may need or prefer.

Another disadvantage can be having very short teaching sessions, making it difficult for the student to become properly focused or complete assignments or tests before being taken back to the set. While union regulations and some state's laws mandate a minimum of three hours of on-set education for each day that school is in session, all of that education does not need to be done in one block. Actual teaching segments may be as short as twenty minutes.

### If you had general advice for parents, what would it be?

Education is the greatest gift that a young person can receive. Whether your child is planning to be an actor, a teacher, a forensic scientist or a game designer, a quality education is equally important. Don't allow anyone to convince your child to take a GED or a diploma equivalency exam in order to "land a role." There are laws and regulations in place that allow for children's education to be provided on set, and it is their right to receive that education until they are 18 years of age or graduate from high school. Encouraging or allowing your child to stop being educated may seem like a lucrative choice in the moment, but it can put a severe damper on the future. Stand up for your child's rights, even if you may not receive proper "thanks" until years later.

### If you had general advice for the children, what would it be?

Enjoy this special opportunity that most others never get! Understand that it takes hard work and dedication, both as an actor and as a student. Study hard and memorize your lines, and above all, have fun with the process. If it is no longer enjoyable for you, communicate that to your parents, as it may be time for a change.

# One-Liners

- Challenge your child to find their passion.
- Help them to reach their highest potential for the sake of their purpose.
- What else can your child do besides his/her obvious talent?
- Challenge your child to find something to love as much as their talent.
- Keep unnecessary people out of your business.
- Only share with others what you are willing to be betrayed with.
- Stop talking so much about what you've done and whom you know.
- No one likes negative stage parents - not even other negative stage parents.
- A good parent who manages sometimes is better than the reverse roles.
- A person who will talk to you about others will also talk to others about you.
- Name-dropping is tacky and does the opposite of what you are expecting it to do.
- Spend quality time with your spouse *regularly*. If you're too busy to do this – you're too busy.
- Diversify: create, give, serve, explore, research, find a need and fill it.
- Commit to community service: find a cause and support it.
- Teach them how to invest in themselves and put additional savings away.
- Buying lots of "things" can actually prove how much money you no longer have.
- Stop competing with the Joneses – they are probably in debt up to their eyeballs.
- Develop a rich full life outside of the entertainment industry.

- Develop a heart of benevolence that blesses others and it will return to you.
- Money is like seeds - it grows if you put it in the right soil.
- Balance faith, family, friends, fun, rest, health and work; and keep balancing.
- If parents create a functional family life *and* industry life for the child they won't regret it.
- Go on regular dates with your children and don't talk about the business.
- Find a hobby that has nothing to do with your child's pending career.
- Diversify your money and your talent and teach your child how to as well.
- Take breaks from the industry and act goofy with your kids for the day.
- If you have no identity when you arrive, one will sadly be created for you.
- Check your mirror and keep checking; so you will always know who you are.
- Let your passions and personal convictions be your driving force in the industry.
- Let your moral compass serve as your GPS and don't make unnecessary detours.

# *The Tag*

I truly hope that this book has been a blessing to you. I hope it has helped, educated, inspired and encouraged you in some way. It is an honor to share this important information with you as if we were simply out to lunch having an honest and open conversation. I hope that you are full and satisfied. I also hope that the insight from the industry insiders were helpful, because I am grateful for their input! It is my prayer that everyone reading this book and the children connected to you will live out your greatest potential and fulfill every drop of your life's purpose. I was created by God to be a good mother, among many other things. I am committed to doing everything in my power to making sure that my children are successful individuals both personally and professionally, and assets as opposed to liabilities in the world. I purpose to do this until the day I die. I don't strive to produce well-known individuals, but rather, well respected and developed men of God and men of high standard. I don't want them to run or rule the world. I just want them to fulfill their purpose and maintain a life without dysfunction. As a result, they will always be wealthy and successful!

If notoriety and tremendous financial resources just happen to come along as part of that highly functional package, then so be it. However, along with fame comes great responsibility and accountability. Now that I realize that a measure of fame is a part of my sons' and my family's future, it is my responsibility to do my part to make sure that we are all properly equipped to deal with that portion of notoriety. We are most successful in doing this as we put our focus and concentration on God. As followers of Christ, we take that priority very seriously. We are people of prayer and fasting. However, like Jesus Himself, we are not religious or legalistic. The book of Proverbs was and remains the key to my parenting skills because I was not bright enough to mother on my own and with my own intellect. Proverbs, daily prayer and fasting have also been my go to source for all things business, ethical and professional. If you are looking for an infallible guide through life and are serious about applying it as a lifestyle, the book of Proverbs, in my opinion, would be it. Following its eternal principles won't be easy, but just as I have, you will discover your devotion to it to be worth the effort.

Again, allow me to warn those of you who are still on a quest to be famous at all costs. Searching for fame and fortune is like shopping at a convenience store when you are hungry. The chips, candy bars and soda may look and taste good while you are eating them, and they offer the illusion of feeling full and satisfied. However, the reality is, you are stuffed with empty calories. You have an abundance of sugar and salt in your system and have wasted your time and money on eating things that will leave you eventually feeling empty, still hungry and regretful. Just like eating healthy food with solid nutrients instead of junk food, nothing satisfies or succeeds like fulfilling your purpose - and if fame is a part of your purpose, then it will always be a part of your destiny. You can learn now how to deal with it and adjust to it properly.

As I mentioned before, there is a difference between the quest for fame and riches and the pursuit of success and wealth. My prayer is that you will have a measure of them all as you fulfill your purpose, but find peace and wholeness in the latter. I hope that you have felt the sincerity in this navigational guide, and that you have felt the genuineness of my heart. My passion in these words were only motivated by a mission to help you. So now I ask the loaded two-part question: Which would you prefer, riches and fame or wealth and success? And what are you willing to do to get it?

*My Three Sons*

# Tylen Jacob Williams

*Photo by Paul Smith*

Tylen Jacob Williams is well on his way to becoming one of the busiest kids in Hollywood. Tylen began his acting career over 13 years ago, at the age of three months old on "Sesame Street," appearing as himself. Since then he has worked on "Without a Trace," "Everybody Hates Chris" and numerous PSAs and National commercials.

He is following the path of his big brothers, Tyrel Jackson Williams: "Backyardigans" (Nickelodeon), "Lab Rats" (Disney XD) and Tyler James Williams; "Everybody Hates Chris" (CW), "Let It Shine" (Disney), "Go On" (NBC), "The Walking Dead" (AMC), "Dear White People" (Feature Film). Tylen currently stars on the family sitcom, "INSTANT MOM" (Viacom Kids and Family Networks), starring Tia Mowry & Sheryl Lee Ralph.

**The Beginning...**

Tylen began his acting career at three months old after being invited by talent casting at Children's Television Workshop to appear on a "Sesame Street" Elmo's Holiday Kwanzaa spot with his brothers, Tyler and Tyrel. From that moment, he seemed to be learning and developing his acting skills by watching his brothers. Tylen was a studio lot and set baby. Whenever his brothers were on set, he was on set. Whatever his brothers were learning, he was learning. They, unbeknownst to them, became his acting mentors and he became their sponge.

*Aside from acting, Tylen is a bass guitarist, artist, comedian, philanthropist, and speaker.*

# Tyrel Jackson Williams

*Photo by Paul Smith*

Tyrel Jackson Williams has been seen or heard somewhere on television for most of the 18 years of his life. He now stars as Leo, the stepson of a wealthy entrepreneur who discovers three super humans with bionic powers living in the basement of his new home, in the Disney XD live-action comedy series "Lab Rats."

Williams has made appearances in a number of television series including Disney XD's "Pair of Kings," Disney Channel's "Good Luck Charlie," "Modern Family," "Community," "Sesame Street" (for several years) and "Elmo's Holiday Kwanzaa."

He has appeared in numerous national commercials for Target, Verizon, McDonald's, Chex Mix, Kraft, General Mills, among others. He has also lent his singing talent to the animated television series "Backyardigans" as singing Tyrone.

His feature film credits include featured roles in "Muppets Again," "Failure to Launch," "The Naked Brothers Band" and "2 For The Money."

**The Beginning…**

Tyrel Jackson began his acting career at 18-months-old when he, with bottle-in-hand, stepped quietly out of his carriage (while his mom was filling out paperwork), and walked into an open and empty casting room door during a callback audition for his big brother, Tyler. He peaked in and quietly whispered "Hi, I'm T. J." while waving at the casting directors inside. His mom rushed in behind him to apologize and remove him from the room when casting asked if he could stay and audition. By the time the family got home, Tyrel had booked the national commercial instead of his brother and was, at that moment, in the entertainment industry.

*Aside from acting, Tyrel is a guitarist, music producer, philanthropist, dancer, singer and speaker.*

# *Tyler James Williams*

*Photo by Lesley Bryce*

Tyler James Williams, the trailblazer, can be seen in Spring 2016 starring in the new CBS spinoff series CRIMINAL MINDS: BEYOND BORDERS. Last season, Tyler guest starred as Noah in AMC's THE WALKING DEAD.

He recently shot a comedy sketch on KEY & PEELE where he played "Steve Urkel."

His film DEAR WHITE PEOPLE opened in 2014. Tyler stars as 'Lionel Higgins' in DEAR WHITE PEOPLE, a satire about being a black face in a very white place.

He was also on the big screen in the Tyler Perry comedy PEEPLES (Lionsgate).

You can also see Tyler in the Emmy Award-winning series "Everybody Hates Chris" where he won a 2007 NAACP image award for Best Actor in a Comedy Series for his performance.

In 2012, He starred in the Disney Channel Original Movie LET IT SHINE as 'Cyrus DeBarge,' a gifted rapper full of self-doubt.

Also an accomplished musician, Tyler recently released a mixtape with his brother Tyrel Jackson Williams titled *Me, My Brother & A Mic*.

## The Beginning...

Tyler began his acting journey at four years old after watching a movie at home on the couch. The long version of the story is found in this book, but after several months of auditioning he landed a recurring role on "Sesame Street" and later co-starred in the animated series "Little Bill." Additional television credits include "Law & Order: SVU" and numerous appearances in sketches on "Saturday Night Live." Other film credits include the feature film UNACCOMPANIED MINORS and ANT BULLY.

*Aside from Tyler's acting and music careers he is also a director, producer, screenwriter, songwriter, musician (drums and guitar), public speaker, and philanthropist.*

# Resources & Research Guide

## Unions
www.sagaftra.org
www.actorsequity.org

## Talent Support
www.theactorsfund.org
www.actorentertainment.com
www.castingsociety.com
www.childreninfilm.com
www.backstage.com
www.deadline.com

## Mental Health
- **Suicide Prevention**

https://teenlineonline.org/
https://www.afsp.org/
http://www.suicidepreventionlifeline.org/
http://www.thetrevorproject.org/
http://www.didihirsch.org/

- **Substance Abuse**

http://www.samhsa.gov/
http://www.addictioncareoptions.com/
http://www.aa.org/
http://www.al-anon.org/

- **Depression, Anxiety, Bi-Polar, Self-Injury, Schizophrenia, etc.**

http://www.nami.org/
http://www.dhcs.ca.gov/services/Pages/MentalHealthPrograms-Svcs.aspx

- **Comprehensive Social Service Support**

https://www.211la.org/

- **Eating Disorders**

http://www.nationaleatingdisorders.org/
http://www.nationaleatingdisorders.org/find-help-support

### Representation
www.agentassociation.com
www.locationmanagers.org

### Education, Child Labor, Laws and Rules
www.onlocationeducation.com
www.studioteachers.com
www.dol.gov/dol/topic/youthlabor/entertainmentemployment.htm
www.minorcon.org

### Money Matters
www.actorsfcu.com
www.ep.com

### Miscellaneous
www.paulsmithphotography.com
www.wif.org
www.mobilfilmclassroom.org

## Documentaries

*The Hollywood Complex*
*That Guy…Who Was In That Thing*
*Showrunners: The Art of Running A TV Show*
*The Writers Room*
*I know That Voice*
*20 Feet From Stardom*
*Casting by*

# *Acknowledgements*

*I am grateful to God for my writing gifts. He is the ultimate COO and I am grateful for His voice, His guidance and His plan.*

**The Genesis:** Donna, Randi and Samantha this journey started with a wallet-sized photo, a phone call and a meeting. I won't forget your contributions 18 years ago. Thank you!

**My Cheerleaders:** Cindy, Paul, and Dawnn you were first to lay eyes on the manuscript. Thank you for your trust, feedback and votes of confidence! Steve, you were the first industry person I told about this idea. You have been my silent cheerleader!

**My Team & Creative Village:** Jennifer, Allen, Dan, Jake, Tom, Jonathan, Allison, Nikkolas, Wendy, Adrienne, Robin, Sheryl Lee, Sarah, Yvette Nicole, Toni, Mary and Jason. You jumped in with your advice, expertise, feedback and creativity. I thank and appreciate you!

**My Industry Insiders:** Cindy, Mary, Kelly, Michelle, Tyler James, Beth, Dawnn, Tina, Tyrel Jackson, Paul, Vickie, Nancy, Victor, Octavius, Tia, Jerry, Kokeeta, Derek, Jurnee, Sarah, Tylen Jacob, and Karin. Thank you for sharing your time, journey and expertise. May you succeed beyond your wildest dreams!

**The Fabric:** To everyone who has become a part of this entertainment quilt of ours, knowingly or unknowingly, I acknowledge you also. No matter how our paths crossed, or for how long, your thread has a place in this book. Aunt Ava, I love you.

*My husband Leroy:* For over three decades you have watched me in various areas and stages of "Creative Mode." Your never-ending, "You got this!" support through the years has made it easy for me to accomplish all of my goals. You are my "comfort food!"

*My three sons* – Tyler James, Tyrel Jackson and Tylen Jacob: Your talents and opened doors created a platform for this book and helped me find a way to help others. I am honored to be your mom!

## To God Be The Glory!